"I'm right here, with you"

A journey in awakening

by Mimi Lutz

ISBN: 1475294492
ISBN-13: 9781475294491
Library of Congress Control Number: 2012908004
CreateSpace Independent Publishing Platform
North Charleston, South Carolina

I dedicate this book
To my daughters Gabriella and Scarlett

For Marcela
Such a great
pleasure to
meet you
Love
[illegible]
April, 2024

Acknowledgements

It has taken me sixteen years to complete this story. I set it aside many times, discouraged and overwhelmed with the task. Then, either an internal push arose or an encouragement from a friend, a teacher, or an editor who gave me invigorating feedback. I am so grateful to all of you, including Matthew Davison and Peggy Payne and every one who helped me at Create Space. I also want to thank Kate Lundell and Mercedes Dorson. They both read, at different times, through the manuscript with such care and discernment and gave me very valuable comments. All the writers in my writer's group moderated by Edith Gilmore gave me buttressing feedback. I thank Dan Halpern, my advisor in a writer's workshop. He boosted my confidence enough to fuel the completion of the book. I also so appreciate the care and support I received from my husband Paul.

"If the reader prefers, this book may be regarded as fiction."

Ernest Hemingway

1

"God guard me from those thoughts
Men think in the mind alone;
He that sings a lasting song
Thinks in the marrow bone."
—William Butler Yeats

It was 1952. Mummy and I arrived in Rio when I was three. We came on a ship from Spain.

"Lilizinha had twelve dresses," my mother often boasted in her boisterous voice, "one for each day of the crossing, and every dress arrived spotless. Passengers stopped at our table to marvel at her tiny good manners." Mummy was a young divorcée who wanted to seem impeccable. She wore her hair parted down the middle, her long black plaits curled into two 'macarons' over her ears, framing her high forehead, large brown eyes, and fire-red lipstick.

While her pregnancy of me barely showed, she went to Rio to visit her sister. There she met a Portuguese banker. I don't know when he became her boyfriend. We moved to Portugal, once she left my father in New York, after my first birthday. "I thought the birth of the baby would change things, but it didn't," she sometimes commented.

The child support my mother got from my father stretched much farther in Portugal. She traveled with her "fiancé," as she called him and left me with her German friends in Lisbon, or with her Chilean friends who shuttled between Seville and Athens. I have a memory of being taken to the gaping hole in the ground where Persephone disappeared, abducted by Hades, god of the underworld in Greek mythology. Most of you know that because she ate three pomegranate seeds while staying with him, she was forced to spend the three winter months in the subterranean world. In spring, she was free to return to her mother to help with the planting and the harvest. Persephone is the goddess of spring. I was in Greece for six months. Persephone's story lingered as I waited and hoped my mother would return for me.

When I was with her, my mother said that "Muñequita Linda" was my song. She sang it to me at bedtime. She spent a little moment with me, just before she went out. She always wore the bracelet, a band made of tiny bricks of gold flexing on pivots at their center, a gold brick highway with a buckle of rubies and diamonds. I could see it in so many ways every time she hugged me or caressed me. Her fiancé gave it to her. She leaned over and hugged me, leaving traces of "Joy," her perfume, on my blanket.

"Too bad it is the most expensive one," she said about the perfume.

Muñequita Linda, de cabellos de oro
de dientes de perlas, labios de rubí
Dime si me quieres como yo te adoro.

(Beautiful little doll, pearly teeth, ruby lips
Tell me if you love me like I adore you.)

She closed her eyes when singing this line, pointed her perfect nose and chin to the ceiling, and ever so slightly fanned her head from side to side.

Yo te quiero mucho, mucho, mucho mucho
Tanto como entonces siempre hasta morir.

(I love you so, so much
Just as before and forever until death.)

"That's your song, my darling Lilizinha."

Riveted by my mother's every move and expression, I clutched my black Raggedy Ann doll made for me by my mother's black Venezuelan nanny, Carmen. I fell asleep, talking and cuddling with my "Nanny Preta" and her wool hair. I lost her on a Pan American flight. My mother had to call so many airports to find my floppy creature. She reappeared, but then, another time, she never returned.

My mother was named the 1939 "Debutante of the Year" in New York City, "The Latin Greta Garbo," wrote Charlie Knickerbocker, a society columnist. She also won a beauty pageant in Miami Beach, Florida, just by being around that particular pool on the day of the competition. She went to Hollywood for a screen test and was offered the part of Maria in *For Whom the Bell Tolls*.

"*Une jeune fille de bonne famille ne devient pas une actrice de theatre ni de cinema. Les actrices sont des putains*" (A young girl from a good family does not become an actress in the theatre nor in cinema. Actresses are whores), my Venezuelan French-educated grandmother insisted.

"I didn't want to hurt Grandmaman; she would have never spoken to me again," my mother defended her choice of not accepting the offer. Her father had died. She didn't notice that her mother would have followed her anywhere, because she herself was also needy.

When I was two, my mother and father attempted to get back together in Bermuda during Christmas. My grandmother insisted on spending Christmas with them even though she knew my father did not like her.

"*Où est-ce que tu veux que je passe Noël, moi*?" (Where do you want me to spend Christmas?) my grandmother quibbled.

"I will be civil with her until Christmas day. After that, I will not speak to her." My mother mimicked my father, as she told me the story, pulling an imaginary cigarette out of the place on her dress that would have been his pocket filled with a pack of cigarettes. "He'd let it hang from his wet sticky lips and then light it with his stainless-steel Zippo lighter and his long, skinny, tanned fingers," she told me. "How could someone be a gentleman for a few days and then just become such a boor, from one day to the other?" The reconciliation did not work. As a result, I stopped talking altogether, even though I had been exposed to six languages and spoke a bit of all of them.

Soon after Bermuda, my mother found out her Portuguese banker "fiancé" was still married, so we sailed to Brazil and stayed with her sister Lili and my uncle Ogilvy in Rio.

My uncle had been the U.S. Naval attaché in Rio during the Second World War. During that time, he realized there were many business opportunities in Brazil. He had graduated from the University of Virginia Law School. After the war, he married my aunt, a divorcée with two small children, Margaret and Bruce. They settled in Rio. He became a very accomplished business innovator. They had many servants. Lela, short for "Mademoiselle," was the governess. She managed the servants and the household.

Shortly after our arrival in Rio, my aunt and uncle moved to São Paulo, a more industrial city. We moved with them as part of their household. This included the governess, the upstairs maid, the downstairs maid, and the cook with her family. The cook's husband was the chauffeur.

The cook also had a son. He was seven, and I was three. He invited me to go into the cellar. Large cardboard moving boxes crowded the space that smelled of mothballs. He sat me down on a pillow, so I could lean my back against a box. He asked me to take my panties off. Surprised and curious by the request, I did.

He showed me a bag with sandwich bread. He gave me a piece. He opened my legs and then very gently the labia of my genitals. He slid the bread on the satin slippery inside tissue and then ate the bread, as if there were some delicious sauce in there. I just kept my legs open and let him have his satisfaction. He gave me some to taste and finished the bread; I pulled up my underpants and climbed up the stairs back into the kitchen. I didn't mention it to anyone. It only happened once.

Since then, in private, I'd rub myself with a big pillow and surrendered to my ecstasies. I didn't know what other people did. I never told anyone about it. Delight was so simple.

Years later, the nuns told us it was a mortal sin to touch ourselves. I confessed it to the priest every time I went to confession. It was a great relief knowing that now I could go to heaven. But as soon as I started again, I was terrified of dying.

In São Paulo, my mother met Victor, my future Hungarian stepfather, at a party. Her glistening black hair fell over one eye, Veronica Lake style. A red satin silk dirndl skirt was held around her tiny waist and on her naked shoulders slid a white cotton lace blouse. She addressed a group of fascinated guests. She flitted her cigarette ashes into the oval glass ashtray, fanned her bright-red, manicured nails back to her lips, her practiced way, for another puff. She lowered her eyelashes for a moment, as she blew the smoke into a haze. Ensorcelled, everyone waited for the pause in mid-sentence to understand the innuendo with the flash of her eyes. Glasses clinked, laughter splashed. Victor played familiar Cole Porter tunes on the piano. He had high cheekbones on a rectangular, chiseled face with wide set green eyes. His handshake was too fierce for some men, and when his lips brushed a married lady's hand—which, of course having been brought up a Hungarian count, he always did when greeting her—he delved into her eyes with his intense gaze of deep appreciation for her female essence. Some of the ladies almost swooned; others probably wondered what this guy was up to. The hostess was his girlfriend: a crisp, American career woman. Victor kept glancing toward my mother as she told a story in her beguiling way.

"Who is she?" he asked a fellow guest who sat next to him on the piano bench.

"She is a divorcée with a three-year-old girl."

Victor had the broadest shoulders, and his bones were massive and dense. Yet his fingers were nimble on the piano keys. He began to play "*Au clair de la lune*" and "*Frère Jacques*" as if it were a Bach cantata, then switched to a Mozart, and then a Chopin style.

He introduced me first to his mother as a mini-ambassador, taking me to her house for tea. Then, he introduced my mother on a different day. A year later, they were married. Mummy said to me, "We both married Victor." I remember her saying to others, "What a pity no one took a picture of Lilizinha at the wedding."

At first, we moved, into a little house in Granja Julieta, on the outskirts of São Paulo. One day, I overheard my mother say to a friend, "I can keep her under control if I spank her once a month." Each time, she sat me down and explained why she needed to spank me and why it was for my own good.

"You must understand that when I explained to you how the black cook became black, that her people came from Africa, where it is very hot, and this is how their skin got so dark, I didn't want you to tell her." The cook had complained to my mother and threatened to leave. I peed all over my mother. I squirmed, wriggled, screamed, and cried.

Then, the next week, she took me to a ballet performance. Immediately after, I wanted to be a dancer when I grew up.

"Lilizinha watched the Sevillanas dance from the balcony of our little house in Sevilla and then imitated them", she often said.

A Russian ballet teacher was found. My mother accompanied me to the class on the crowded city bus, even though she was pregnant. Mme. Leepolska strutted up and down her dance hall hitting her staff on the wall. She also tapped her students' calves and knees with it. Her demanding, strident voice sent us into tremors. For warm-up, while switching our feet in the fifth position, we jumped to Strauss's "Radetski March" played by a live pianist. She told my mother, "Herr knees arre too weak, and she will neverrr be able to stand on herrr toes."

My mother pulled me out of the lessons, and I began dancing on my own. My stepfather played the piano, and I twirled through the room in my smocked cotton, pale-blue nightgown. I pretended I was close to the stars. I could skip from cloud to cloud, gather the sparks of light in my skirt, and toss them to passersby. I was a tree with branches fluttering in the breeze, some of them drooping and swaying, others jubilantly opening their arms to the cajoling sun, the swelling moon, the rain and thunder too. I became a little sparrow perched for a few instants on my windowsill. In many dreams I flew around the house and my mother couldn't ever catch me.

I was six when my first brother, Alex, came home. To have the privilege of holding him felt very grown up. I was asked to sit comfortably in a white wicker rocking chair with many pillows supporting my arms. Once he was in bed for the night, I knew how to get him to sleep by softly patting him on the back and singing, "*fais dodo mon petit frère, fais dodo, tu auras du gâteau, tu auras du chocolat.*" (sleep my little brother, you'll have some cake, you'll have some chocolate) I had dreams of eating chocolate ice cream and lots and lots of chocolate.

One morning, I noticed my mother had left her red and gold brocade evening purse open on one of the chairs in the living room while she was sleeping. Under her silver cigarette case were neatly folded bills resting on the scarlet satin lining. She called it "mad money." "Always take some, in case you have a fight and need a way to get home."

I felt the slippery softness on one side and the cold steely touch on the other as I slid my small fingers in. I listened and quickly glanced around the room. I clutched the money. A smoky smell of used, thick paper wafted up from my hand. I marched into my room. I hid it under my doll's mattress. "*Sonhos de Valsa*" (Dreams of Waltz) wrapped in their purple-pink aluminum foil and covered with cellophane. A sphere-shaped wafer dipped in milk chocolate mixed with hazelnuts. How would I hide so many wrappings?

When my mother checked her purse, she got frantic. She asked everyone in the house for her money. Both my grandmother and mother chimed, "*Le mieux, c'est dire la verité, on a confiance en toi.*" (To tell the truth is the best prize. You are trustworthy.)

"*Rafaela, voce pegou o dinheiro da minha bolsa*?" (Did you take the money from my purse?) My mother's voice was taut as she tightened the knot of her royal blue, satin dressing gown and retraced her steps of the previous evening.

"*Não senhora, eu não vi o seu dinheiro.*" (No, madam, I did not see your money.) Rafaela came in every morning at seven. She stood wide-eyed and at a loss on the kitchen threshold.

"*Como é que desapareceu*?" (How did it disappear?) Her shrill voice was an accusation.

After long moments of quiet and trembling hesitation, I sputtered the words. I said, "Here, Mummy, here is your money. I took it this morning out of your bag. I wanted to buy chocolates." I held it up to her, my arm and hand shaking.

"*Je te félicite, Lilizinha, d' avoir dit la verité*," my grandmother intervened.

I wasn't spanked that month.

2

"Those who can't laugh at themselves leave the job to others."
—Anonymous

We moved into Higienópolis, a residential section of São Paulo, when I was seven, shortly after my second brother Samson was born. We lived on Rua Alagôas, the same street my aunt and uncle lived on, a few blocks away. I spent days at a time with them. My cousins and I attended the same elementary school. My mother and my aunt made their school choices together, and my aunt and uncle's chauffeur could drop us all off at the same time. My aunt and uncle were richer than my mother and stepfather. The food was better at my aunt's house. There were little thin steaks well done with a lot of fried onions for the children and a different desert every day. Breakfast was always with real butter.

My mother, out of economy and a good sense of nutrition, served lentils and beans and rice, kidneys that smelled of pee in a sherry sauce, or breaded fried brains. For desert, it was bananas or papaya. Her household operated with margarine.

My mother often said that the reason I was sent there was because my cousins were closer to my age. I was happy to go. She was busy with my newborn baby brother. Yet, yearning for my mother was a constant underlying feeling. I got accustomed to the feeling that I wanted her more than she wanted me. I started believing that's what I deserved or needed.

My aunt and uncle's house was a large Victorian house built at the beginning of the century by the gentrified landowners who came to São Paulo, after accumulating enough revenues from crops, to enjoy the luxuries of the city. Wide-rounded marble steps led to the entrance. A columned veranda with a high ceiling and black-and-white diamond tiles reached to a heavy black baroque wrought-iron door coated with thick glass. Every room had a stucco molding in a floral pattern around the high corners and was painted in a pale pastel color.

After breakfast, Petunia and Ogilvy and their youngest brother Malcolm, my younger cousins, and I were herded into the spacious children's bathroom that smelled of freshly laundered towels and bubbly mineral water. My older cousins, Bruce and Margaret, Tanti Lili's children from her first marriage, were exempted from this ritual. We were obliged to sit on our respective potties. I often got to sit on the cemented one. We could only get off after Lela had dutifully wiped our butts.

During that wait, I began entertaining them by telling stories about the inhabitants of my world.

"Sh, sh, sh, sh, sh. You see, when you enter into any one of these shadows from the tree on the wall there, you will see the tiny silver door." They nodded as their gaze seemed

linked to the rhythm of the breeze outside. "I will meet you on the other side. I can take you to a few places I know." I pointed to the swaying shapes. They stared at them, mesmerized by the promises of novelty.

We slipped in and could hear the flowers whistling as they opened their purple, velvet petals.

"You see the little metallic-blue kangaroo creatures emerge?" They beckoned with their eyes; we followed them. They leapt high above us and arrived at an open field of cropped grass. Then, they disappeared into button like holes in the earth. We gaped at each other, puzzled. Out of each of those penetrations, a jabuticaba tree appeared. Just like the one there was in the back garden, with minuscule petrol-green leaves and where the bark was studded full of wine red fruit filled with succulent white jelly. Monkeys lulled themselves from the branches, speaking Portuguese, "Você quer uma jabuticaba doce?" Yorkshire terriers named Tiradentes and Bingo yapped on the surrounding grounds in French. They were my aunt Lili's dogs.

"How did they get here?" Petunia asked

"Mais qu'est-ce vous faites, les enfants? Nous voulons aussi jouer!" (But what are you doing, children? We also want to play!)

"Why are we here? What is all this about?" asked Ogilvy, who in spite of his astonishment, still kept an inquiring mind.

As we walked farther, knotted vines unfurled and stretched themselves out, side by side, like a bridge into some more fields. We ran and smelled lavender everywhere. There were orchards with peaches and plums all so ripe we had to stop and pick some to slurp and savor, until our chins were dripping with sweet juice.

"This is great," exclaimed Ogilvy, as he skipped and rolled himself on the damp, soft, emerald grass. We were so happy we didn't notice, as we pranced, a stone with a life of its own; a pulsation that made us trip and roll into an unexpected gargantuan hole. Bumps and scratches later, in the gloom of this cavernous place we smelled pungent odors of dead carcasses. We stared in horror. "What animals could these be?" Ogilvy said, as he got closer to touch the bone "Don't touch," I cried, horrified that it might be dangerous or dirty. It was too late. The bones slithered and stretched into branches; little pale-green leaves sprouted from its cracks; the main stem sank into the earth. As the plant expanded, greenish-white flowers emerged. They were sweet-scented ladies of the night. Caestrum Nocturnum. Tiny white blossoms in cone clusters danced to the notes of an ethereal lute.

A monstrous belching goat leaning on his hind legs on a perfectly fitting rock played a harp with his front hooves. When he stopped, Ogilvy whispered to me, "I wonder if he can talk, too?"

"Of course, I can. You need to want to express yourself to learn to play an instrument. What do you want to talk about?"

"What is going on? Why are we here?" Petunia asked.

The goat bleated, "To find 'Le Renseignement *(The Revelation).'" We nodded. A succession of Bs at different octaves rang from his strings and brought us right back onto our potties.*

My cousins and I echoed our increasingly frantic cries from our entrenched position. "*Lela, j'ai fini. Leehla, j'aaai fiiini. Leeeehla, j'aai finiiiiii.*" Our voices vibrated through the long, carpeted corridors.

"*Qui a fini*?" (Who's done) asked Lela as she marched onto the blue pentagon tile floor, with folded toilet paper in her hand.

Lela was our big Swiss governess with a determined gait, who loved to knit and bake brioches. She could, simultaneously, read a book and knit a sweater for one of us in less than a week. Her clear blue eyes always had a sparkle of tenderness that could break into a smile if you squeezed her in any way. She took us on innumerable picnics and helped organize delicious birthday parties laden with *brigadeiros,* fudgy chocolate candies. We each had our own can of sweet condensed milk in the refrigerator that we could suck on. At night, she plunked us all together in the same bathtub. As she scrubbed us gently, she told us we were beautiful and wonderful and smart. She allowed us to set the alarm clock for a midnight snack. We were cared for as prized pups.

Yet, I always knew I was the cousin. With these cousins, I felt totally accepted. Petunia was four years younger than I was. We had a constant bond. She was so petite and perfectly beautiful. She was my live doll. We went to guitar lessons together and played for the grown-ups in unison.

Lela spoke to us mostly in French, sometimes in Portuguese or English. She spent time untangling my honey brown hair after it was washed. It was very long. She said in her Swiss accent, "You have beautiful curly hair, Lilizinha." Then she braided a plait on each side. She taught me how to knit and showed me how, with babies, "If you have to take something away from them, at the same time give them something new, and then they won't cry." She made fun of opera, wrinkling her nose and opening her mouth wide to belt out a wild vibrato yodel until we burst with laughter. She was part of our family for years.

My cousins never came over to my mother's house to play or for a meal. They were sent over to play once when my brothers had chicken pox so that they would catch it and get it over with. Petunia, my cousin, says she was amazed at how messy my room was and that it looked like fun. At her house, everything was in place. We went to their house for the important festivities: Christmas, Thanksgiving, and Easter. Those were the times we were allowed to eat with the grown-ups. In both houses, we ate in the separate children's dining–room.

The house where my parents lived was always in reconstruction. There was inevitably a new installation going on: a different window, a new door, tearing down a wall, building an extra bathroom that might give you an electric shock when you turned on the shower, a spiral staircase from the outside terrace down to the patio, making the garage into a bedroom and in front of it a tiny pool covered in Spanish tile.

There were piles of bricks, bags of cement, and messy construction debris. The first time my mother showed me the house was from the inside of a taxicab. "You see?" she said. "It's the little white house, and we are going to fix it up. Isn't it adorable?"

It was a drab, white two-floor townhouse with a flat roof. It was maybe from the art-deco 1920s. My mother transformed it into a house from Sevilla, Spain with wrought-iron windows and gates and antique wood doors.

She and I and her mother had stayed years before in a very similar little house rich with bright red geraniums flowering from the window boxes. It was behind the Giralda in Sevilla. That house was her model. She made pilgrimages to the demolitions of large patrician houses, looking for the perfect piece that fit into her vision. She planted the red geraniums and forgot to water them. The front door was a thick stained-wood gate that spanned the width of a car and was eight feet tall. It had a tiny portal, shoulder high, which allowed one to see who might be at the door without having to let them in.

Many religious paintings of the Cuzqueño schools in the Venezuelan and Peruvian traditions lent a somber formality to the living room: St. Michael, with gold and scarlet wings stabbing a dragon, a Madonna or two with or without the baby, Jesus as a young man sewing his cassock. There also was a nineteenth century European painting of God explaining to Adam about Eve who is sitting there beside him.

I checked my conscience before I approached my mother. Had I written the letter? Had I reminded the maid to change the baby? Had I finished my homework? Had I tidied my room? I had to guard myself because she inevitably found something I had done wrong or needed to do differently. Or else she said, "You look green around the gills; you need to go wash your face." And I would dutifully go.

After a while, maybe I got too big for my mother to handle. I remember Victor holding his discolored suede slipper, slapping me all over. I can still feel the warm pee running down my legs and filling me with embarrassment. I squirmed and cried and wriggled powerlessly at age seven. I don't remember what I did wrong. At other times, I overheard my brothers being beaten by their father in the garage. Nothing was ever said.

3

"I have never been interested in any power except my own power in the theatre."
—John Gielgud

At my Tanti Lili's house, I read all the Tintin books aloud to my cousins, and we put on plays that I directed. In the mornings, before school, my cousins ran into my uncle's dressing room; he picked them up in his arms, hugged and kissed them, talked and joked with them. I stood in the doorway not daring to enter the room. My uncle shyly said hello to me from a distance.

He was a tall elegant man, impeccably dressed in a business gray, gabardine three-piece suit with a pale pinstripe and a homburg hat when he went out. His dressing room smelled of lemony aftershave mixed with fresh coffee. Early in the morning, he had on his navy blue silk dressing gown over his freshly ironed pants and shirt, his fine hair slickly combed back, and was usually having his first tiny cup of coffee, brought to him on a silver tray by the upstairs maid dressed in her morning uniform in pale pink cotton with a white starched apron. Sipping his *cafezinho*, he always held his body in a very erect posture, as if the admiral were about to march by.

He wrote lists and kept them in every room, taped to the inside of a closet door. They informed the servants where to place certain objects and how things worked.

I sometimes ventured into his impeccable library, a spacious room with French doors out to a private garden. Here the New Yorker magazines were piled in rows, on a slant, like fish scales, covering the surface of the square coffee table. I loved to leaf through them and try and figure out the jokes. I couldn't. On the sidewall were shelves filled with books. Among the mahogany brown leather bound ones, there were some with no embossed titles. I opened one to examine it. It stated the names of slaves and families that uncle Ogilvy's great grandfather had owned before the civil war in Virginia. It mentioned which slaves were then sold, to whom, and the price. I felt such a dizzy feeling that I never went back to explore them again.

Uncle Ogilvy's strides were perfectly measured. His sonorous voice had a touch of amusement. He taught us how to sing old Western country songs, mostly about little old ladies who ended up in ridiculous positions. He had grown up in Marshall, Texas. Photographs and etchings, portraits of six generations, beginning with his father at the bottom, then grandfather, and up through time, hung in a tidy column on a wall of his dressing room. Each one looked more regal than the next. They all had the same nose, turned up like a glorious trumpet.

A mysterious cloud shaded the ancestors' photographs. Hovering was a rumor his father had killed himself when he lost all his money after the 1929 stock market crash.

I must have overheard it in some adult conversation. I never saw my uncle sad. He seemed sure of where he was going. Sometimes I ventured in to give him a little peck on the cheek. He responded with a tidy double pat on my shoulder.

"Good morning, Lilizinha," he said, in his more formal tone.

If I had thoughts about my own absent father, they were very private or just below my conscious awareness. I knew he was rich and handsome and was traveling with another wife. I had the memory of only one picture of him with a radiant smile. He wrote me an occasional letter in printed words and very short sentences. Sometimes it included a twenty dollars check for a Christmas or birthday present. I never questioned his absence at that time. I never discussed my father or stepfather with my cousins. My moments of awkwardness or confusion were very private. I didn't think anyone was interested in them, except my invisible friend, Nanny Preta. She returned in a dream, dressed in white, held my hand, and asked me if we could play together. She wasn't a rag doll anymore. She was a beautiful milk-chocolate skin-color girl with yellow bows in her braids and large brown eyes. When I felt misunderstood or falsely accused, I hid in a room or bathroom and cried, pulled my hair until it hurt, and banged my head against the wall. I could hear her soothing voice inside my heart. She was about my age. She wanted me to understand it from a different point of view.

"You can't expect him to hug you as if you were his child."

"Who are you?" I asked, trying to check if she was the same one from my dream.

“I am another part of you. I’m right here, with you. Call me Joan.”

“I can still wish for that kind of hug.”

“You are Lili Luar. You are wrapped by the moonlight, until the right person comes along.”

She spoke English, French, Portuguese, and Spanish. She could switch in midsentence, as we all did. To hear her softened the jagged moments.

After school, we were taken swimming, riding, or to play guitar or tennis. Then back to their house for tea. A little time was assigned for homework, and then it was bath time before dinner. My cousins changed into their fresh pajamas, beautiful dressing gowns, and red leather slippers from Best & Co. Often, if I was going to be picked up later to go home, or even if I wasn’t, I changed back into my same clothes of the day. There were differences between us, yet my grandmother was a unifying presence.

There were two official guest rooms downstairs. In one, my grandmother, Marie Thérèse, stayed. She alternated her time between Venezuela, where her son lived, and Brazil. When she arrived just before Christmas there was a flurry of excitement: I heard my mother and my aunt say in a sing-song: “*Oye, trajo ayacas. Ai! Que delicia que trajo ayacas!*” they all huddled at tea time and savored the cornmeal mush with vegetables and meat wrapped in banana leaves as if it were chocolate ice cream. I tasted them once. It wasn’t my favorite.

On our way to the children’s dining room, we could see my grandmother through the slightly open door, sitting at her dressing table, her head hanging down over her knees, brushing her long gray silver hair. She brushed it endlessly every morning and evening.

"By brushing the scalp oils into the hair one hundred times in the morning and in the evening, the hair shines." she said in French, when we stepped in to greet her.

My grandmother made a large knot at the base of her neck. She wore sensible shoes and comfortable tweed or seersucker suits, depending on the temperature. Once, while walking through the park with her, on our way to church, I suddenly noticed she gingerly stepped out of her underpants. There was a tidy crumpled pile of skin-colored silk on the cement ground. The elastic threaded through the waistband must have broken. She walked on nonchalantly, as if they weren't hers. When she needed to go to the bathroom she said: "*Je vais chez ma tante.*" (I'm going to my aunt's house.) My grandmother only spoke to us in French, although she was Venezuelan, and only responded to us when we replied in French "*En Français*," she repeated tirelessly.

I stared at her horn-rimmed glasses, her amused eyes behind them, silver hair, and rounded powdered nose with one drop of water about to drip off her nostril as I struggled to find the right word. Just in time, she wiped her nose with a handkerchief. As soon as I uttered a half-baked sentence, she smiled and corrected me. Slowly our French improved. At night, she showed me how to wash my handkerchief and then spread it wet on the bath-tiled wall so by morning it would be dry and ironed flat by the stretch on the flat surface.

When we didn't want to eat our food, she hovered her right hand over our plates rubbing the bottom of her signet ring with her thumb and saying, "*Voici la petite poudre qui le rendra delicieux*" (Here is the little powder that will make it delicious.) I remember bending my neck to look under her hand. Where was this powder? When I sampled the food again, it tasted better.

In between meals, when she wasn't at her book-binding lessons, she was in the kitchen teaching one of the maids how to read. She spoke every language with a French accent. She was educated in England and mostly in France. Her father owned ships, four of which he named after his daughters, Mercedes, Theodora, Maria Theresa, and Josita. For several years, while he disagreed with the Venezuelan government in power who confiscated vast stretches of his land, he moved his family to Neuilly-sur-Seine, where his wife had grown up. We heard about those confiscated *terrenos* all our formative years. There were many lawsuits powered by many dreams. He delivered his girls to the convent of the Holy Child together with their bags of rice and beans. The Order of the Holy Child had schools in France, England, and the United States. He had to make a special request that they be allowed to bathe daily in hot water. My grandmother was one of the first women to drive a car in Caracas. She told the story that her chaperone had to raise her voice while she was playing tennis. "Marie Thérèse, *ne courez pas tellement, on voit vos chevilles*!"(Don't run so much; your ankles can be seen!)

I heard all four daughters had to elope to get married because their father never thought any of their suitors was good enough. I was named after my grandmother and nicknamed after my aunt. My grandmother created a system to teach people how to read and write. In 1926, she proposed her method to the first radio station and to newspapers. The newspaper could publish a new lesson every day, and she could teach the lesson over the radio. They told her they didn't want so many people reading and writing.

When she and my mother argued she would say, "*Je me sens touroulata, touroulata, touroulata,*" and sometimes faint. My mother rushed into my room pleading, "Lilizinha, get a glass of buttermilk; we were having a discussion, and now she is lying on the bed, and she won't talk."

Grandmaman, as we called her, often said to us, her grandchildren, when she heard us interacting among ourselves, "Nobody will understand you because you don't speak any one language. You're mixing them all up." We didn't care because we understood each other.

She taught me how to read and write before I got to first grade; I was first in the class. In second grade, I was twenty-eighth in the class because I didn't understand about having to make an effort.

My grandmother spent a lot of time encouraging me to memorize and dramatize many songs and the "*Fables de la Fontaine.*" She had a strong influence on me, as did Tanti Fargo.

Tanti Fargo stayed in the other guest room. She came after her divorce and lived a long time in Uncle Ogilvy's house until she got her little apartment. There was a running legend about her. Uncle Ogilvy, her brother, loved to tell us the story of how she was born with two heads. These two heads argued so much, their mother had to have one cut off. This explained why Tanti Fargo always wore a scarf around her neck. I remember eyeing her neck as closely as I could, to see where the scar could be. She was often sighted mumbling to herself. She didn't notice people were watching her, and she'd become quite emphatic, waving her hand like a flapping wing, attempting to convey a point. Yet, who ever she was arguing with was invisible to us.

She gave us implicit permission to have a passionate internal dialogue with ourselves. Tanti Fargo had a way to let you know she understood what was going on by winking with her right eye while making a noise sucking her saliva with her back teeth, as if she were egging on a horse. She had been an excellent horsewoman in her youth in Marshall, Texas. She also lifted her right shoulder all in the same rhythm. She alternated the horsy sound with a, "heh, heh, huh." It was a riveting experience every time.

She was one of the few in that group of women who went to college and the only one I know who had gone to therapy after her marriage collapsed. She had a boyfriend or two. It was never obvious who he was. She held a job in a paint company that belonged to a friend of Uncle Ogilvy's. She was often at Tanti Lili's five o'clock teatime. Mostly familiar ladies, including my mother, dropped by, and their husbands or boyfriends came to pick them up after work. Somebody always said, "It's after six," and they all laughed. My stepfather, with a big grin on his face, rubbed his palms, sliding them up and down at great speed, he was so thrilled. "Let's have a drrink!" They switched to dry martinis, which I learned to make very well by observing and rarely being allowed to mix. The opportunity to have a little taste of gin on my fingers and also a bit of Cinzano dry vermouth. Why not?

Tanti Fargo never had children. She chatted with all the ladies and was well informed. She had an educated bite to her statements, which could be interpreted as edging on the supercilious. She told me once: "I wanted Ogilvy to include me with his friends. I wanted to be like him, not pushed away like the annoying little sister."

The ladies shared tidbits, gossip, and their discoveries about the children.

Tanti Fargo also wanted to be up to date about the children at these gatherings. She diligently asked us many questions. What did we like about our school? Which teachers were our favorites and why? What did we like best to do? Who were our friends? What were we reading? We sometimes thought she was "nosy." She wanted the most thorough report on any one person in the family. Yet, when she died, I realized she also helped us define ourselves, as we had to articulate our experience. She was great to talk to because she really listened. I always felt she was standing in my shoes while I explained something to her. She accepted me. Even though she had a horsy kind of manner, she was elegantly dressed and a great model for me, a combination of femininity and internal independence.

Although my mother commented, "Fargo walks as if she just got off the horse," and showed us all how to walk gracefully, like a model, Tanti Fargo never changed. She never followed my mother's rules. I loved her for that.

We threw her ashes into the sea off the coast of Northern Massachusetts, because my cousin Ogilvy has a house and a boat by the sea up there. Her ashes floated away together on the surface of the sapphire-blue ocean, a wafting ghost taking its time to dissolve. At her service, several people were forthcoming as to how Tanti Fargo helped them with either emotional or financial support to get through school or through life. She has become bigger and more important by her absence.

After Lela, there was a sequence of governesses. I befriended most of them. They listened and were playful with me. I felt included.

Petunia often said to me at the table: "*Se come pra mim*?" (Will you eat it for me?) She didn't like food. We sat side by side. I was thrilled with the food there. It was either the seasoning or the greener grass. I'd eat it for her. When nobody was looking, she grabbed the food with the napkin and passed it to me under the table. She was forced to stay there until she finished her food. Once she threw up, and one of the governesses made her eat it again. I wanted to protect her.

There were many games: "Maria Cristina;" "*Mamãe e Papai*;" "Cowboys and Indians;" or "*Cidade*," which was a town we built in the sand, next to my aunt and uncle's beach house on Praia Pernambuco. Big square holes were covered with palm leaves and paths connecting them. I was the mother, Ogilvy the father, Petunia and Malcolm the children. Malcolm was the one assigned to go to the kitchen to get bread so we could eat. He was the small one with white blond hair and watery blue eyes. We used his cuteness as a lock -pick on the maids, who always said yes to him. We also played in a tiny, white wooden playhouse with bottle-green shutters in the back garden of the house in the city. There, all invented dramas were played out. Mostly the worry was if one of the children got sick. Then, we had to call a doctor. Ogilvy would double up as the doctor while the father was away at work.

If ever there was a complaint about what the children were doing, that we hadn't obeyed the governess, that we'd taken too much food between meals, if anything went wrong, I was accused as the instigator. Tanti Lili called me a hypocrite when I denied it.

"You are so sweet when your mother comes around. But I know you. I have a mean streak in me. Nobody fools me," she said. In private, I prayed to somebody invisible: "help me show her I wasn't the sole cause of the trouble."

I did help them steal food from the kitchen, and I did help organize a rebellion against one of the governesses. Miss Elizabeth was from Iraq. She always had a cigarette in her mouth and an ashtray in her hand. A rancid smell wafted around her. Tanti Lili announced one evening at dinner that she was placing two large deodorants for everyone to use after the bath. We, the children, chuckled because we knew she meant Miss Elizabeth. At the summerhouse, she limited our expeditions to the beach because she was terrified of the ocean. I tried taking walks with her to familiarize her with it. It didn't work. Before, we had often been allowed to go to the beach and I'd watch over my cousins. I was a good swimmer. They often called me, teasing, "*Mme. La Gouvernante*." I didn't like it, although I guess I got pretty bossy sometimes. To this day Malcolm says I was the one who taught him how to make a bed. I don't know how useful that has been for him. Miss Elizabeth had short, black curly hair, a strident voice, and beady black eyes. One day we locked her in one of the bathrooms from the outside and took off to the seashore. It was a joint plan. Miss Elizabeth resigned.

Sometimes we got up at dawn and walked down to the low-tide beach where the first rays were dipping themselves in the sea. Glistening sand and gurgling waves greeted the daylight. The clean scent of the ocean breezed through our hair. We felt part of the village when we could help pull in the soggy, prickly, seaweed-smelling rope. Heavy twine was attached to the fishermen's net they had laid way out into the ocean the evening before. Whoever helped pull in the net got a free fish. There were lots of people from the villages nearby pulling it in with us. It was a satisfaction for each of us to come back with a fish in hand. My Tanti Lili was thrilled. We felt so powerful, to be able to feed the family, just by being in the right place at the right time. Maybe because my Tanti Lili was so petite and radiated so much contentment when we contributed in any way, we wanted to please her. She could be critical and bossy, especially when she insisted we pull out from the grass a boxful of weeds before a meal.

In the photographs, as a young girl, she was a perfect porcelain doll with blond curls. She had smooth legs and fine ankles. My mother, five years younger, always felt a twinge of jealousy. My grandmother was told when my mother was a baby that she would not live beyond the age of seven because of liver problems. Maybe my grandmother didn't get so emotionally involved with my mother, from the start, for fear of losing her. My mother, therefore, needed her that much more.

"I was the ugly one with the straight black hair, big teeth, and the enormous forehead. Lili was always shielded from what was going on. Our father died. It was during the Depression. We had no money," Mummy told me. "For a time, Grandmaman was living and working in a dingy rooming house on the West Side, trying to find a job."

"*Ne dit rien a Lili,*" (don't say anything to Lili) my grandmother said to my mother. My mother continued: "Lili was at boarding school, and Tanti Josita, my grandmother's sister, took care of her during the holidays. She took care of both of us. But I was the one who, at fifteen, came to New York at Easter to see my mother. Upon finding her in such drab surroundings, I decided to drop out of school, get a job modeling, and find a nice little apartment on the Upper East Side. I took care of Grandmaman," my mother emphatically reminded me. "We had no phone. There was one down the hall. When one of my beaus called, and a girl from another apartment picked it up, I said, if he asked, she was my visiting cousin." My mother filled me in on the details of her childhood. I asked her to tell me the story of her life.

"I was born with a 'bad liver,' "she noted. "Tanti Josita insisted on taking me to France every year to drink the waters at Vichy. It was thanks to her that we both came out in the Tuxedo Park Debutante Ball. My mother became more energetic, as she spoke with indignation. "Tanti Lili has had it much easier than I did."

Tanti Lili didn't participate in any of our activities. The station wagon picked us up at school late, when she and my mother had been doing errands. She was mostly busy with arranging her house, her social life, and probably some charity. She had her breakfast brought to her bed late every morning. Some mornings we were allowed into her room to greet her. We each kissed her on both cheeks. She sat in bed in a dainty petal-pink bed jacket with a droopy yet freshly ironed satin bow around her shoulders. Her Limoges breakfast set and a pink and yellow rose were placed on her white wicker H-shaped bed tray. She smoked incessantly and inhaled the smoke with great vigor, opening her mouth wide as if to make sure she got every last bit of it. A collection of tiny antique baroque angels hung above her bed. Two graceful photographs, one of my mother and another of my grandmother, hung on the sidewalls. Two closets, one on each far corner, had narrow doors and thirteen shelves, each with a different candy-coated color set of high heel simple pumps.

She liked to decorate rooms and paint ceramics. We ate on plates painted with fish and corals and plants. There were little bluefish with smiles and big brown fish with frowns. She had her workshop over the garage, and her friends could come and paint with her.

When I was sick, a governess threw an antibiotic down my throat because I could not swallow it. She aimed very well. I opened my mouth wide, exposed my throat as if I wanted to sing from my belly, and she tossed it in and let the sip of water do the rest.

I remember my mother showing up. “Ooo, ooo, ooo, darling, how are you? You look pale and still feel hot,” she said as she patted me on the forehead and in the curve of my neck. “You have to perspire the fever away.” When I had a temperature, I was never worried that she might criticize me. She lifted the covers up to my neck, tucked me in tightly, and asked me to sleep. A few times she read to me either *Alice in Wonderland* or about Joan of Arc from Tanti Lili’s Encyclopedia Britannica. She kissed me on the cheek and left. I yearned for her to stay longer.

4

There is a vitality, a life force, an energy, a quickening that is translated through you into action, and because there is only one of you in all time, this expression is unique. And if you block it, it will never exist through any other medium and will be lost.
—Martha Graham

When I was eight, surges of passion and longing overtook me sometimes. My heart raced, my arms felt driven to hold someone. I embraced my bent knees while I sat on a green garden chair. My bones buzzed. Sounds of "oouuh" and "aaaaaoooh" would ooze out of me. I had the much older, lanky Brazilian neighbor, Sergio, in mind. He flirted with my baby brother's babysitter and had no idea what was happening to me. My cousin Petunia was the only one who witnessed these "*crises d'amour*."

Surprised, she asked me, "Lili, what are you doing?"

"I'm hugging, the neighbor. Oooohhh," I moaned as I squeezed my knees with my arms wrapped around them. "But you can't tell anybody I do this," I added as

I recomposed myself. Petunia chuckled in amusement at the power of her knowledge.

When my mother came to visit, and we had a moment alone, and I could say, "Mummy, *j'ai une crise d'amour.* Oouuhh!" She took me in her arms and would echo, "*Ooooh, une crise d'amour.*' "Then, my passion was for her.

I remember my mother saying, when I was eight, "Lilizinha, you cannot climb all over gentlemen when they come to the house. A young lady doesn't do that, "*ça ne se fait pas. Ce n'est pas comme il faut.*" (It isn't done. It isn't as it must be.) Her words and tone felt sharp and cold. I had committed a mortal sin. I felt so much sticky shame.

I was putting her in an awkward position. I must have longed for physical contact. If the gentleman was older or full of self-importance, it didn't even occur to me to get close. Yet, when they were younger, more relaxed, and easygoing, it felt safe to jump on their laps or ask them to carry me on their shoulders. I wanted to play.

"You must curtsy to any adult who is of our class," she ordered. She demonstrated exactly how to put one foot behind the other and ever so slightly genuflect in a very swift upbeat movement while holding the adult's hand and greeting that person. I did, until I was eighteen. It became automatic.

Grown-ups had very strong odors. My mother, when she awoke in the morning, had a decayed smell. Children had a powdery scent when they woke up; unless they had a dirty diaper or thrown-up milk. The scent that I liked was of certain blankets. Some of these I could cuddle with and suck my thumb, while I smelled a piece of blanket.

Grandmaman had a clean fragrance wrapped around her. My stepfather had a stench of cigarettes, sometimes mixed with whatever he had been drinking.

My parents were my mother and stepfather. My older cousins and I were the only ones I knew whose parents were divorced. Everyone else had their mothers and fathers living with them. I felt embarrassed about being slightly substandard. Nobody knew my father.

My father was living in Bermuda and later in Ft. Lauderdale, where he died. I was his only child, supposedly. After he died, I heard he'd had an affair with a married woman, before he married my mother. She became pregnant. He gave the husband money to adopt the child. No one would tell me who that was.

He never came to visit or seek me out. I only wondered why much later. Maybe he was angry with my mother. They wrote curt letters to each other about money. "Money doesn't grow on trees, you know," he wrote more than once. He had calculated what I needed as a one-year-old baby: $150 a month. He never increased the amount; my mother had to make due.

He traveled a lot with his other wives. He sent me postcards written in crisp tiny print. As a child, that seemed all right to me because that's the way it was. My mother made a point of taking me to the United States three times to meet him. The first time, I was ten. We arrived in New York City and stayed at the Lowell Hotel. He called, and I picked up the phone:

"Is that you, Lili?" he said.

"Is that you, Daddy?" I replied, savoring with gusto the fact that I was saying the word "Daddy" to the right person, for the first time. One of my favorite books at the time was *Daddy Long Legs*. In it, the heroine shares her feelings through letters with her adopted father/benefactor whom she never meets in person until the end of the book.

I clearly remember the lightness in my stomach as I climbed those steps. It was 1958. The first time I saw him was at the Palm Court of the Plaza Hotel in New York City. He was very tall. He smiled. I was dressed in a black watch-plaid skirt, vest over a white blouse, and shoes covered in the same fabric.

Daddy was there with his third wife, Audrey. She had a pearly-gray mink stole around her shoulders and dyed platinum blonde hair. She spoke with a high-pitched voice. All the grown-ups chatted among themselves, while sipping dry martinis. The violins played their dusty tunes. The ceiling was so high with its luminous stained-glass skylight, the palms so languorous. I wondered if any one of the grown-ups was jealous of the other. That night he took me to dinner at Trader Vic's and then to see *The Secret Life of Walter Mitty*, a Danny Kaye film. Daddy laughed a lot. I didn't get why.

That same year, I traveled with him and his wife on his seventy-two-foot yacht, *Saggitaur*, down the inland waterway from Baltimore to Jacksonville, Florida. He was moving from Bermuda to Ft. Lauderdale. There was a captain on board and two maids. We saw lots of spooky hanging moss on massive overhanging trees along the shoreline and many soggy rice fields, as far as the eye could see.

I had a stateroom to myself. The closet was filled with my stepmother's different mink jackets and coats. I got seasick for the first time. It gave me a few days of respite from the homework I didn't want to do. I was missing months of school to be on this trip. My mother said there were many ways of learning, not only in school. I played a lot with Barbie dolls given to me by my stepmother, and the maids made a lot of new clothes for them. I watched the other boats from the top deck, with my father.

It was during that visit, when we were alone, over the only banana split I have ever attempted to eat, that he voiced with a nostalgic gaze: "You have your mother's big brown eyes." He had never talked to me before about his feelings. It was the first time I felt his heavy heart. He was still in love with my mother. I felt sad they weren't together any more. I knew he and my stepmother slept in separate staterooms. I felt an abyss of powerlessness. I tried mixing the chocolate ice cream with the whipped cream but it all seemed too much.

My mother left him when I was one. I failed at saving the marriage by being a girl. My mother's obstetrician had assured her she was carrying a boy. When I was brought to her, after the birth, she shrieked in horror.

"Take that girl back. That's not my boy. I want my little boy! Where is my little boy?" The room was filled with pink carnations by my grandmother who had to convince my mother that I was her baby. When my mother confronted her doctor:" How could you lie to me? I trusted you."

"Fifty percent of the time I'm correct and my patients think I'm a genius, the other fifty percent think I'm a kook." He replied, impervious to the disappointment of the mother and the rejection the child might absorb.

I don't know if my father was aware of any of that. I just know he said, as I slid the ice cream with the plastic spoon into little valleys on my plate. "I hated my mother." "She dressed me as a girl until the age of seven." He was her only child. She had him at age forty-five.

After a few bites, the banana tasted too slippery. It was hard to listen to the story and eat. Daddy continued: "Father was like her puppy dog. Her boudoir was so crowded, it was like Grand Central Station. She always arrived wherever I was with my tuxedo, so I could dress for dinner. I just wanted to be a regular guy."

He had graduated from St. Paul's and from Harvard. As an adult, Daddy only read the *New York Times* and *Reader's Digest* books and magazines. He played tennis and drank many very dry martinis with tiny pickled onions cradled at the bottom of the glass. He spent hours looking for old vintage coins; he sat at a card table by his pool and, with a magnifying glass, studied penny after penny to find the ancient one. He liked to fish.

When we were about to check out at a supermarket, he avoided the registers that were manned by African Americans.

As we stepped out onto the sidewalk, he spoke in a muffled tone, so only I could hear: "I hate Jews and Blacks. They talk and smell funny. Have you noticed?" I shook my head in silence. I was confounded and embarrassed.

When I was thirteen, the second time I saw him, he picked me up from the airport in Miami with Audrey. Our first stop on the way to his house in Ft. Lauderdale was a bar.

While we were waiting for the order to come in a well-shaded booth, he asked me, "Do you know what necking is?"

I'd never heard the word before.

"It's what a girl and a boy do when they hug and kiss in quiet places." He giggled in an uncomfortable way. I didn't understand why he wanted to make sure I knew that.

"What do you think of Ft. Lauderdale?" he asked me as we approached his house.

"Too clean; everything looks too clean," I replied as I smelled the leather upholstery of his car.

When he gave me a watch I didn't particularly like, I embraced him as a girl and as the woman that I could imagine myself to be. He was the only one I could allow myself to pretend about in silence. I treasured the gift that was from him.

One morning, I sneaked into his bedroom while he wasn't there. The bed was unmade. I smelled his pillow. It had a musty scent of sleep and lime. I wiped off the little curly hairs abandoned on his sheet and stretched out the top sheet. I never told him.

Toward the end of that stay, after I asked him a lot of questions to which he did not always reply, he said to me in a solemn way, while driving his Mercedes Benz, "I am a low-brow, and you are a high-brow." I didn't understand. Sometimes he said: "Hey, Brazil nut, you're my Brazil nut," as he chuckled with a twinkly smile and put his arm around my shoulders for a few seconds. "Do you live in a mud hut? Ha, ha. Ha." I stared dumfounded.

Three years later, I saw him for the third time. I was wearing a rose pink Pringle of Scotland lamb's wool knitted matching skirt, and sweater. In an elegant restaurant on the Long Island North Shore, over a lobster Newburg, he said, looking straight at me, "I wish you weren't my daughter, so I could fuck you."

Shocked into silence, a part of me was flattered, and a part of me was sad. It was an initiation into womanhood and a loss of a protective father.

When I was seventeen, I was living again in New York City. While he was driving me around the city, I mentioned I would like a car and a college education. His response was, "I'm not sure I am your father."

I reeled inside into a confused spin. At that moment, I wasn't even aware of what those feelings were. I felt extremely uncomfortable and unsure of myself. A frozen geode of silence. Who did I belong to? Who had been my father? Was this his cheap way of avoiding the cost? I never questioned him further on the subject. My father did support me very minimally and gave me away at my first marriage. My husband and I moved from New York to Madrid. He came to visit me once.

When he came to Madrid, because he often spoke with sexual innuendos, I felt free to ask him which books spoke of sex. He sent me a box of erotic literature: *Lolita*, *Candy*, *The Tropic of Cancer*, *The Tropic of Capricorn*, *Lady Chatterley's Lover*. I only read *Lolita* and *Candy*.

I was twenty-two when he died. He was brushing his teeth one morning after having gone dancing the night before. His wife went to the kitchen to prepare breakfast. She wondered why he was taking so long to join her. She found him dead on the bathroom floor. He had had a massive heart attack. The doctor said he was dead before he hit the floor. She called me in Madrid.

We arrived the next day for the service. Alone, I sobbed, wishing I had asked him more questions.

That night, after we cast off his ashes into the Atlantic, I spent time with my stepsister. She was my stepmother's daughter from her previous marriage. We had developed a gentle friendship during the prior few years. Her mind and her features were handsomely chiseled. She confronted her mother fearlessly on many issues, and her mother always remained calm as she retorted her points of view. It was a lesson for me to watch them.

After my stepmother went to bed, I explained to my stepsister about the séances we had attended in Spain. She was willing to try it. We sat around a three-legged table. We placed the tips of our fingers on top of the table with our little fingers and thumbs touching. I made sure there was no one tipping the table with their knees. We meditated and asked for a spirit to come and identify him or herself. One did. One leg of the table lifted and dropped. Each time it did, we voiced a letter of the alphabet out loud in alphabetical order. Then, it came to a full stop. The table spelled out Warren, my father's name. We asked him if he had any message. He said, "Yes, for Lili." When we asked him what the message was, the table spelled out, "I love you." He also left me a smidgeon of financial freedom.

As I understood how our experiences with our parents predispose us to be attracted to boyfriends or husbands who can provide similar experiences, I decided to imagine a different story had happened with my father.

I wanted a relationship with a man who could be understanding and caring; a man with whom I felt a shared priority of values. Instead of trying to transform the man I was seeing, I changed the story about my father: I meet my father before he dies. I imagine him loving to spend time with me. He talks to me. He takes me out for a meal or to the theater, movies, or to a museum. I imagine he comes to Brazil several times to check out how I am doing as I am growing up. We walk down a sunny street and stop at a bookstore to browse and read little bits of borrowed pages to lighten our day. We sit. He orders a coffee; I have lemonade. We comment effortlessly on what we have read. He loves to talk about his favorite authors and how he learns from them.

We often take long walks in the rain on a beach, or even in a blizzard in New York. I candidly share my experiences. Some shock him, and some move him. Sometimes in Florida along the beach, we sit at the edge of the sand with the water and observe the little curves of the bubbly waves.

He often comes into my room, sits on my bed, and asks me questions. What do I need? He wants to know. He often allows me to sit on his lap and lay my head on his chest. I follow the rhythm of his heaving lungs mixed with the beat of his steady heart. He sings me a song, and I can feel his breath travel through his vibrant vocal chords and pour out a light from his heart. I know my father is a man who understands the ephemeral and ineffable nature of the present moment and is willing to savor it. I ask him questions: What were the ten most important discoveries he made in his life, and why were they so pivotal? What did you value the most when you first went away to school? How did those values change when you went to college? What scared you the most when you graduated? Why did you decide to marry your first wife? And your second, my mother, your third and fourth? What in a woman do you cherish the most? What was the most important conversation you had with yourself? And how did it reflect into changes in your choices or your values, if at all? Did you think about what you really wanted to accomplish or contribute before you died? I listened. I heard and savored his soothing tone of voice and clearly well chosen words. They nourished me in unseen ways.

5

I merely took the energy it takes to
pout and wrote some blues.
—Duke Ellington

Once, while I played dolls with Margaret, my eldest cousin, in her bedroom, she rolled her pupils into the sockets of her eyes and breathed heavily, slithered her twisted body all over the bed, tumbled onto the floor, advancing toward me, contorting her salivating mouth. There was a rank smell in the room. Her disfigured features froze; I yelled. The house was too big to be heard. I rushed to the door and struggled to twist the slippery knob. I couldn't open it. I banged on the door, my heart thumping. When the governess opened the door to announce a meal, Margaret's demeanor was completely normal, fitting a dress onto a doll and asking me in a matter-of-fact tone of voice, "Do you like this pink one or the yellow one better?"

She was jealous, because the governess spent more time with me untangling my long hair and complimenting me on it.

On one occasion, Margaret began repeating to me in a whining teasing tone, “Your mother is thirty-three. Hee, hee, hee, hee.”

“No,” I said. “She’s twenty-nine, that’s what she told me.”

“She is not; she is thirty-three. She is thirty-three. That’s what my mother said,” searing her brown eyes, framed by straight brown hair, into my brain. I bustled down the stairs. She followed me, repeating in a nasal staccato, “She’s thirty-three; she’s thirty-three.”

It was tea-time in Tanti Lili’s pale yellow with purple stripes damask-upholstered sitting room. Gold taffeta curtains framed the windows down to the carpeted floor. There was an antique desk, yellow roses, and a steaming silver tea set with watercress sandwiches and cinnamon toast presented on a gleaming tray fitted with a starched white lace doily. I approached my mother, eyeing the goodies, hoping we’d get offered some, and asked her. “Mummy, isn’t it true that you are twenty-nine?”

My aunt was right there, so my mother had to admit, “No, darling, it’s a little white lie. I thought you liked me better younger. I am thirty-three.”

The truth was that she was older than my stepfather, and she didn’t want me to repeat that. I couldn’t speak. I felt betrayed. Could I ever trust her? I ran out of the room and hid in a bathroom and sobbed. I reverted to talking to Joan, my invisible friend, and hearing what she had to say.

On the weekends we were often picked up from school and driven directly to my aunt and uncle’s beach house on Pernambuco Beach. There, I could take off for a walk alone on the beach either at dawn or in the late afternoon.

It was a refuge, a sanctuary, a way to feel transparent, as if I belonged to all the colors and shapes I could see, all the whispers I could hear. I found a sharp stick and wrote on the very edge where the sand was soggy enough to indent the mark and close enough to the next stretched out fan of smoothing water, so the sign dissolved into the shiny surface of the sand. I wrote over and over again these words in large capital letters. Was Joan whispering them to me?

"HUMANITY IS A WILD BEAST THAT NEEDS TO BE DOMESTICATED." As the foam came over it and I watched the letters slowly disappear, I wrote again with great conviction.

"HUMANITY IS A WILD BEAST THAT NEEDS TO BE DOMESTICATED." I stared at the words and wondered what this phrase meant and why was I driven to write it out on the wet sand. Then I skipped a little further up the beach enjoying the coppery rays on the shallow waves.

It was my secret. I ran back through the rustling palms. Later, I dismissed it as child's play.

6

"There is nothing either good or bad,
but thinking makes it so".
– Shakespeare, Hamlet, (Act II, Scene II).

Subjected to another "I'm the only one who is right" tirade, I was sent to my room. I pulled my own hair out on purpose when I banged my head on the wall. I wanted to scream but always kept silent.

"You like feeling sorry for yourself. You are a spoiled, ungrateful little girl."

I pretended I wasn't there. I observed her strident voice as part of the lights and shadows of the room, the funny shapes her lips would make. I saw her bottom lip as if it were her top one and the top one as the bottom one. My mother seemed to be speaking a foreign language I didn't understand.

"Why do you just stand there and stare at me? Why don't you say something?" she yelled, after a pause.

In her presence, I had nothing to say. My mind was a blank. The stretch of my scalp, the thumps on the wall, the pain let me know I was there. It provided relief.

Another moment of respite was tending to the red geraniums in the window box under my bathroom window in my mother's house. I watered them every day and peeled off the dead stems and leaves. The plants thrived and flowered over and over again. They even sprouted new plants if a thicker stem was simply stuck in the earth and watered. A few times I watered my mother's geraniums. It was a much bigger job. I took pride that mine were thriving and hers were dry.

One afternoon my mother arrived with five large boxes of books.

"Look what I found at a bargain price from the American who is leaving Brazil!" She pulled out one of the heavy majestic tomes of deep blue faux leather embossed in gold letters on the spine. She presented me with our own Encyclopedia Britannica.

"It is a great source of information since I had such a limited education. But I got a lot of stimulus from all the travelling with Tanti Jo. Everything about anything is in here."

She opened, as if it were a box of treasures, the Jerez to LIBE, book 13. She showed me how to alphabetically find, in this case, Joan of Arc. With fervor she read aloud to me about this young girl who heard voices of angels. They said her mission was to save France. "Go to the Dauphin, have him crowned King of France."

Inspired and determined to the point that she convinced others to follow her, she managed to have the King crowned in the cathedral of Reims. All this she accomplished in spite of being an illiterate shepherdess from Domremi.

France and England had been at war for one hundred years. It is called the Hundred Year War. The English were trying to dominate the French territory and name one king for both England and France. The English captured Joan of Arc, imprisoned her and finally burnt her at the stake as a witch. That was horrifying. Nevertheless, she did change the history of France.

As I lay in bed that night, all the shapes and shadows lurking in the corners became geometric designs. Kaleidoscopic chunks seemed to slide further and further away into some endless invisible tunnel or down a massive drain, where all my reality was sucked up and away. Strings pulled in my stomach, and my limbs paralyzed. When I wondered if there would be anything left, I heard a whisper, "Even if it all gets consumed, we still are here."

"Who are you?"

"It's me, Joan."

"Joan? I don't see you. I only hear you."

"That's enough. I'm right here, with you. You might see me sometime."

"When? I'd like to see you now. Maybe I'm just imagining you."

"Your imagination is your way to communicate with me."

At that very moment, the chunks of light and dark that had been traveling at surprising speed toward an invisible center slid back toward me. The edge of the floor and the wall swallowed up all the shapes.

"Have you noticed how it's changed?" I said, hoping the voice would still be there.

"What are you talking to me for, if you think I'm only your imagination?"

"To make me feel I'm not completely alone. Hush, someone is coming."

"Your mother and stepfather are shouting. He hit her. She is crying and running up the steps."

Everything in my room was recognizable again: The white bookcase under the double window, the roll top desk, my blanket's comforting scent.

"Are you still there?"

"I'm right here, with you, whether you see me or not."

"How can I see you?"

"I am a shadow in the moonlight."

"How long have you been with me?"

"For all of eternity."

"What does that mean?"

My mother stormed into the room. The clicks of her silver-studded heels sounded sharper and pointier by the second. She sat, with a sigh, on the bed next to my tucked-in body. Her hair was disheveled. I could see the droplets of tears collecting on her lower lashes. Her face was swollen, with dark streaks. Her silver lamé blouse reminded me of the moon on a lake at night.

"We're leaving," she blurted. "I'm taking you and the boys. I must go."

We never left.

7

"Take your life into your own hands and what happens? A terrible thing, no one to blame."
—Erica Jong

We had a very black cook, Silvania, who lived in the garage with her husband and their little boy. Her spine leaned forward at an angle from her coccyx. I liked all the fried foods she made. She took me out walking by the cemetery, along a street that cut our street diagonally.

Against the outside wall of that Catholic colonial burial ground, there were many makeshift altars with daisies and mums dangling, like exhausted dancers, over the edges of the vases. Candles were burnt down to the cement side-walk. An annoying sweetness of cheap perfume wafted around dead waxy decapitated chickens. Silvania, the cook, never let me touch them because she said that the *macumba* (black magic) that they had thrown on certain people might get on me. We weren't supposed to interfere.

We had a cleaning lady called Natalina who came in once a week. We nicknamed her "*naftalina*," which means mothballs. Natalina always impressed me. She seemed even taller than my stepfather, very voluptuous and strong. She had curly hair, an African mouth, and a pointy aquiline nose. Her skin was the color of creamy coffee. When she came to clean, she picked up all the furniture and moved it so every corner of the house was spotless. When she sat down to eat, she had a plate piled up high with rice, beans, and vegetables, fried banana, and a fried egg, sunny side up at the tip of her mountain of food. She curved her powerful torso and leaned over so much that the bulbous mound of food could hide her face. It was fascinating to watch her eat, because she shoveled it in. Any grains that didn't quite fit into her mouth bounced right back onto the remaining hill of food. She never laughed or smiled. Her eyes were slit in an Oriental way. Her voice was thunderous. Her caramel skin was always glistening with perspiration. She smelled of cleaning fluids, mostly wax. At that time, I was reading a lot of mythology. I thought she was a Titan, one of the giants who existed before the gods of Olympus and who begot the gods.

Natalina was someone to be reckoned with if she felt thwarted. She got angry with Silvania. I overheard her complaining to Silvania, "You didn't have to go and tell my boyfriend how smitten I am."

Natalina's boyfriend was a friend of Silvania's husband. Natalina left our house saying she was going to put the *macumba* on Silvania, and we never saw Natalina again. Silvania said she wanted to go find out what she had to do to protect herself from Natalina's *macumba. Macumba*, she explained, was the dangerous "*candomblé*." *Candomblé* comes from the joining of the African mythology and rituals with the Catholic saints and parables. I wanted to know more.

"Where do you find out about all this?"

"At the *candomblé*."

She took me one afternoon. *Candomblé* is one of the many rituals from the African religions that were brought over by the slaves. It was at her cousin's house way out in a suburb of São Paulo. Mostly women and some men came dressed in white, with their brown heads wrapped in bright white cotton scarves. They brought candles and food and flowers and *cachaça* (the alcoholic sugar cane drink). They placed it all on an altar for a virgin coming out of the sea, Yemanjá.

They asked me to sit at one side of the room. There was a chair, but I wanted to stand. My eyes so open, I didn't want to miss a thing. I was the smallest one there. They all had darker skin, each one a different tone. The rhythmic shuffle of their feet moved in a circle. There was a man with a drum keeping the tempo alive. They waded through the sound, allowing their bodies to become disjointed while chanting in chorus their refrain to Yemanjá, the goddess of the sea. Incense smoke filled the room with dry scents and swirling curves. They shuffled and danced until their eyelids began to droop.

Suddenly one of them contorted herself. She let out cries of unleashed surrender. Her eyes went white. Her body flung itself all over, like an unraveling tightly wound elastic. Then she collapsed with a thud on the floor. The others picked her up and sat her on an elevated chair, put garlands of flowers around her neck, and gave the woman *cachaça* and a lit cigar to puff on. When the woman began to talk, she now had a man's voice. It wasn't the same person talking; it was the spirit who had taken her over. This spirit is the "*caboclo*" from the line of "*umbanda*"; it is an old Indian man's invisible spirit that is available to help us, Silvania explained to me.

Umbanda, Silvania had explained, was the Afro-Brazilian ritual of using the power of the spirits for good intentions. All the other women lined up in front of her. They all wanted their turn to ask for whatever they needed to heal or to change in their lives. The man's voice in the woman's body would give each one a different recipe for health and satisfaction. Someone wanted more money; another, her husband back. Others wanted to get rid of the ache in their back or in their belly. He would tell them to drink a tea made with a weed or a flower from a specific place or to boil a root or an organ of an animal. Many recipes. It went on and on. Every person had his or her turn. Each left a gift: flowers, perfume, more *cachaça*, dead chickens, cakes, chocolates.

When everyone had made a request, the *caboclo* was rewarded with drink and smoke. The chanting swaddled the room with a reassuring constancy. The chair was placed in the middle, and the others danced around. At first, there had been several taken by the *caboclo*, but only one was chosen as the healer. The others were granted the space to have their convulsions and lie on the floor with no special attention. None of those ever spoke. Slowly, everybody came back to their normal selves; the *caboclo* left.

I joined a group of my cook's friends talking and getting ready to go back into their regular lives. Silvania adjusted her white cotton headdress. Her eyes looked peaceful and strong. She didn't say much on the way home, except for, "*Gostou?*" (Did you like it?)

"*Gostei,*" I replied, feeling slightly dazed as if I had come out of a dream.

No harm ever came to Silvania from Natalina's *macumba.*

I wanted to experiment with my cousins contacting the invisible. Could we create some harmless chaos that could make us laugh. Grownups were so serious.

We dressed in white and danced in a circle conjuring the scene. We lit a fire on the beach, enhanced the rhythm with tambourines, and pranced around the smoky flames.

We imagined one adult throw a whole dish of food on top of another adult's head. We talked and giggled about it. It seemed so preposterous because grownups were all so *comme il faut*. This was one of my maternal family's pet phrases: *comme il faut* (as it must be).

A couple of weeks later in town, we were ushered into the vast marble-floor dining room where uniformed servants with white gloves served my aunt and uncle and my parents. We were there to greet them before we were chauffeured to a birthday party. We didn't know that just before we walked in, my uncle had made a comment on how the spaghetti was too sticky and that my aunt had to teach the cook to make it *al dente*. My aunt must have been fed up with my uncle's criticisms. He was a perfectionist.

Right before our very eyes, in a very uncharacteristic way, she picked up the serving platter out of the maid's hands, walked over to my uncle, and plopped all the spaghetti on his head. His face was of utter astonishment when my uncle realized that his impeccable gray pinstripe suit was covered with sticky red sauce! There was a lead silence of amazed shock and a scent of food gone rancid.

My aunt sat back down at the table and calmly said, "When are you going to start appreciating something around here?"

No one knew what to do or say. My uncle, giggling nervously, went upstairs to change.

We, the children, were speechless. So was everyone else. Yet, we knew that there was something more to this event than what met the eye. Later that afternoon we had to confer.

"How could it have actually happened the way we imagined it?" asked Petunia with her eyes wide open as violets.

"Do you think there is a connection?" Ogilvy added.

Malcolm, Ogilvy, Petunia, and I were spooked. We sat huddled together upstairs on the thickly carpeted playroom playing jacks, passing them around, like prayer beads.

"We must only imagine the events we want to happen," I suggested in a whisper.

They all nodded together in silence.

8

Perhaps nothing is more valuable for a
child than living with an adult
who is firm and loving.
—Margaret Meade

"You must never feel embarrassed; feel proud of who you are. You have outstanding ancestors," my mother said, never allowing me to have a pedestrian sense of myself. I was enrolled in a larger historical picture.

"Your great-grandmother was a Savelli, an old Roman family who can find several popes among its lineage. The first Savelli pope lived in the eighth century."

Images of rotund old men dressed in crimson satin robes and pearl-encrusted miters swaying to the rhythm of the swing of the gleaming silver incense holders in magnificent basilicas drenched in Gregorian chants came to mind. I felt faint with the acrid scent of the invading incense and the interminable length of the sung masses.

"My grandfather," she went on, while she was getting dressed to go out, powdering her nose and sliding the buttery scarlet lipstick to define her lips. She owned a large collection of twenty different tones of lipsticks all standing up like soldiers in a triangle formation on her dressing table. I only dared to try them when she was out of the house. "My grandfather was a ship owner and a Ladrón de Guevara. For several generations, the male Ladrón de Guevaras in Venezuela followed the tradition of going to Italy to find their wives so to avoid risking the mix of races."

This was presented to me as the absolute and only right thing to do. I saw the tall masts of the ships anchoring in some quaint Italian port and the tall ship-owner being welcomed with wine and music into certain families, hoping their daughter would be the lucky one to spark the fancy of the visitor and be chosen to bear children in America.

"One of our ancestors, along with Simon Bolivar, the great South American liberator, signed the Venezuelan Declaration of Independence from Spain."

I could see the swish of the brocade tails as the gentlemen sat on the gold damask, silk-upholstered chairs. He was given a gold-tipped pen and inkwell on a silver tray; the great document was unfurled for all those powdered-wig gentlemen who had left their wigs at home to sign with great pomp and circumstance the independence from the mother country with their natural hair and their black three-cornered hats. A few candelabras were lit, or maybe it was in the stark daylight in the sight of the cheering crowds.

Another ancestor was a Grand Inquisitor of Spain. He is depicted in El Greco's painting dressed in rich scarlet robes, with dark shadows around his eyes and a cynical twist at the corners of his mouth.

"The title of *Ladrón* [thief]," she continued, "was given to the lord of the castle in Guevara, in the North of Spain, in the Basque country. This was in the ninth century, when he stole into safety the heir to the Spanish crown during an attack by the moors." My mother told the history with great relish.

"The story goes that he cut the royal babe out of the dying queen's womb. In the dark, damp stone-walled room, the lonely queen drenched the cotton sheets in wine-colored blood. He wrapped the child, tucked him under his cape, and rode into the mountains. Disguised as a shepherd, he cared for him until he grew up enough to be brought to his father the king."

I could see the king's astonished face when he understood this boy was his long-lost son whom he believed to be dead. Yet, the resemblance was too obvious to deny.

My mother's father had been an American diplomat stationed in Venezuela. Later, he became president of the Cuban Electric Co. in Havana. He died very young; my mother was twelve.

"I remember," she said, "when he returned from a trip from the countryside how he complained about a lump on the back of his neck. The doctors pierced it repeatedly. Yet the lump kept growing back, larger. They said, 'Only cows get this disease.'"

My mother once suggested that someone might have poisoned him because he was endorsing too many workers' rights.

My father's grandfather had come from Germany as a stowaway and then worked on a ship that belonged to the Williams family of Rhode Island, descendants of Roger

Williams. My great-grandfather married the boss's daughter. My father's mother was a Daughter of the American Revolution. She inherited a lot of money from her industrialist father and moved to New York from Chicago when she married my grandfather. He graduated from Harvard Medical School and never practiced medicine so he could be available to "play" with my grandmother. Yet, at the end of his life, after my grandmother died, he offered his hands to be used to test different dosages of radiation and establish the beneficial parameters. He stopped playing the violin and died with his hands bandaged.

I savored these details of all the connections that had ended up becoming me. Yet, they did not provide the inner confidence I craved.

My mother's self-esteem was based on her social position and her ancestral pedigree. She did show strength of character at fifteen when she found a job modeling and moved with her mother to' the only acceptable area to live in Manhattan.'

My stepfather is a Hungarian aristocrat who came to Brazil as a refugee. He grew up in a castle in Hungary until the age of 15, when they had to flee. His father who had been a member of Parliament was taken prisoner by the Russian communists. He was a child prodigy on the piano and tinkered at fixing radios and televisions. That's how he supported himself when my mother met him in Brazil. He took her out wherever he could play the piano in exchange for dinner. Eventually, he trained as an insurance broker. All this was interesting, but it did not give me a deep enough anchor.

There was another force looming. It was 1956, the Hungarian revolution. Thousands of homeless and jobless Hungarians were arriving by ship or by planes.

My mother only spoke about the help these refugees needed, how to place them in the correct places, so they could start their lives again. It had been a spontaneous revolution of the younger generation against the totalitarian government of the Russian communist takeover. I saw pictures of Russian tanks running over young people or shooting at them. I was horrified. In my family, "communist" was a bad word. The Bolsheviks had started with a lot of idealism wanting equality for the people, I was told. In fact, they became a controlling centralized government that didn't allow any freedom of speech, thought, or enterprise. She helped these desperate people who ran away from their country. Their properties had been nationalized, and they had to start from scratch.

My mother saved my allowance, and I knew what she owed me. It was CR $ 354. I asked her to give it to these families. I don't know if she did.

9

"I sought my god, my god I could not see
I sought my soul, my soul eluded me
I sought my brother and found all three."
—Anonymous

My grandmother and the American Chapel School connected me to God, the Virgin Mary, and the whole Catholic liturgy. In church, I felt faint, between life and death, while kneeling with the acrid scent of the incense, especially during the Stations of the Cross.

My grandmother took me to Mass almost every Sunday. After Mass, we'd go to the bakery on Praça Higienópolis, and I'd get a cake. Mass and cake became one. My grandmother taught me how to pray.

Petit Jesus, qui êtes aux cieux
pardonnez-moi tous mes pêchés
bénissez ma maman, mon papa et
toute ma famille
Aidez moi à bien me porter
Merci pour mes petits frères et toutes les autres bonnes choses

Bonsoir, Petit Jesus.
(Little Jesus, who art in heaven,
forgive all my sins
Bless my mother and my father
and my whole family.
Help me be well-behaved.
Thank you for my little brothers and all the other good things.
Good night, Little Jesus.)

Many catechism classes given by the nuns prepared me for my First Communion. Through baptism I was cleansed of "original sin" and welcomed into the Church. Why were we held accountable for something some distant cousins of thousands of years ago did? I did not understand this "original sin" even though I knew the story. The second sacrament was First Communion. They spoke a lot of blood and suffering. We were redeemed by confessing our sins and by eating his body and drinking his blood.

Eat the body and blood of Christ, I thought. *What does that mean?*

If he were alive, I would have him in the refrigerator and slice off his flesh anytime I was hungry and drink his blood? What am I eating? What is actually becoming my body? Is it his ability to suffer, be crucified and then resurrect? Is it his gift of knowing how to make the dead come alive, or how to multiply a few loaves and fish into enough food to feed a multitude, or to cure a leper, or to turn water into wine? Am I capable of such amazing feats? Or was this memorable ceremony only a celebration of the longed-for union with the invisible? My grandmother often talked about "*les petits miracles*." If she wished for something and prayed for it, she was led to it "miraculously."

This First Communion gave me the right to do it over and over again: not only hold that thin wafer in the ceiling of my mouth, but also let it melt so quietly into a pond of warm saliva until it completely disappeared. I took it all, the preparations and the attention, very seriously. Cousin Margaret's white organdy First Communion dress and Spanish lace mantilla gave me permission to be strong and beautiful. This sacred, out of the ordinary experience represented the link to the transforming invisible power of Jesus. Through any suffering, whenever I might need it in the future, I could resurrect.

I have wondered: Did it glorify suffering? They said he suffered for us, so we would not have to suffer. But we do suffer. Is it a punishment? Is there a purpose? Is it to be capable of feeling a wider drop of compassion? Do we make ourselves suffer? Can we suffer and then resurrect? What does it mean to resurrect? How do we revive? Are we never stuck in our suffering? Do we always have the option to transcend?

If one is starving and begging in the streets, it may seem insurmountable. Resurrection seems like something very good and gladdening to the hearts of many. As a child, I definitely wanted to know and needed to know how to resurrect.

Father Supple was the headmaster of the school. He had married my mother and stepfather. For him, I must have been an illegitimate child. My mother had not married my father within the Catholic Church.

When I was eleven and twelve, he often came into the school cafeteria at lunchtime. He stood right next to me in his long black cassock, with a big putty smile, and caressed my shirt over my chest with tiny budding breasts. I felt so awkward and embarrassed because he was doing this in front of everyone. Was it meant to be harmless affection? Yet, I felt so self-conscious about my breasts I wanted to shrink them and make them disappear. They were very sensitive at that time. I was very uncomfortable but could not admit it or say anything. I did ask my mother for a bra. She ordered some almost flat ones from Best & Co. I felt completely powerless to change the situation with the priest. Maybe this is why my breasts remained infantile, while I watched my girlfriends wearing more and more copious bras.

I observed a girl named Janet at the same school. A little older, with brown silky hair, Janet always had the starring role in most of the school productions. She could dance and lip-sync any song. She had no shame. Her performances were big and compelling. I wanted to be like her. Often I asked myself, “Why aren’t I outgoing like Janet? What is stopping me?”

Most of the time I felt tied up in knots. I learned to play the guitar, and it took a lot of practicing to allow myself to play and sing with a little abandon. It still was easier to play a song that I had memorized than to speak my mind. I even wondered if I had a mind or a point of view. I knew I was mostly taking on my mother’s. I hated myself for that. I wanted to have an opinion of my own. I didn’t know how.

All those miracles seemed amazing stories but so distant from the reality we lived in. Except when I remembered the “*caboclos*” and how we imagined an event that happened. I wanted to test my inner friend.

My parents went out a lot in the evening. My room in my parents' house was upstairs. My brothers' room was downstairs near the maids' rooms. It was the converted garage. When my parents were out, I felt alone and vulnerable.

Once, while I was doing my homework, I heard the clicking of very high heels on the wood floor. I thought my mother had come home. Maybe she'd forgotten something. The sound got louder and louder. I glanced down the stairs and could see nothing. By now my heart was pounding in my throat, and I did not dare look again. I armed myself with my rolled-up umbrella. I stood behind the closet door, as the sound grew louder and sharper. I called, "Mummy, is that you?"

No reply. The noise kept tapping up the stairs. I was ready behind the door to hit someone, if necessary. Then silence. Vast, limitless silence. I tiptoed slowly out into the hallway, holding on to the doorway and the walls as if they were a security blanket. There was nothing there. Before re-entering my room, I had a sense there were spirits in there. I felt them: gigantic pieces of transparent marshmallow slipping and sliding silently. So I called out:

"Are you there?"

"You know, I'm right here, with you."

"What is your name?"

"Joan."

"How can I know it's always you that answers me when I call you?"

"Because you hear me coming from your heart."

"I want to see you."

As soon as I started talking with her, all the jitters dissipated. I began to ask for small miracles and big miracles.

I needed to know how far my Joan was capable of helping. I asked for a sister.

My mother got pregnant a fourth time. I went to Mass and Communion every morning to pray for a sister. My sister, Ilona, was born.

"Do you want to be Ilona's godmother?" my mother inquired. My sister became my new doll. As a baby she looked like Romy Schneider, the actress. She also slept upstairs. Often I took care of her. If at night she couldn't sleep, I picked her up out of her crib and brought her onto my bed. She climbed on top of my waist as if I were her horse.

"Lie down." She flattened herself on the mattress and then opened her eyes and started giggling. She mounted me and pretended I was her galloping steed. We slept together. If she cried sometimes during the day, I took her for a little walk up and down our street to change her ideas, and she felt better.

My grandmother taught me how to sing and act out several songs with dance. It was a way to tell a story disguised within another story. I could disclose whatever I wanted, and nobody could prove me wrong. I performed for her friends or my mother's.

Nevertheless, I grew up feeling fidgety and scared of grownups. Some adults asked me why my eyes were so sad. I bit my nails and picked the broken ends off my hair. I didn't dare talk much, except to my cousins and the maids who believed all my stories. One day sitting next to me on the sofa in the living room of my parents' house, my mother turned to me; I was about twelve, and she said, holding me by the shoulders, “Lilizinha, you are so beautiful, except for that nose of yours.”

From that moment on, I became self-conscious about my nose. I spent time observing my profile. The curve on the outside of my nostrils was very pronounced. Because my nose was on the long side, it seemed to me it was hooked. I looked as if I were Indian from India.

It had never bothered me until she said that. From then on, every time I felt someone was looking at me from the side, I raised my hand and covered my nose, so that he or she could not see it. With time, it became an obsession. I complained to my mother several times that I didn’t like my nose. She asked me if I wanted plastic surgery, I didn’t really know. It scared me. I don’t think I had ever thought that was an option. But, then, why would I complain to her? I must have thought she could help me.

10

"Stories are medicine. ...They have such power; they do not require that we do, be, act anything. We need only listen. The remedies for repair or reclamation of any lost psychic drive are contained in stories."
—Clarissa Pinkola Estes, Ph.D.

In Brazil, I went to an English kindergarten, then a Brazilian elementary, American middle, and French high school. My mother composed my letters to my father. I copied them. I hated it. I never argued nor rebelled. I pulled my hair. Her excuse was that I didn't really know my father; and that although I spoke and understood it, I only learned to write in English at age ten in an American Catholic school. They all went out. I had to stay and copy a letter that didn't mean anything to me. I often said to myself and sometimes even to her: "I don't believe you are my mother."

She stared at me with a deadpan face and walked away in silence. Maybe she was hurt by what I said.

I reported the events or routines of my life in Brazil. It seemed like a litany of the same thing over and over again.

Maybe that's why my father never developed an interest in me.

Dear Daddy,

Thank you for your newsy letter. I am glad you have had a good time on your trip through Europe.

I have been having a good time too. My cousin Petunia and I have restarted our tennis lessons, and we are getting better at it. I have begun to attend the French Lycée and am very excited about learning how to write in French. I also go horseback riding with my cousins every week. I really like the horses. On the weekend I go with them to their beach house and we all get very sun tanned and swim better every day. Once a week, after school, we go to swimming lessons and we are learning to swim the crawl.

I hope to hear from you soon. Love, Lili.

I abhorred the tennis lessons. The school, the cousins, their beach house, the horseback riding, I did enjoy. We never mentioned feelings except for "very excited."

My mother always was confused about the spelling of the word excited.

"I can't remember whether the 'x' or the 'c' comes first," she said every time she looked it over. "And, do you know, Lilizinha, if in receive, it's the 'e' or the 'i' that comes first?"

She laughed at her own forgetfulness. I showed her my spelling book from the American school.

"I want you to be able to write thank-you notes in as many languages as possible," Mummy said.

When I was thirteen, I remember writing one clandestine note to my father.

Dear Daddy,

I miss you. I wish I could see more of you. Sometimes I even wish I could live with you. I am afraid to say it. It might hurt Mummy's feelings too much. I wish we could talk more. I wish I could ask you more questions. I wish you would be more interested in what I'm doing. I wish you would come and visit me. Please answer me. I need to talk. Love, Lili.

I can't remember if it was ever mailed. I asked his widow years later if he had ever mentioned it. My father apparently never received it. Maybe I gave it to my stepfather to send, and he intercepted it. Or maybe I didn't dare mail it.

At that time, I was switched over to the French Lycée. Even though I spoke a little French, I did not know how to write it. They had to put me back two years. My classmates were eleven. They huddled, whispered and giggled when I recited a poem. They treated me as if I were a clumsy idiot.

"*Eh giraffe!*" they called me and burst out laughing.

For the first time ever, I was getting zeros on a lot of my work. The math was in the metric system and I had learned the American system.

I was developing bunions on my feet, and the doctor suggested I wear these very high arches inside clunky boys' shoes. My cousins were in even younger classes. I played with them and their friends. Thank God, they liked me. I organized games for them. The one they loved most was "freeze." They moved behind my back. When I turned to look, they had to be immobile. Anyone who stirred was out.

I grew accustomed to not speaking. To say "I don't agree" was unthinkable. Whenever, quivering inside, I did express any opinion, it was mostly received by my mother with a tone of ridicule and logical proof of how I was totally wrong and probably, therefore, an idiot. To say "I was disappointed," "*ça ne se fait pas*" (this is not done), she said. "How ungrateful!"

My mother often expressed her theory of child rearing: "Children are born *'tabula rasa'* and everything has to be inculcated into them."

A few times, I remember blurting out responses that must have come intuitively because I did not understand what I was saying, and yet my stepfather's face would light up as if I had said something wonderful. I remember this happening only when it was just the two of us. There was an alliance with him in that we both loved chocolate and cold cereal, and sometimes I sang while he played the piano.

In bed alone, at night, I felt free to be myself. I had my imaginary radio show; this was before I ever saw a TV. "And now we can tune in to Lili's special hour of 'Inclination.'

They were mostly stories of disdained love and also the development of villages for all the children who were homeless in the streets.

In São Paulo, there were many children begging on the streets. Those big eyes watched us go by in our chauffeured station wagon. The imaginary villages I was creating had facilities for teaching these children different skills, so they could eventually make a living or prepare to study further.

There was a family who lived in a small park diagonally across the street from our house. They lived inside cardboard boxes and begged for food. It was part of the scenery and so unreachable at the same time. Very poor people came to the door. My mother insisted on giving them no money, just food.

One day, I went out with my brothers, to be picked up by the station wagon that took us to school, the whole sidewalk in front of the house was smudged with food, a white unctuous paste that smelled of rancid cheese. It was shocking and deeply troubling to see. There were thousands of homeless people who came from the North of Brazil where there are many droughts. They came to the city looking for work.

On a cold day, I felt so guilty for having a coat. I wanted to give it to a begging child whose clothes were in dirty tatters. Terrified of my mother's reprisal, I never did. It was a sticky, heavy feeling I could not rid myself of nor explain to anyone. These fantasies of being able to help them someday somewhat relieved me of my shame and guilt.

The love stories on my radio show were like the soap operas on the radio that I listened to with the maids, while they taught me how to iron a man's shirt. My shows were different in that when someone was mean to someone else, there was a fairy godmother who turned them into a pig or an anteater. A lot of value was placed on the victim who did not show her feelings and braved the situation of rejection with grace and a superficial smile. "Smile though your heart is breaking" were lyrics to a song I used to love. What an ode to a contradiction.

11

"It is sown a natural body; it is raised a spiritual body. There is a natural body, and there is a spiritual body."
—1 Corinthians 15:44

When Bruce was thirteen and I was eight, he cornered me in the garage and kissed me passionately.

"You're such a woman, such a woman," he whispered, as he pressed me against a wall. I could smell the damp concrete. I squirmed and struggled out of his grasp. I didn't dare scream. Maybe I'd be accused of something. I pulled myself out of his grip and escaped.

Once, after our bath time, we were all in pajamas running around the upstairs, getting ready for bed. I was ten. Bruce called me into his room to show me something. It was the same room that Margaret had been in a few years before, the one where it was hard for me to open the door. After I stepped into the room, he slammed the door and pushed me onto the bed. He pulled my pale blue flannel pajama pants off and then proceeded to pull off his pajama pants. This was the first time I saw an erect penis. It was rather stiff. He wanted it to get close to me. I struggled, kicked and pushed him away; I wanted to call for help, yet I was sure that they would blame me, so I didn't.

It took titanic concentration to open that door. I confessed it to the priest as having sexual moments with my cousin. He asked if we got naked. I said he took off my pajama pants, but I ran away before he did anything. He told me to say four "Hail Marys" and four "Our Fathers" and gave me absolution. I also told Charity, my best friend, about this incident. She listened, fascinated. Then, we played doctor together; she was the doctor. It puzzled me how even though she was younger, I felt she was older, more in control.

Charity's mother was a devout Catholic. She asked her guests when serving coffee: "Do you take sugar, or are you giving it up for the souls in purgatory this week?"

We prayed the rosary out loud, with her whole family kneeling on the concrete pathway facing a cement virgin placed in the bushes.

Her tone of voice was eerily calm, as if she were holding something down, hidden somewhere. She showed me how to light a match after I pooped so it wouldn't smell. Her husband was the head of "The Seven-Up Company" in São Paulo. Her chewy brownies and the endless supply of 7UP were treats we never had at home.

The richest memories of growing up in São Paulo were the three magical months of summer vacation I spent with my cousins at their house on Pernambuco Beach. The luminous mornings on the beach's subtropical sunlight bleached our hair and tanned us as dark as the local children we sometimes played with. We aspired to be so dark skinned so as not to be distinguished. We practiced walking barefoot on pebbles and stones until the bottom of our feet became as leathery as theirs. We swam to a raft anchored a hundred yards off shore and practiced our diving endlessly. We made pools in the sand and filled them with as many living creatures we could find, mostly baby jellyfish. We built gigantic castles covered with dripping steel-gray sand forming Gaudiesque shapes. Then, before our late Brazilian lunch of black beans, rice and farofa, fried bananas, sliced oranges, sautéed kale thinly sliced, joined by some fresh fish off the grill, Tanti Lili came for her swim. We scrubbed our skins as she did with the soft wet sand and then rinsed off splashing each other and giggling endlessly. Bruce called me "hyena" because sometimes I couldn't stop laughing.

One morning my parents arrived unexpectedly. They marched on the sand with a dark expression on their faces, from the house to where we were playing.

"Pack your bag. We're taking you back to the city. Be quick," they ordered me in a brittle and dry tone. I had no idea why. The two-hour drive back to our house in the city was silent. Something was very wrong. Finally we arrived at their house. "Go sit in the smoking room. We're going to discuss something in there," they commanded.

I felt my mind and heart frozen in fearful anticipation of what might be about to happen. I sat on the edge of one of the leather chairs. I didn't dare lean back. The antique desk encased in bookshelves. The walls were dark ocher with paintings of leaping horses and prints of Roman warriors. A small love seat covered in brown damask was across from the desk. That's where my mother sat. Her lipstick was fire engine red, and her brown eyes seemed darker than usual. All the familiar objects seemed different.

"Charity told her mother that you showed her dirty pictures. Where did you get them?"

"Dirty pictures?" I repeated in a daze, at a total loss, because if Charity had told on me, I thought it might be about what happened with Bruce. Yet I responded whispering in disbelief. "I don't know of any dirty pictures."

"Well, this is disgraceful, Lilizinha, you have embarrassed us so degradingly. What an ungrateful little girl you are. Don't lie. Where did you get these dirty pictures?" They didn't believe the truth. I wasn't going to talk about Bruce. What was I supposed to do?

"I promise you, I don't know of any dirty pictures," I repeated, terrified, with all the conviction I could muster.

"You don't have to lie to us, just tell us exactly who gave you those dirty pictures."

I thought that perhaps, if they didn't believe the truth, maybe they would believe a fabricated story. So I began: "When I was at Mackenzie, there was this girl, Cristina, she gave them to me. I kept them for a while and then gave them to Charity to see what she thought of them."

"What kind of pictures were they?"

I didn't know what to say, so I improvised.

"There were women without clothes holding their babies."

"That is impossible," said my mother. "I would have noticed them here in the house. This is a ridiculous story. Maybe you thought pictures in the book I have on the coffee table of those aborigines were dirty pictures. Did you?" Her strident voice insisted.

"No. I know that's how those people live. The truth is, I don't know any dirty pictures."

"You are such a liar, Lilizinha."

It seemed as if the interrogation went on for days and nights. I did invent a couple of other stories. None of them worked. In their eyes, I was odiously guilty. There was no way that I could redeem myself. I was a lost, cornered rat.

"Go up to your room and pray."

There was a painting of the Virgin Mary on the wall. The figure was in a cloud of mist. I asked her to help me convince them of the truth. About half an hour later, my stepfather came into my room and ordered me to come into their room with him. I stepped in terrified. He showed me their bathroom with his hand and said, "Go, undress."

The shorts and the top were all one piece. It was pale blue cotton. I took it off. Then, I had to walk back into and across the room naked. I felt sullied by his thyroid eyes.

"Kneel down at the foot of the bed," he rumbled, with his thick Hungarian accent. I did. The bedspread was bottle-green velvet. A painting of pink roses in a ceramic vase painted by his mother hung on the wall. He pulled off his belt and began to whip my back, my buttocks, my thighs, over and over again. This time, I decided to be silent. I would not give him the pleasure of any sound. Every searing burn across my back strengthened my determination to be silent. Every whipping disconnected me even more from my body.

Years later, when I asked them about having beaten me, my mother said, "We never put a hand on you." Yet, I still vividly remember all the marks, blue and purple stripes across my back and buttocks and thighs, when I observed them in my bathroom mirror, for days and nights after that.

"Get dressed," he commanded when he finally stopped.

I got up, in a daze. He stretched out his hand, staring into my eyes, to congratulate me for not having cried. I gave him my hand to shake. Without realizing I sealed a contract to hate him, all men, and myself.

"Get dressed. We want to take you to church to go to confession."

I wasn't quite sure what I was supposed to confess. When I got there, I invented having stolen an apple at the market. Maybe I had touched myself sexually recently. So now I had a completely clean slate. After that, they drove me over to Charity's house. Her parents were having a cocktail party. Her mother received us at the door with a warm embrace and said: "Oh! You know those dirty pictures that Charity talked about; she finally remembered who really showed them to her; it was Abby Edrich," and without missing a beat she went on, "Lilizinha, Charity is in the back garden, why don't you go and play with her?"

Nothing more was ever said. Nothing. As if it never happened.

"Are you there?" I said inside of me, looking for Joan. "I don't want to play with Charity ever again," I kept mumbling under my breath to her.

"Just go over there and find out what happened," she responded faithfully.

The front of the house was full of people. My parents floated into their social pitter-patter. I reluctantly walked to the back of the house.

"What do I say to Charity, when I see her?"

"I have no idea. When you see her, you will know."

I found Charity sprawled on a pale blue quilt, surrounded by the scent of freshly cut grass. She had long dark brown hair, wide almond eyes, and very full lips. She also, like her mother, always spoke slowly and softly. Her mother had brought out her inimitable brownies and two bottles of 7UP. It was a balmy breezy Brazilian afternoon; I had stepped out of a battle into a tea party.

Joan whispered inside of me, "You'll feel better if you talk to her."

"What did you tell your mother, Charity?" I said in a quiet tone.

"It was before my tonsil operation. She sent out for a priest to perform Extreme Unction. Before he does that, he asks you if you have anything to confess."

"Charity, how did you get around to telling your mother about dirty pictures?"

Ignoring my question, she continued: "After I had done so, my mother came by my bed and asked me if there was anything else on my conscience that might be troubling me. So I told her about what happened with you and Bruce and about the dirty pictures. I was clearing my conscience."

I noticed Charity's gaze looking down at her hands, as she spoke. She couldn't meet my eyes.

"Clearing your conscience means releasing what you feel you have done wrong, not what somebody else has done." I stared at her face as I spoke. I never wanted to be her friend any more.

Charity gave me a dumbfounded look, as if this had never occurred to her and then shook her head from side to side, implying some kind of misunderstanding. Then she picked bird sized crumbs from her brownie and fed them to herself as she stared at the grass in an awkward silence.

"Joan, I don't want to be with her anymore."

"I understand."

"You understand?"

"Yes, tell her how you feel."

"I don't want to, I feel my best friend betrayed me."

"From your point of view that is true. From her point of view it might be different."

"You're just playing with words. I know what happened."

"The sooner you talk it out with her and forgive her, the sooner you can let go of the whole uncomfortable experience."

It took me years to understand what Joan was suggesting right there and then. The feeling of being betrayed by my best friend remained buried inside of me.

12

"There is nothing so secular that it cannot be sacred, that is one of the deepest messages of the Incarnation."
—Madeleine L'Engle

When I was at my parents' house, I spent a lot of time in my room alone. My mother said, "What's the point of getting good grades at school, if at home you stare at the wall?" I felt shamed and confused; what was she implying? She was not curious of my inner experience.

"I had a dream about you, last night," I once ventured to share. "Do you want to hear about it?"

"Yes, of course, darling."

"I saw you come up the stairs, with a dark look around your eyes. You had a large pair of black scissors in your right hand. You were very serious."

"Uuuhh! How horrible, how could you see me that way?" she cried in disbelief as she powdered her nose and carefully filled and outlined her lips with scarlet red lipstick, in front of her bathroom mirror, readying herself to go out.

"That's the way you were. You came up slowly, staring at me. I was standing barefoot, in my white cotton slip, barely awake from a nap. It was cold on the old purple tile bathroom floor at the top of the stairs. You approached me, bent over, and cut off my right foot, at the ankle. I woke up with such a sharp pain."

"Oohh! Lilizinha, what a terrible dream! How could you think that way of me?"

"I don't know," I said. "That was my dream."

My mother was silent. She needed to go out. I was left with my thoughts, my fantasies, and the books I was reading.

What got me reading were the Nancy Drew mysteries. From there I went on to *Desiree*, *Rebecca, The Agony and the Ecstasy*, *Wuthering Heights*, *The Count of Monte Christo*, and all the Alexander Dumas books. My aunt Fargo subscribed me to a book club. I loved to melt into a book. I had a book of myths from different parts of the world. My mother had bought it from a departing foreigner. I read that book over and over again. My grandmother knew this was my favorite book. She bound it in leather for me. I also loved the books of Monteiro Lobato. He wrote fabulous, surreal Brazilian tales. Later I enjoyed as much of Graham Greene and Somerset Maugham I could find.

I knew there were ghosts and spirits. I often walked through the cemetery that was a block away from us. There were impressive baroque sepulchers with life-size marble angels, from the eighteenth and nineteenth centuries. The walkways were so neat. Dried dusty flowers brought by family or friends were the wake of their losses. When I looked in through the clamped shut gates of the gray mausoleums, I could hear yearning whines of souls waiting for their day of reckoning. It smelled of cold marble and formaldehyde. The maids felt uneasy in the graveyard, especially if there was some gaping hole waiting for a body. A journey awaiting to be made.

When I was ten, my parents took me to Lima, Peru, then Panama, and then to the United States for the first time in my conscious life. We went to Cuzco and Machu Pichu in Peru. What most impressed me was the harrowing bus ride, on the narrow road at the edge of the mountain, from Cuzco to the tip of very high peaks where the Incas mysteriously built their sacred royal enclave. They enticed the Spaniards to settle in a naturally continuously foggy area, which eventually became Lima.

The bus was filled with indigenous people, called Quechuas. They traveled with their live chickens cackling and fluttering their wings. They held them by their legs. Their children sat wide-eyed with colorful hand knitted caps with tasseled flaps over their ears singing their favorite rhymes. The bus seemed to be a few inches away from the edge of the cliff. At every curve, the rest of the road was invisible. I sat in the front to keep a close watch on the driver, who seemed detached from the bustle around him. The ravines, the sharp edges, the mysterious stony ruins attached drama to the stories my mother was reading.

After sleeping through my first uneventful mini earthquake at the Hotel Bolivar in Lima, we flew to Panama City. My parents left me for a week in Panama with a friend who had a pool in her living room. She had broken her hip parachuting out of a plane into China during the Second World War. She needed to exercise it constantly and eat a lot of cottage cheese, she said. It was so steamy hot in Panama City that it was more comfortable to be inside the pool than out. All her friends had pools. I then decided that I liked having a pool to swim in all the time. Everything seems so wobbly and buoyant when you look at it from under the water.

When I was thirteen, my mother bought a trip to Europe for the three of us on a lay-a-way plan. Because of the very high inflation, the local currency was worth less and less if one sold dollars to pay in 'cruzeiros'. My brothers and sister were considered too young to travel and stayed for a while with our German cook and her family. They took me all through Europe in a little Volkswagen Bug with my cousin Margaret. She was articulate and occupied a more validated position because she was going to college. We arrived in Lisbon, drove through the south of Spain to Madrid, then to Pamplona to see the running of the bulls, then to Barcelona.

For three months, we stayed in *pensions* or camped along the way on freshly harvested fields. We looked for "little *caminitos*" (little paths) as my mother called them, to guide us off the highway. Once, on the Cote d'Azur, we couldn't find a field or a *pension* that had any room, so we stopped by the side of the road where it seemed very green and unpopulated and pulled out our inflatable mattresses right there. It was dark and very late. We were all exhausted. In the morning, a gentleman on his horse greeted us. We were camping on the driveway of his estate.

In one of the fishing villages, my mother bought me my first bikini. I remember looking at myself in the mirror and feeling happy at how pretty, thin, and dainty I looked. My mother confirmed it and said, "You look adorable."

We had a large picnic basket in the space behind the back seat. Sometimes the local cheeses reeked in the warm car. Once, my cousin and I were slicing salami in the back seat as we were driving through the north of Italy. I remember my cousin saying, "Could you slow down? The salami is flying out the window!"

We were immersed in European history and art; museums and more museums, cathedrals and castles. I began to distinguish styles of painters and epochs and their architecture. At the Uffizi Gallery in Florence, my mother said I looked like the Botticelli Venus. I didn't quite agree with her but was flattered that she saw me that way. My mother is well-versed in European history, especially the intrigues and the love stories that wove through it. She and my cousin were reading out of two volumes about the history of the popes and discussing them in the car. They were especially fascinated by the stories of two medieval popes who had the same last name as my great-grandmother. My mother and Margaret got into arguments where the underlying intention was to prove, "I know more than you do." They were tiresome. At those times, I'd pretend I was asleep and go off into my fantasies.

Once my mother and stepfather got into an argument. I don't remember what it was about. My mother was so furious with him she put out her burning cigarette onto the back of his hand while he was driving. The car came to a full stop.

13

"Love is the joy we feel when we share our heart authentically with another person."
—Tim Heath

I was fourteen. The grown-ups were planning a party at Punch's house. She was my mother's best friend. Punch was from the Mainline outside Philadelphia. She came over almost every afternoon, fresh from the hairdresser. She had blond streaks in her hair and looked like a blue-eyed version of Jackie Kennedy. She was skinny and always wore a different color *tergal* skirt. Those pleats never wrinkled; it was a new synthetic material that was fashionable. My mother mentioned to me that she would like as many of those skirts in different colors as Punch had. Punch and her husband Martin were around every weekend. My parents bought a little farm together with them. There were vineyards and lots and lots of lemon trees. Very often the four of them stayed up singing, drinking, while my stepfather played the piano until dawn. When I got up early to do my homework, they were all still giggling downstairs. Sometimes they took their mattress off the box spring and all four slept in my parents' room. In hearing a lot about the party, I expressed the desire to go.

"Darling, it's a grown-up party. Well, if you want to dress up like a servant and pass around the canapés, I don't see why not. It could be amusing. You'll have to wear the whole black uniform, the white headdress, gloves, and lacy apron."

The surprised faces made me smile inside. I didn't get paid for it; it was only for the fun of being there. There were a couple of male friends of my mother's whom I knew liked me. One of them had said to my mother that if they ever had a daughter they wanted someone like me. I have just realized that's why I wanted to be at the party, to see them and their smile when they saw me.

It was a big sprawled out sunset-pink brick house near Chácara Flora, with different levels of shiny, waxed, oak floors and French doors opening out onto manicured lawns.

There were down-filled pale yellow sofas and lots of fresh flowers. Everybody chatted away and drank a lot. Eventually, my stepfather played the piano, and the braver ones sang their favorite songs.

A few days after that party, a heavy gloom filled our house: my mother cried, didn't want to talk about it and the piano was silent. Those friends from Philadelphia stopped showing up.

As the gloom began to dissipate, I overheard my mother talk about "that woman." I knew she meant Punch. My mother discovered Victor had an affair with her, and she threatened to leave with the children. She showed up at my stepfather's office.

"Either you call that woman and tell her it's all over, or I'll jump out the window right here, right now." It was the twenty-third floor. Besides her inevitable tragic death, it would create an outrageous scandal that would affect his work. He must have called. My mother did not leave. They never entertained the Philadelphia couple again.

Nevertheless, through the years, this loaded story was implied in many conversations to infuse the atmosphere with a vigorous dose of guilt and emotional manipulation.

"We know how you have behaved in the past," she said, like a hunter stretching his bow, gloating over the emotions she could elicit, as she let the invisible arrow fly and pierce.

I thought my mother was the innocent victim of this situation. It was only in my mid-twenties that I heard some other bit of gossip. The Philadelphia couple's eldest son was and still is a friend of mine. On one of my trips to Brazil, we had a chance to hang out, and he told me he had heard, at the time, that my mother also had an affair with his father. Maybe that was what his mother told him to excuse her own behavior. I asked my mother, she denied it. Recently, she admitted:

"Yes, I did it out of revenge," she said with a naughty giggle. "He was an architect, and he gave me good advice on how to make the changes on the house. Then, we had our little moments."

14

"I learned long ago that being Lewis Carroll was infinitely more exciting than being Alice."
—Joyce Carol Oates

When I was sixteen, my mother suggested I go away to school. I wanted to get away. My father didn't want to pay for private school in the United States. My mother didn't want me to go to public school.

"In public schools, girls just stand on street corners counting their lipsticks," she said.

She got me into a private school in Neuilly, France, with the same order of nuns who educated my grandmother in France and England. My mother had attended their school in New Jersey. I was thrilled. I would continue in French and make new friends. I had been studying at the French Lycée for three years. I was doing well. I skipped half a year going forward. Excited to get out of my house, feeling grownup, now I could leave behind these childish fantasies I had for such a long time, like talking to Joan, my invisible friend.

Before dropping me off in Paris, my parents took me through Rome, Greece, Turkey, Lebanon, the Arab side of Jerusalem at the time, and Egypt. From the unimaginable pain of Michelangelo's Pieta in the Vatican, to the immense, mysterious ruins in Thebes and Luxor, from the majestic and trend-setting Acropolis to the pyramids, from the secret initiations of Eleusis to the Roman ruins at Baalbeck: all these places, all this art, the timeless oracle at Delphi, the temples and stones, every experience widened my understanding of how small I was in relation to so much knowledge and skill.

The endless wars and hordes of warriors and women and children had been crushed by time into disregarded dust. I was being fed pages and pages of numerous history books and art books, yet hidden inside my quiet shapes, I felt the changes of reflections as you notice when you turn the kaleidoscope. The "*Son et Lumière*" at Ghiza at the foot of the Sphinx, pyramids in the middle of the sand, and the starry sky stayed with me through time. I imagined myself as a conscious grain of sand being blown from one camp to another.

In Damascus, I had a rude awakening. When walking with my stepfather in the middle, between my mother and me, the Syrian men strolled nonchalantly right into me so that their left arm could feel the middle of my body. They were quite shameless about it. It happened twice. I had to huddle close to my stepfather to protect myself. There was a gentler young man who talked to us at a museum and invited us to his living room filled with mother-of-pearl encrusted furniture. Every Louis XV chair was heavily inlaid with luminescent scales. The seats, upholstered in white damask, had a plastic cover to protect them. He graciously served us mint tea, and we chatted about the beauty and the history of Damascus. After we left, my mother joked that he probably liked my nose.

Then back to London, where I took the train and the ferry on my own to Paris. There was a residence for young ladies attending other schools in Paris and there was a day school. I lived in their residence and attended their day school. Soon I made friends with my first roommate, a Nicaraguan girl named Teresa. A photograph remains of us at the Sacré Coeur in Montmartre together. She was only in the residence side of the establishment. She had a giggle that sounded like water running fast over smooth stones. I've seen her by chance more recently. We planned once to meet in the big reception room at the United Nations. She worked there representing Nicaragua. She was late. I was pregnant and had some sort of panic attack and left in a rush. I felt overwhelmed with the crowd of people in that room. Later I apologized.

There were two Somoza girls. Somoza was still in power in Nicaragua. They arrived every day with a new shopping bag from beautiful boutiques, with stylish hats, sweaters, shoes, bags, and scarves. A little jealous, I managed to vicariously enjoy their new fashionable accessories.

Initially, in the day school, I found it difficult to make friends. There were many French aristocratic names like La Rochefoucauld and de Polignac. I was the odd ball, the only foreigner. I got good grades, so I was considered the goody-goody. Some of them did invite me over to their houses for lunch. One close friend, Isabelle Florianotovska, was a swimming champion. Florianotovski was a well-known name in French politics, and one of them had been one of Napoleon's generals. I was invited and attended some luxurious French parties with endless tables of pink, green, brown petits fours. I roamed alone from room to room; they all stuck together. I was the weird one.

A French girl, Sabine was a friend from Brazil. Her parents were divorced. Her father remarried in Brazil. She came to visit her father for the summer in Europe, the winter in São Paulo. She had a head of dark short curls and the cutest profile. We met when I was ten and she was twelve. I hardly spoke French. Today, she says she taught me to speak French. When I saw her in Paris, her life was more involved and complicated. We saw each other from time to time. She was ahead of me, painting her nails, knitting, and socializing; I was doing my homework and being shy. Our interests were out of sync at the time.

My body went into shock when I found myself so far away from my family. I didn't get my period for six months and was accompanied by a nun to my first gynecological examination. She stayed in the room next door. The doctor left the door open.

As soon as the classes were over for the day, I rushed to the local market and got myself a large piece of Emmental cheese. Frenzied, I ate it walking through the streets of Neuilly, trying to get a change of scenery from the focus of the school. I started gaining weight and was afraid of what my mother would say. At the time, I gave myself a hard time about eating too much and gaining weight. I struggled with the attempts of disciplining myself not to eat. I began to smoke Gitanes. It was very French and somewhat cool. It also curbed my appetite. I had to do it in hiding or outside of the school. Today, I understand that I was so severed from my private inner world that I only experienced the dizziness of an enormous hole. Schoolwork and the search for friends were not enough to nourish me.

The girls I made friends with more easily were the ones who lived in the residence as I did. There were two other boarders who also attended the day school like me. We ended up as roommates and allies. The first one, Nanon, invited me to go for the weekend with her mother who was divorced. It was with this roommate that I had ontological discussions. Nanon looked like a boy with short-cropped hair and a sturdy, wide build. She often said in her clipped tone, "As long as anything is mysterious and we don't understand it, we call it 'God.' Then, time goes by, and we do understand it scientifically, and then it is not God anymore. So God is only what we don't understand."

She had me convinced that God did not exist. He was merely a convenience of our intellect to label everything we cannot explain. Other girls pointed out that God was a way to comfort people who were frightened by the mystery of death. I subscribed to these ideas for a while because I did not want to think of myself as a weakling. I put the whole matter on a shelf waiting for further understanding to show up and move me from those positions. Even though we were attending a religious school, all the rituals were deprived of meaning or substance for me. They were taken for granted and performed by rote. I didn't give the nuns' explanations credence.

On my first Christmas vacation, friends of my parents invited me to Geneva. I got a round-trip ticket on a train. On the return trip, I found a seating compartment with five other people. Among them was a philosophy student and a philosophy professor. The philosophy student asked me if I thought man had a soul.

"Of course man has a soul. That's what shows up in his art even from the days of cave men; they had the need to express themselves, so that they could reflect upon themselves. That is a movement from the soul."

I couldn't believe I had spoken with such certainty. When I looked at the philosophy teacher, she was nodding and smiling enthusiastically. That moment gave me a feeling that there was someone deep inside of me who knew answers I was not aware of. I felt excited and puzzled, and relived that moment to tune into the part of me that seemed to know.

The second roommate was a Lebanese girt with the most beautiful green eyes I had ever seen. She received and shared rolls and rolls of pressed apricot. Her father was powerful in the Lebanese government. She introduced me to two of her cousins; one was very studious, the other showed us how she separated each eyelash with a pin after she had darkened them with mascara. This gave them a feathery feel. They provided a contrast between superficial and profound knowledge. I had a longing for both and wondered if it had to be a choice or could I combine them.

After that first year in Paris, I returned home to São Paulo for the summer. As soon as I had unpacked my bags, my mother showed me pictures of women with beautiful profiles and asked me which one I wanted. She explained she had found the perfect plastic surgeon, and his clinic was around the corner from our house. In São Paulo at that time, there was a plastic surgeon on almost every street corner. The next morning I was in the clinic. They anesthetized me. My mother stayed in the operating room supervising the plastic surgeon. At some point during the operation, I could hear them all say, "Oh! She looks like Catherine Deneuve."

I could feel the cutting of the tissue and the sliding thread of the inner stitches, but no pain. I had the feeling I was lying under the table. When I woke up, my whole face was bandaged. After a couple of weeks, when they took off some of the bandages, my eyes were black and blue, and I was very swollen. It took a long while before I started to look normal again. They predicted a year for the swelling to disappear. My mother wanted me to tell my friends that I had fallen off a horse. I didn't mind telling them what happened. My mother said we wouldn't have to tell my father, but wanted to see if he noticed. Nobody noticed, or nobody said so. I did. I liked it.

By the time my summer vacation was over in Brazil, we were packing to go to Caracas and then to New York. We stayed in the magnificent "Hacienda La Meiga" with my mother's cousin. It was a colonial farmhouse, which had belonged to the family for several hundred years. Every room was vast, with high ceilings. There were graceful antiques and compelling art, patios with gurgling fountains, flowering jasmine, and many servants. The family showed us picture albums of when they spent time with the Prince of Wales and Greta Garbo. They spoke of Venezuelan history and how our family trees intermingled with the best families in Caracas. They told stories of surprising moments with eccentric relatives. There was a terracotta terrace all around the house with nineteenth-century white wicker furniture, sunset pink and yellow hibiscus, and gardenias everywhere. Freshly cut flower arrangements filled the rooms with scents of roses and golden fields. The bedroom assigned to me, for the week we were there, had purple wisteria murals.

Every night we dressed for dinner, and after dinner Victor, my stepfather, played the piano. My mother and her cousin chatted all through the evening. She had two sons and a daughter. The youngest son, Marcos, was very shy and quiet; the older one, Andrés, was good-looking and well-spoken. *Town and Country* had profiled him as one of the most eligible bachelors of the year.

"Oh! Wouldn't it be wonderful if Andrés and Lilizinha fell in love? Why not, I got married at sixteen," my mother's cousin emphasized, waving her soft rose petal white manicured fingers. She was a beautiful woman with auburn hair and lightly powdered ivory skin. It was very far-fetched. He was sweet with me. He called me "Ondine." He was very articulate and witty. Once during that visit, he invited me to his room to hear some music. There was a very highly polished mahogany French Empire commode and bed. The chairs and the bed were upholstered in deep Bordeaux damask. I can't remember which piece of music it was. All I can recall is how petrified and shy I felt and how impossible it was for me to say anything at all while I sat in his room.

The last night we spent there, I decided to sleep naked. My only nightgown had been freshly washed and ironed. I wanted to pack it that way. In the middle of the night, my cousin's father came to my bedside with a lit candlestick in his hand and began to pull down my covers asking me for a hug. I was stunned.

"Let me just kiss you goodnight," he kept repeating. I held onto my sheet under my chin and wouldn't budge.

"No, I'm sleepy, go to your own bed." I persisted several times. I could hear his heavy wine-flavored breathing on my cheek. He didn't give up.

"Let me just give you a hug before you leave, tomorrow." He whispered into my ear.

Determined he was not going to see me naked, I said,

"No, go away." That was that. "I'm sleepy; go away."

He insisted and pulled at the covers even harder with his free hand and kissed me on the cheeks and on my earlobe.

"Just a little hug, I *need.*"

"No," I whispered as loud as I could. I felt my stomach tighten in a knot and my knuckles go white as I clenched the covers close to my neck. He got fed up and left. I heaved a sigh of deep relief.

The next day I didn't dare mention it.

By the time we left Caracas, I had a silent "crush" on Andrés. His parting words were, "I'll call you up in Paris, when I go."

My school was in Pauline Borghese's villa. She was Napoleon Bonaparte's sister. Every time I heard the phone ring, I stretched my ear in hopes that it might be Andrés. It never was.

When my parents moved back to New York, his mother wrote to me saying that he was in New York and was looking forward to seeing me. It was wishful thinking. Nevertheless, it motivated me in part to go back to New York. He was in love with a beautiful divorcée, and his mother didn't approve of that. He ended up marrying her, and their marriage is strong. She is a world-famous fashion designer.

When we got to New York, my father didn't notice my new nose. In Paris, my friend Sabine asked: "What's happened to you? You look prettier." I told her, and we giggled about it. That year I took some acting classes with Christian Stengel. He had been Simone Signoret's teacher. I got the courage to produce, direct, and act in a school production of "*Les Précieuses Ridicules*." I made more connections.

I called Gertrude, my parents' friend. She worked for the American Embassy and shopped at the PX where she got me bags of candy. At her apartment, she introduced me to an American psychiatrist who worked in Paris. I learned that it is imperative for psychiatrists to go through analysis before they begin their practice.

"It's a requirement to graduate." She said.

I toyed with the idea of becoming a child psychiatrist when I grew up.

15

Be the change you want to see in the world.
—Gandhi

I wrote to my father. He was going through his third divorce. "Please, come and live in Paris for a while."

We would have time to become friends, going to the theater, concerts, and museums together. I imagined taking wonderful long walks through the Rive Gauche, the Jardins du Luxembourg, and sitting at cafés discussing the events of the day.

It was too far-fetched a dream. He didn't have any friends or any Francophile interests, although he had spoken French as a child. Maybe it was possible. "No," he replied.

I was lonely in Paris. When my mother and stepfather decided to move back to New York after almost two decades in Brazil, I asked if I could move in with them there.

I independently transferred myself into the French Lycée in New York City.

At first, I was recognized for French composition. I was entered in an international competition among French

Lycées representing my grade for creative writing. I wanted to apply to Georgetown University. I thought I could go to the Foreign Service School and become a good diplomat. I had a vague, romantic idea of being someone with a lot of "*savoir faire*" talking to many different people. As I got acquainted with American culture and began to prefer social life to student life, my grades suffered.

At about that time, I met the son of friends of my parents. They met through my stepfather's work. They were Cubans who left a year after Castro took over. My mother had lived in Havana as a child and recognized the name. After I'd been seeing him for two weeks, my mother and I went to visit my aunt in Nassau. She was summering there. My mother, after explaining all of the above to her sister sitting on the brick veranda overlooking the sea, asked me in a velvety tone, "Did he ask you to marry him yet?" as if boasting that I could attract someone from a good family—meaning well-educated and with social standing. They were comfortable. Maybe in Cuba they were rich.

"No," I said, taken aback. It had not occurred to me. Was this her way of giving him her stamp of approval?

He babysat two parrots that my brothers brought from Brazil. Honório, named after one of the popes in our ancestry, and Maria Fernanda, named after a famous Spanish actress who was related to my great-grandfather. Before we called Henry to inquire about the parrots' wellbeing, my stepfather hooked up the phone microphone to the amplified stereo speaker so everyone in the house, and probably three houses down, could hear my conversation with my new "beau," as my mother called him. My protests went unnoticed. What they all teased me most about, especially my cousins, was how Henry kept repeating in his good English with a flurry of a Latin accent: "The parrots are fine; the parrots are fine." He rolled his *r's* and seemed very eager to please. I had told them that Henry wore "Old Spice" as his cologne. Someone had a bottle of it in the house. My cousins ran after me spraying the cologne and crying, "Here, have some Henry juice!" as they leapt up and down with excitement and giggled.

When we got back to the city, Henry and I continued to get to know each other.

He danced well and was articulate. He had graduated from the University of Pennsylvania Wharton School of Business and was looking for a job that would send him to Spain to avoid being drafted to Vietnam. He resembled the Venezuelan cousin; both had brilliantined dark hair, although Henry was chubbier and shorter. We saw each other more and more.

He drove me to Washington, D.C., to visit Georgetown.

"Come to Spain instead, and marry me," he said.

I had been asked in marriage twice before, and liked one of them. But my mother didn't know them, much less approved of them, so the possibility was completely remote. Marriage seemed possible and satisfying, given my father's reaction to my request for going to college. My mother certainly wasn't encouraging nor paying for it.

Henry finally got a job with an American insurance company in Madrid. They were expecting him in May.

"At first, you had said it was all right that I get my baccalaureate in Madrid; now you are changing your mind?"

I retorted to my mother, when she complained that the wedding dates would interfere with my graduation.

"If he wants to marry you, he'll come back after he has installed himself in Madrid."

"He won't be able to come back right after he starts a new job! You had agreed that we could get married in the spring. You said I could finish the baccalaureate in Madrid and you would explain it to my father."

"Yes, I know, but I talked it over with Victor, and he's the one who has insisted we cannot allow you to get married until you finish your baccalaureate."

In the French curriculum, the last two years of studying are an equivalent of "junior college" beyond high school. There used to be a baccalaureate exam at the end of each one of those two years. Now they had changed it to one single exam at the end of the second year. I was about to take that exam when all this drama of the marriage dates broke out.

At school, I was crying most of the time, not knowing why. It never occurred to me to talk about it to anyone. I didn't think anyone was interested. I couldn't concentrate anymore.

Yet, when I spoke to Victor on the phone, while he was in Europe, I repeated Mummy's words about him to him, he said, "Darling, I just want you to be happy."

As soon as he got back from Europe, my mother convinced Victor to invite Henry for lunch down on Wall Street and maneuver him to change the dates of the wedding. When I heard about it, I couldn't believe it. It was a "*fait accompli.*"

"It's our marriage, not theirs."

Once I felt certain that we were going to be married, I agreed to tell my mother I was spending the night at Sarah Lawrence with another friend and instead spent the night at the Plaza, the first naked night with Henry. He had a room for himself for the night, a small rectangular room with chintzy bedspread and curtains to match and a tall window opening onto 58th Street. We undressed each other slowly. When he took off his underpants, I felt nauseous. I thought it was my problem and I would have to grow out of it. I faked an orgasm. Before we fell asleep, Henry said to me: "I don't believe you are a virgin, because you didn't bleed at all." I had seen a little thread of blood in the john, but felt that whatever I said, he would not believe me. "I don't know what happened. Maybe because I rode a lot of horses."

Why didn't he believe what I was saying? It wasn't a question I was asking myself at the time. The cuddling and embracing was too satisfying to open an inquiry in my mind.

This is a letter my mother wrote to me during that time.

New York, Jan.1967

Dearest Lilizinha:

I am writing you a letter, for it seems so difficult for you and me to "talk" together these days, and also, I confess, because I have terrible saudades of those times, not so far back, when you and I were still "best friends"—when we told each other our dreams, our plans, our fears, and when we trusted each other as a matter of course.

In the meantime you have decided to be "independent." If you were to give it thought, you'd realize that is an enigma, for who among us is independent? We are all interdependent of one another in innumerable ways! If you agree with me this far, we could go on to analyze what it is that you are really looking for, or trying to become.

When you say that you are trying to become independent, you mean of me. Quite right, and I have been trying to achieve this end! You don't suppose that your going to Paris at the age of sixteen was accidental? I started planning that when you were barely fourteen, when I wrote to Mother Mary Boniface. We went to Rome with you in 1961 to visit M.M.B. at the Mother House, especially for her to meet you, and for her to be in contact with M.M. Osmond and arrange for your entrance at Neuilly in 1964. I want you to be "independent," to be "you" as much or more than you do. I don't mean to hurt you, but it is because you are not grown up enough that you don't realize this.

But Lili, you mustn't blame or resent me for the bits of dependence that you may still feel now and then! It is not only normal but also right that a child should depend upon parents. Indeed, whom else should it depend upon? During the child's upbringing, parents do everything possible so that when she is grown up, she will able to look after itself, support herself, and her family if necessary. Since the beginning of time, we are called "minors" until we are twenty-one years old, I suppose, because only by then have we reached complete maturity. Young men, for instance, are urged not to marry before that age, for they then assume the responsibility or the dependence of the young bride, which before that rested upon her parents. So, if you depend upon your parents until you are twenty-one or married, it is not only right but also normal.

You have not depended upon Popi and me for money since last October, but you do morally, spiritually, and even physically in a sense. To behave as if you did not, as if you were no longer a member of our family, is not only ungracious and rude, but also ungrateful and ignoble. As I am your mother, as well as your guardian, I dare to say these strong words as I dared to lay a strong hand on your "po-po" when you were a small child and needed to be corrected, so please read them and accept them with the same love that they were given. The mother who does not correct her child is not a loving mother.

Look around and notice who are those "revoltados" who "divorce" their parents? What do they accomplish? They misconstrue filth for existentialism, existentialism for independence, ignorance for courage, and weakness for strength! Although you are not revolting against society or the system, your revolt is against your mother, who, in your mind, seems domineering and frightens you into silence!

In my defense, I say that the last time you were spanked was ten years ago by Popi, who adores you!

Sometime early in 1965, you wrote to me saying that when you observed young ladies at parties, that you realized how right I'd been when I tried to impress upon you how much more "rafinée" were the ones who neither drank nor smoked. You told me that the ones who did were betraying their "ill-at-easeness," that it was not sophistication they were "putting on," and yet, only a few months later, you arrived in São Paulo smoking like a chimney. Tell me, were you showing your strength by defying the suggestions of your parents? (You must remember that Popi had always been "d'accord" with me on everything to do with your education, and all these decisions were carefully discussed between us. I am trying to share the credit!)

You knew that the scientists have established for a fact that smoking is conducive to cancer in the respiratory tract, that it is a vice that people seek to rid themselves of, that it is not an asset of any kind, and yet you had the "courage" and the "strength" to take it up! And I, your domineering mother, just smiled sadly and said, "Well, it's your life, Lili, but at least smoke like a lady," and the only time that I did get angry is early last year when you were imitating that French girl, and behaving like you-know-what.

I think that anyone would agree that rudeness, insolence, and ingratitude are despicable. They are not synonymous with independence, and that some independence could be achieved through strength of character, constructively applied in everyday life, with characteristics such as humility, a sense of honor, a sense of duty, a sense of humor! And giving rather than demanding and ever taking more and more. These are strengthening qualities. Even to Mother Earth we must return in order for her to continue giving. If you were to read the ancient writings of the old religions, of the thinkers of antiquity, you'd find that what I'm saying are very basic, elemental truths, very necessary for the development of a healthy mind and soul and body.

When you wrote from Paris that you wanted to come, you told me, "I'll help you, Mummy, in every way I can," and I felt that I would need you, that I could count on you, depend on you, lean on you. Here was your golden opportunity to be the woman that both Popi and I fully expected you to be, for we both knew that this was going to be a very difficult year for us all, but instead you behave like an ill-bred little girl, untidy, selfish, rude, and inconsiderate, things you had never been before (you had always been untidy, but now that you were grown-up, I was certain that you'd have the self-discipline to correct yourself!).

I am almost certain that as long as you continue to be overly vain, you will continue to feel dissatisfied with yourself and envious even of people not as beautiful as you, for you will envy the qualities that they have that you do not. As long as you do not seek to recognize where your duty lies, you will not gain the admiration and respect that you desire. To be admired for your physical beauty only is an insipid and short-lived cup of nectar; besides, you'll find that the competition gets tough sooner than you think.

Then my parents bought a house in Tuxedo Park, a gated community, with rolling hills covered in pines encrusted by beautiful lakes and vast stone Victorian houses built at the turn of the century. It included a country club where young promising debutantes were introduced into society at the cherished Tuxedo Ball. Before moving, I had the opportunity to clean out my bedroom on 75th Street. I found all of my father's letters in his teeny skimpy phrases. In a surge of detachment, I threw them all away, except for one. It was addressed to my mother and he said, "Where is my daughter?" I loved that little phrase. Recently, when hearing what another father had written his daughter from far away saying he wished he had been there her first day of school or for her first performance or dance. I realized my father had never wished nor cared about anything like that, or if he did, he never wrote nor spoke about it.

On my birthday, in the new house, after several drinks, my mother spoke in her husky voice, "It was so funny when I was down in Rio, pregnant with Lilizinha; every night I teased Uncle Ogilvy, made him think that a different man was the father of the child I was bearing. It was so amusing. I had him so confused."

I was not amused in the slightest. Tears ran down my cheeks in the kitchen. That was the night that Henry and I planned my escape.

The next day, I was dropped off at school. Then, I went to Grand Central and took the train to Larchmont, where Henry's parents lived. That night Henry convinced his parents to go talk to mine and let them know that we would elope unless we could decide the dates of our marriage on our own. I left school two months before the last exam.

My philosophy teacher at the Lycée wrote me a note saying that maybe I had made the better choice to get married instead of getting my baccalaureate.

So they gave in.

A few days later, we went to my parents' house to get my belongings. I was moving out and going to stay with my girlfriend Amanda in Greenwich Village. When we arrived, there was no one there. So I packed and Henry carried things into his car. I came across my old diary. It was fire engine red fake leather with a gold-plated buckle. The outer covers were slightly cushioned so they felt malleable to the touch. I had recorded different events and mostly feelings I had for boys that I knew at school. When Henry began to read it, he got very upset and belted out, "You won't need this anymore," and, wearing a grimace on his face, proceeded to tear it all up into small pieces so it could not be pieced together again. I was dismayed. That was my diary. Who was he to tear it to pieces? I was so eager to please him, I didn't complain at all, and laughed it off. I did not know how to confront him.

At one point my mother called. I was so scared of speaking my mind to her that Henry wrote some words in block letters, so that I would say them to my mother over the phone: "WE'VE CHOSEN THE CHURCH AND THE DATE OF THE MARRIAGE."

By the time we finished packing and were about to leave, my parents arrived in the driveway. It was snowing heavily. It was more than a foot deep, purple-white icy powder everywhere. My mother barely said hello and marched into the house. Ten minutes later, she stormed out so furious, fuming white smoke, hot air mixed with cold, an unstoppable engine. She came up to me and slapped me on the face. "Get out, both of you. I don't want you here anymore. Just get out."

She may have found Henry's written message to me. I ran away.

"My mother hates me. My mother hates me. My mother hates me," I cried, trudging through the snow along the lake, sobbing, "My mother hates me. My mother hates me," until I collapsed on a snowy bank of the lake. Henry eventually picked me up and drove away with me back to his house. I never lived with my parents again.

This is one of the letters my mother wrote to me at the time:

> *Dearest Lilizinha:*
>
> *On the day following your nineteenth birthday, you left home with Popi and the boys to go to school, and instead of doing so, went to the Janfuls and told Olga that you couldn't stand living here any longer. That evening, she and her husband came here to get some clothes for you and to acquaint me with the details of your deep-seated resentment and the communication barriers that existed between you and me.*
>
> *They, of course, had no way of knowing that we had been talking, laughing and crying together affluently and fluently in four languages—until very recently—so I listened in stunned silence.*
>
> *You have authorized your fiancé to dare to hurt your grandmother, who has loved you and looked after you so tenderly, by saying to her, "Lili has*

been unhappy since the day upon which she was born!"

You have uttered with your own lips, here, in front of this house, in front of your brothers and your little sister, that you have never trusted me! That was the last time I saw you—March 25th.

All the calumnias were forgiven even before you said them, for, as one day you will discover, a mother forgives all and can never do enough for any child of hers.

I emphasize this because one of your complaints, according to Tanti Lili, is that I did too much for you; I must confess that you have convinced me. You are right; I have done too much for you, but would probably make the same mistakes again, being a mother.

You have hurt me very deeply, Lilizinha. In fact, you could not possibly have hurt me more than you have. And Popi is wounded beyond words. But I have managed to re-find my calm, for my conscience, thank God, is clear. You say that you love your mother, but you don't want to see me, speak to me, or even write to me! You say you don't want to hurt your mother, but you go right on doing so willfully and knowingly!

All these things are evidence of such a confused mind and soul that I pity you with all my heart and am all the sadder because I cannot, may not, come to you and hold you close and wipe away the tears and the fears and the anguish that must be tormenting you.

But which imaginary windmills are you fighting anyway? I have not tried to impose my wishes on you.

After the initial shock of your having quit your studies only three months before getting your baccalaureate, and advancing your wedding date to the week before you would have finished your studies, I capitulated entirely!

Then, I decided, and Popi with me, to go along with anything and everything you decided to do, and I told you so. "Just keep me posted, and I'll try to do whatever I can to help you and to make you happy." Your happiness, finally, is my only concern.

But I am so tired. I am not begging you to come home, or to do this or that. For you must and will do exactly as you wish.

But what are the advantages? Whose respect are you gaining by making such an ungraceful departure from a home in which you have always been pampered by parents who adored you?

It is because it is so difficult to envisage a marriage that is happy with such a senseless three-month period preceding it, for a foundation, as it were. It is because of this that I am writing to you once again.

For your own good, Lilizinha! For the sake of your future happiness, consider and reconsider the path that you are following. Seek the advice of third parties who are not emotionally involved.

Perhaps a priest could help you. Consider your pride! How can you hold your head high after insulting your family so ignobly? Consider the Janfuls, how you must be hurting them. They, who were so overjoyed about their oldest son's engagement to you. What a happy occasion your wedding day, and all the days leading to it, was to have been. But you are robbing them and yourself (not to speak of me) of much of that joy, by your inexplicable behavior. And all this sadness to no advantage at all!

I have also been told that you "expect" me to appear at the church on May 27th, calm and dignified, not having seen you for two months, because you wish it so, that you expect me to come to your wedding and be able to smile at you affectionately, as if you had not been insulting me with your actions and with your lies for four months, that you expect me to kiss you and give you my blessing; give my blessing to you, who have publicly rejected me, your mother.

And these things I will do because it is no matter what you do, or what you say, you cannot change me, your mother.

God enlighten you, my poor daughter.

With all my love, as always, Mummy.

During a discussion with Henry over the phone, I must have said something he didn't like at all, he yelled at me at the top of his lungs: "I wish I were there so I could crush your skull against the wall and see its contents dripping down to the floor." I was shocked, but not enough for it to dawn on me he could be serious.

At first, my mother had been delighted because Henry was from a good Cuban family. Soon she must have felt he was controlling me more than she was. She never actually said that, I only suspect it. If she noticed something she didn't like about him, she never told me what it was. I never felt she truly opened her heart to me. She refused to send invitations. When my stepfather tried to arbitrate between us, she said curtly to him: "Stay out of it. You are not her father."

My grandmother had the wedding dress, because she was going to make the few adjustments it needed. When I called her to pick it up, she said: "I feel like burning this damned dress and throwing it out the window. You have hurt your mother so much; you don't deserve it."

Everyone in my family saw it only from my mother's point of view. Or maybe they didn't want to argue with her because she always had to be right. Nobody in my family asked me what was going on and why was I so unhappy. The only aunt who seemed to have a sympathetic ear was Tanti Fargo, but she also didn't want to get into trouble with my mother who was indefatigably loud and outspoken when she was annoyed. I had to call Tanti Lili.

"Tanti, do you think you could convince Grandmaman to give you back the wedding dress?"

She sounded a bit upset, yet not as intransigent as my mother and grandmother.

"Yes, I probably can. Why don't you come and pick it up on Thursday afternoon?" When we did go, I felt we were tip-toeing because our welcome was counted in seconds. We left immediately, dress in hand.

A few days before the ceremony, Henry and I got into a discussion. There were many, because I had left my house and now was staying in his parents' house and at my friend Amanda's. In the middle of all this, I started crying hysterically and Henry slapped me across the face. I lost my balance and tumbled to the ground. We were out on the street in front of his house. I was stunned and quiet. I could have stopped the whole relationship right then and there. Instead, it seemed quite familiar. He said later: "It was for your own good; you were hysterical, I had to bring you back to normal." Just as my mother used to say to me, "It's for your own good," and I believed her. I had to wear extra makeup on my wedding day so that the black and blue under my eye would not show.

Years later, I wished my parents had seen that play that has been running in New York for thirty years or more, *The Fantastiks*. It was about two couples. They were next-door neighbors and very good friends. They wished that the son of one would marry the daughter of the other. So after all four together planned their strategy, they began by forbidding their respective child to seek or frequent the company of the other. That's how they sparked the interest of one for the other. Finally, their children did get married to each other.

By my mother's opposition to the dates of the marriage, she unconsciously pushed us both closer together.

I spent the night before the wedding at Amanda's place. She was my best friend and a successful actress. We had been friends since we were babies. Our mothers were best friends. They had met in New York and later in Athens, Seville and Lisbon. We had Earl Grey tea, late at night, while talking and giggling as usual in the large first floor kitchen of the turn of the century townhouse. Then I went up to bed repeating: “Tomorrow I’m getting married. Tomorrow, I’m getting married. Tomorrow, I’m getting married. Everything is in place, everything is happening.”

On a cool and sunny May morning, my daddy picked me up in a black Lincoln Continental limousine. My future mother-in-law came over to help me with the antique Spanish mantilla that had been in her family for years. She also lent me a beautiful diamond brooch to pin on the dress right at the seam of the Empire dress, centered between my breasts. I stepped off the steps of 66 Bank Street, into the chilly spring May noon; I was in a daze. My mother came dressed in a dark gray shantung suit to the church. They wore gray faces too. In the pictures, they forced the smiles. Victor’s back was ‘killing him’; we had heard because he worked with my future father-in-law. My little sister was one of the bridesmaids. My brothers both came in their red jackets. My youngest brother Samson shed tears during the wedding. A picture of him in the church shows his reddened eyes. They showed up; that is what counts.

My grandmother did not come to my wedding. I remember there was an old woman there. A lot of people asked who she was. I wasn’t quite sure if she was an elegant bum or a disheveled guest. She was in a purple wool hat and a bottle-green tightly fitted jacket; her hair was short and gray and curly, it seemed windblown. She wore bright scarlet red lipstick. She got into a few of the pictures. Her eyes were so wide open. She looked pleasantly surprised. Maybe she was my grandmother’s spirit.

The last time I ever saw my grandmother was at my cousin Margaret's sumptuous marriage. When I approached my grandmother, she abruptly turned her back on me and walked away in a huff. While I was living in Spain for the next five years, she died of a brain tumor. I was surprised I didn't cry.

16

"See the light, and your life will reflect it. Deny the light, and in your blindness you will create chaos. When you choose to open your eyes again, the chaos will be no more".
—Marianne Williamson

In Madrid, at first, I felt listless. We stayed at a hotel for two months until we found a place and furnished it minimally. We didn't have much money. We had spent the day looking at different pieces of furniture. The sofa for the living room seemed to be the priority after the bed. One evening we were discussing this in the hotel room.

"Which sofa did you like the best?" Henry asked me as he took off his shirt and sat at the edge of one of the beds in his T-shirt.

"I liked the blue velvet ones; they were the most attractive but also the most expensive," I said, letting my voice trail as my eyes watched Henry and focused on what he was thinking.

"I know," he said. "We not only need the sofa but also an armoire and everything for the bedroom and furniture for the terrace." His tone became more exasperated and nasal at the thought of needing so much and not having the money for it. I could smell his accumulated deodorant-scented rancid perspiration.

With the desire to alleviate the pressure, I said: "We don't have to buy the furniture all at once. We can buy it little by little."

I barely had time to breathe before I felt a sharp burning punch across my face and head. It felt like thunder exploding in my skull.

"You are thinking like your mother, poverty mentality. I can borrow the money from my employer and pay him back slowly. We will have a respectable and perfect apartment."

It was a good idea. I hadn't thought of it, but I did not need to be hit to get the point across. When I said, "I'm sorry," hoping to calm him, it only exacerbated his rage, and he threw me across the bed and hit me all over my body. I thought I better stay put like a pillow. The next day my face was swollen, with blue marks, so I stayed inside until I could mask it with makeup and would be able to face the people outside. I was in shock, yet I did not question his right to do this. Years later, my ex-mother-in-law wrote a letter to her son admitting that she had overheard the hitting, from the room next door, and telling him he must treat me with the kindness and respect I deserve.

Once he got the money from his employer to furnish the apartment, he said to me one day: "We need a carpet for the living room. I'm working all day. Why don't you go and pick one out?"

I was trembling inside because I didn't know what was beautiful. "Okay," I said tentatively. After looking around an exquisite shop, I chose a carpet that I felt would work well with the other furniture. I bought it and had it delivered.

I was thrilled when I saw Henry pleased with how well it blended with everything else. The choosing and buying of that carpet was a cornerstone in the building of my self-confidence. I promised myself: when I have children, I would allow them to pick out their own clothes and make decisions about the decoration of their rooms. As teenagers they will easily recognize what is beautiful for themselves.

After the apartment was all furnished, when we walked in together, he often said: "Look, how beautiful, the neighbors' apartment is!" We giggled together. He couldn't own it in his heart. It was a façade.

On our honeymoon, I told him I had been faking the orgasms and I didn't want to do that anymore. His reaction was to go to the kitchenette, pull out a bottle of whiskey and a glass, sit at the kitchen table, shoulders drooped, head hanging over his glass moaning and repeating: "I can't believe I married a frigid woman. I married a frigid woman." He sat at the kitchen table for a good part of the night, chugging it down, feeling powerless. Once, while we were attempting to make love, and, as usual, I couldn't have an orgasm, he slapped me in a rage.

I wasn't seeing what was happening. I had bouts of conjunctivitis. Henry often said to me in a wistful tone, "You don't know who you are, and when you find out, I'm afraid you will leave me."

My first inkling was after reading *The Doll House* by Ibsen. Henry's cousin lent me books. I was riveted by it. I identified with Nora, the heroine, and was shocked at how mindless my position was. I truly felt as though I were Henry's doll. He chose most of my clothes, asked me to go to the hairdresser twice a week, and showed me off to his acquaintances and business associates. He never inquired about my interests. When I expressed the desire of wanting to learn how to drive a car, he replied he would be too scared thinking about me driving around. I was there to satisfy his needs.

He must have been satisfying some of mine. At least, I had the quiet time to read and explore my feelings about what I was reading. My curiosity for reading sharpened. I considered going back to the Lycée. I walked by the one in Madrid but never went in to apply. Instead, I spent many afternoons at the Prado fascinated by the Hieronymus Bosch triptychs and the dark tortuous Goyas. In many of the books I read, the heroines mentioned Dostoyevsky, I found *Crime and Punishment* and could not put it down. What a whirlwind of detailed emotions from premeditated survival-driven murder to shame and guilt and remorse. The author was so thorough in his description of emotional turmoil, I felt I had met my brother, my soul mate, I also felt all those feelings of hate and despicable horror at myself. The novel's old lady upstairs, for me, was my mother. I too had killed her in a symbolic way, so she would have no more power over me, but that was an illusion. Dead, she still had power to manipulate through the guilt I felt at having done that. I also understood that I needed to break away, so I could find out whom I was and was not, independent of her.

Three years later, my mother and stepfather called. They wanted to visit us. On the dates they were coming, Henry was leaving on a business trip. I didn't tell him about it, not until after he came back and they were gone, so he wouldn't be nervous while he was away. They came. We spoke politely. We had a few meals together. They left. I felt apprehensive throughout their whole stay. We never mentioned one single word of the past. All we spoke about was the present: what was happening with my brothers and sister, the rest of the family, about my grandmother's death. Apparently, just before my grandmother died, she told my mother, "*Quand Lilizinha reviendra, ouvre-lui les bras*." (When Lilizinha returns, open your arms.) So I'm guessing my mother took that message to heart and came to extend peace and understanding between us. I thank her for that.

17

Just be what you are and speak from your guts and heart—it's all a man has.
—Hubert Humphrey

The Spanish that I relearned was so *castizo*, my Cuban in-laws and friends were jealously amused.

"*Habla como una madrileña.*" (She speaks like a *madrileña.*) They teased me.

We had a few lovely Spanish friends. With them, we began having séances because they enjoyed them and showed us how. Spirits emerged and spelled out vivid messages. I was spooked and fascinated. The first time it happened, we were in the north of Spain spending some summer holidays near Santander with Henry's family. We were invited to go for the evening to a friend's place. This was a beautifully trellised Victorian house, with purple wisteria dripping all around. An Englishman brought over an English architect to design his house and the grounds and built it at the turn of the century.

The story goes that this Englishman had come to the north of Spain to make his fortune ten years before the house was built. He began working in the coal mines, and eventually owned one himself. When on a visit to Paris, he came across a young English girl sobbing in distress in a café. She had answered an advertisement to be a governess to some children in Paris and now could not find the people at that address.

The Englishman invited her to come with him to the north of Spain where initially she had to disguise herself as a man so the miners would not be distracted by the presence of a woman. Eventually, the Englishman married the girl called Charlotte and had many children with her. The Englishman asked the English architect to live with them while he built his new house.

Six of us were sitting in the study of this house around a three-legged table with all our fingertips touching the top of the table and our thumbs and pinky fingers lightly connected. I kept double-checking that nobody's legs or knees made contact with the table. We were silent for a while, praying and asking for a spirit to come and then waiting to see what would happen.

The table began to move by itself. One of the legs lifted up and tapped the floor. Keeping my fingers on the table, I bent over, my eyes focused under the table, to make sure no one was moving it. We asked the spirit its name. The table spelled out Charlotte. The first tap being A, the second B and so on. When this name showed up, our hostess told us Charlotte and the architect had an affair. We asked the spirit who was moving the table when she was born, and later it checked out to be correct. One of our friends said to Charlotte's spirit, or to the table, out loud, in a tantalizing tone: "So, tell us about how much you liked that architect, heh, heh, Charlotte."

Suddenly the table spun riotously and directed itself toward our friend who had been so indiscreet. We all cried, "Say you're sorry; apologize, please."

The table seemed to want to attack the girl who had challenged it. Yet, as soon as she said, "Forgive me, please don't get so upset; I'm sorry, I didn't realize it was such a sensitive issue," the table subsided. I shook and giggled nervously incessantly. My body curled over my knees in a fetal position. The giggles kept erupting until I cried. After I composed myself, we went on to ask her how many of her children were buried in the grounds. Later, the numbers were checked with the records and were correct. These events changed me forever. That night Henry and I slept huddled together in awe at what we had experienced.

From then on we participated in many séances, whenever we were together with the same group of friends. Once, my father's spirit came along and told me I was too ethereal. He was right. I didn't feel grounded and was most of the time in my thoughts wrapped in a veil of dazes.

I learned how to play bridge with the Spanish women. It taught me how to think ahead and keenly observe. I pulled out the silver tea set my aunt Lili had given me and placed it on a silent butler tray. I made moist egg salad or cucumber sandwiches, cut up in small squares after trimming the brown edges off. I also got buttery crumbling almond and chocolate cookies. We sat around the card table reveling in our concentrations and the bits of gossip that would dribble in between games, smoking mentholated, long, slim cigarettes. I gained confidence. I practiced on my own for hours while Henry slept late on the weekends. I had a little plastic board that played the other hands while I worked on mine.

With Henry I often traveled through Spain. Toledo and El Escorial were the two closest places to take friends from the States. We also explored in many other directions.

At one point, I asked: "When do you want to have children?"

"I don't want to have any children. I am too selfish."

I was stunned. I had been taking the pill since before we married, expecting at some point to stop taking it. I had not asked him before getting married, but if he didn't want children, I certainly would not have them with him.

Most of the time, I read. Ayn Rand became a passion. She inspired me to take responsibility for myself and not pass the buck. Yet, every time I thought, "He hasn't beaten me in a month or two," feeling relieved and hopeful, within the following ten days something clicked and he went black.

He came home one evening and inquired whether I had bought a certain *eau de cologne* he liked and had asked me to buy. I hadn't. "When are you actually going to get something done around here?" he hammered. He observed himself in the mirror as he gesticulated with his harangue.

"You think you look attractive, when you talk this way?" I quipped. That did it. He hit me so hard my brain felt like beans in a maraca. He grabbed my head by the hair and banged my head against the wall, until I passed out. Then he got scared. When I woke up, he was crying and carrying me back to the bed. My hair fell out in clumps. We didn't talk for a day.

The following afternoon I confronted him in the kitchen. I was quivering barefoot on the cold tile. He was standing naked.

"How can you say you are the 'good man' you think you are and also beat your wife?" Trembling inside, I continued. "It doesn't make sense! It's such a contradiction! How do you explain that to yourself?" His face was blank. He was silent.

Then he walked over to me, shook my hand, and said, "Congratulations." I was taken aback and thought now he would change.

18

"To live is to be born every minute. Death occurs when birth stops. Physiologically, our cellular system is in a process of continual birth; psychologically, however, most of us cease to be born at a certain point."
—Erich Fromm

The day I heard Joan's voice again, my feet were perched on the parapet of our spacious terrace on Maria de Molina. This is a main thoroughfare in Madrid. Our apartment faced the French Embassy, a sumptuous estate with flowering gardens and high gray stucco walls. I was about to jump off the eighth floor.

My face was black and blue from having been beaten the night before by my drunken husband. I felt there was nothing to live for. I had spent the morning sobbing. I had no one to talk to.

I climbed onto the black wrought iron chair, held the wall behind me, and stood on the wide green painted metal railing of the wall. The cars were rushing by down at the bottom. I wondered how it would feel falling through the air and crashing either on the pavement or on one of the cars. Or worse still, on the road and then being run over by a surprised driver, before he could hit the brake. The pain I would incur seemed less than the agony I was already experiencing. To be alive and to be treated as nothing of value is worse than to be dead and to be acknowledged as dead. At least, it's the truth, and truth begets more truth. My heart felt battered. My brain numbed. My skeleton was barely worth holding up.

This way I would go into a continuous nothing with the advantage of not being conscious of it. I thought of my mother; she seemed so far away, as if she didn't care. What difference did it make to anyone? The world would go on forever. I had been a little ant that had disappeared. I think my father was still alive. It didn't even occur to me to call him. He could have been dead by then.

Slipping through the air, nothing to grab onto, and the inevitable disintegrating crash. I could see my limbs twisted in soggy, bloody clothes. My face disfigured, flattened by the pavement; people rushing to the horrifying sight. Traffic immobilized, yet only for less than an hour. It would end as a two-line obituary; a grim funeral; shameful, guilty, despairing silence.

I let go of the wall, stared at the traffic below, and began to lose my balance. "Maybe there is more to life than this." Screeched a voice inside of me,

I grabbed the wall again in that last instant, heaved a sigh of relief, and crawled down to the ceramic floor. Shaking, feeling faint, nauseated, I felt my bones trembling like a young tree wobbles in the cold wind. I crouched on my knees by my potted roses and smelled the damp earth. I stared at leaves drying up and new ones sprouting in neat little green conical envelopes edged in regal purple. The red and pink buds pressed together like tight lips holding on to their silence.

How was I going to leave this whole life, all organized and orderly, and start somewhere else, in a completely different place? It seemed impossible, insurmountable. Then, I heard the voice again.

"It can be done; you can do it."

Where was that voice from? It was the same voice that grabbed me and pulled me out of my deathly stupor.

"Who are you?"

"You remember me. I am Joan. You sent me away."

"I can barely move or think or speak. I feel I'm starting all over again."

"You are."

"What am I starting?"

"A new vision of yourself."

"How do you know I can?"

"You know what you want."

"I don't. I just don't want this anymore."

"How do you imagine yourself feeling happy, peaceful?"

"I've never done that."

"Now is always the best time."

"Where are you from, and how come you always seem to have the right answer? Why didn't I listen to you? Where are you?"

"I'm right here, with you."

There was a new feeling in the air. I stayed up all night to see on television the astronauts step on the moon for the first time. There were many people in Spain, simple people who thought it had been rigged as a show, but that it wasn't true. It is hard to embrace how powerful we can be. It was the first time the Earth was seen by man as a celestial presence.

September 13th. My stepmother called. They went dancing the night before. She was making breakfast. He was brushing his teeth; massive heart attack. Dead before he hit the floor. I never saw him dead. We arrived for the sprinkling of the ashes in the ocean off a friend's boat. I cried and sobbed on the bed in private. I hadn't got to know him. Now it was final, sealed. Was it engraved in my brain cells? Or could I ever change that perception of him? My stepsister, my husband, and I had a séance at his house two days after, and his spirit came. He spelled out that he had a message for Lili: "I love you."

A few months after we returned to Madrid, Henry and I were in a bad car accident. Neither of us remembers what happened. We were each in and out of a coma for a week in the same hospital room. I woke up once for a short while. I was shown a mirror. My face seemed to have been swallowed by a black and blue balloon. I did not recognize myself. Another time I woke up to see Henry peeing out the window; another time he was hitting the nurse, and they had to tie him down to the bed.

We know Henry was driving and that our car was totaled, even though we didn't hit another car. We had been on our way to spend the weekend in Portugal. We stopped for lunch. After we got back on the road, the car was found turned over, at the bottom of a small cliff, at the edge of the road on the way to Portugal, near Talavera de la Reina. They suspect Henry fell asleep at the wheel. When he woke up and tried to control the car in the rain, it skidded abruptly off the road. We were sent home to sleep for a couple of months: Valium in the morning, afternoon and evening. We woke up for the bathroom and a little food; then, back to sleep; the way to heal a brain concussion. I got better sooner than he did and went out. I took up horseback riding. I was getting another chance at life.

Whenever Henry talked about the accident, he made it sound worse and worse. He felt he couldn't go back to work. His right arm was trembling. He was stuttering. We decided to have him checked in New York by a doctor who only recommended rest. Henry sounded disappointed when he spoke about the diagnosis. He had been expecting surgery to be required. I felt nauseous whenever he walked into the room.

When we visited my stepmother in Florida, I shared these feelings with her. She said: "Whatever you decide you want to do, I will help you. Your father is not here. I am your father."

When I got to New York, I told my cousins' governess, "He has been beating me for years."

"Lilizinha, you cannot allow that to happen. You must leave. That is totally unacceptable." She fixed her serious large brown-eyed gaze upon me, so I understood what an intransigent position I needed to free myself. She pursed her lips and shook her head from side to side in silence to continue her statement. She was showing me the attitude I must take.

Until then, I thought it was part of marriage, to be beaten! I had heard it at home and took it for granted.

We were staying at Tanti Lili's house in New York. Petunia, my dearest friend and cousin, turned us on to the first joint we ever smoked. She was a senior at the University of Pennsylvania.

"I have an inexplicable urge to eat," Henry said a few moments after taking his first and only puff. He also wanted a shower. He couldn't turn on the hot water. When I went to help him, by mistake, I forgot to mix it with cold water initially, so he yelled, "You're trying to kill me." I realized then I didn't want him physically dead, but I was fed up with him.

"I am not stoned, yet, I have this inexplicable urge to eat," he kept repeating.

When one starts wishing someone dead, it's time to start leaving.

I begged Petunia to come to Madrid when she got to Europe for Spring break. I couldn't bear the idea of being in Madrid without anybody to talk to. She came and it was wonderful. We got stoned and went to the Prado where the Velasquez became three-dimensional. Especially the dogs—beagles or pointers—stood out as if they were panting and were about to jump out at us. When we walked through the streets of Madrid stoned, I felt naked, as if the roof had been blown off my house by a hurricane; the Spaniards on the sidewalk did not seem to notice. It was still warm, the end of the summer, and I was shivering.

While Petunia was there, a Cuban polo player who had been flirting at parties with me for years called from Marbella, insisting that I come down, so we could see each other. We had bumped into each other several times at 'Puerta de Hierro', the country club where I began to ride horses regularly after the accident.

"Are you happy in your marriage?" he asked as soon as the conversation could subside into a closer exchange beyond the usual formalities and initial chit-chat.

"Yes," I said, not very convinced.

"Why do you always have such a sad look on your face?" he insisted.

I looked away in wistful silence wondering how I felt about this marriage. Sometimes we're so accustomed to a discomfort, it becomes second nature to us, and we feel resigned to it, until someone points it out to us as something unacceptable and opens our eyes to our forbearance. How does the caterpillar feel when it cannot tolerate its chrysalis anymore?

Horseback riding was a good way to get back into the world, after those months of sleeping. It was a way to breathe the balance of nature back into my cells and allow myself to be guided by its rhythms.

Alone, I kept thinking about this man and wishing he would call. I was starving for affection.

Petunia suggested that I go and find out how I felt about him. Also it would allow me to get away on my own. I called my parents' friends who took care of me in Athens and in Seville when I was two while my mother traveled with her Portuguese lover. They now lived in Marbella. Their youngest daughter was Amanda's sister. She was there visiting her parents. They were happy to hear from me. I felt soothed and protected to be with my family's friends. She was a wonderful painter, and he, a diplomat for the United Nations. Their house on the hills towered over the village and the ocean beyond. Life was teeming below and the quiet hill was studded with blossoming peach and apricot trees and scents of oranges and limes. My room opened into the garden. I made them a *ropa vieja*, ('old clothes'), a Cuban dish with stringy meat in tomato sauce and lots of fluffy white rice. They liked it. I stayed a few days.

I arrived in Marbella and was able to see my friend, the polo player, that same evening. The attraction was very strong, partly the forbidden fruit, partly the man who seemed to care about how I felt and who desired me intensely. It was hard not to surrender, in the car, after dinner when he kissed me and wouldn't stop, as if sucking at a delicious ripe fruit. His hands caressed me with a fervor I had never felt before.

"What is going on there?" A floodlight began to light the car from behind. "What is happening here?" said a gruff voice, as the shafts of light kept swinging through the car. We could hear the grinding of rock and rustling of bushes as they approached.

"Nothing, officer," He said, as we scrambled into more presentable positions. "We were looking for a lost earring. That's why we stopped." Our faces shone with perspiration. We were hoping it was too dark to see the redness of our blushing.

The officers shone the light into our faces and asked for his documents.

Then they let us go. He took me back to my friends.

It was great to be lavished with attention. He was steeped in the horse world; I was still searching for myself. I didn't think I was in love and told him so.

Back in Madrid, everything seemed senseless. I wasn't meant to be there anymore. I didn't exist. I had no one to talk to. It was hard to see Henry, except for my past experience of him.

I couldn't envision myself leading a double life. My polo player friend was proposing I wear a wig and meet him in the afternoons for the movies! It wasn't my style. I called my mother in Brussels and asked if I could see her. She said, "Of course." My mother and stepfather had moved to Brussels a few years earlier. He was the head of the multinational company he worked for in Europe. I called my stepmother, in Florida, who immediately had an airline ticket issued for me.

I went to my in-laws to say good-bye. They had moved to Madrid a few years before. I told them I was going to Brussels to visit my mother and then to New York. My mother-in-law took me aside into her bedroom to ask what was going on. I said, "I feel nauseated when he walks into the room. I must leave."

"Are you sure there is nothing I can do to help?"

"It's over."

"I understand," she said. "I had been suspecting that he was hurting you. I'm sorry to see you go."

Henry asked for my engagement ring back and a gold necklace his mother had given me. I slipped them off and handed them to him. Whatever I needed to do to free myself was worth doing.

Henry cried, sobbed, and with his face slobbered and reddened with tears, he begged me to stay, saying he would change. I said it was too late. I packed and left for Brussels.

19

'The quality of mercy is not strained.
It dropeth as the gentle rain from heaven
upon the place beneath. It is twice blessed:
It blesseth him that gives and him that takes',
—Shakespeare, *The Merchant of Venice*

My mother and I had a friendly and cautious exchange. She was eager to befriend me and emotionally support me. I wanted to develop a new relationship with her where we might eventually understand together why we had become so estranged from each other. I yearned for a mother with an unconditional embrace. I didn't know how to reach that dimension with her. We never spoke of the very difficult time before the wedding. I didn't feel equipped to handle that depth of interaction. Our exchanges remained pleasantly superficial.

While staying with her in Brussels, I started to plan to go back to New York. I could stay with Tanti Lili until I got settled and found a job and a place of my own.

She gave me a lot of phone numbers of friends of hers who would be happy to help me find a job or anything else I might need. Among them was the name of Bertrand Smye.

"He was in love with me," my mother explained, as we sat around her kitchen table after breakfast, "when I was leaving your father. I couldn't stay with him because he was married. I was his wife's friend. He would have left his wife for me. How could I have lived with myself? So I left," she said, giving me an unrequested explanation of her relationship with Bertrand Smye.

I stayed a week with my mother exploring a few of the outstanding sites around Brussels. The boys were away at school. Ilona my younger sister loved to draw caricatures of her favorite and least favorite people. She was fluent in French with the Flemish accent and had us belly laughing with her vivid imitation of how the cleaning lady and the vendors at the market spoke. I felt welcomed and distanced by the years of separation and misunderstandings. My father-in-law headed the Madrid office for the same company that my stepfather represented in Europe. Yet, my father-in-law had specifically requested not to have to report to my stepfather, because of all the family tensions we had in the past.

"Do the Janfuls know you are leaving?" my mother asked with circumspection.

"Yes, I went to their apartment and explained." I held back the details, as I washed the breakfast dishes.

Tanti Lili in New York also welcomed me with open arms and offered for me to stay in the apartment up on the fourth floor of her townhouse on 92nd Street. All her children were away at college. She was very generous lending me clothes. While I slipped them on and off, choosing one for that evening, we talked about what happened in Spain and whom I was meeting now in New York. The room I stayed in had high ceilings, a white wicker desk, and Mycene blue and ivory cotton curtains and bedspread that gave the room integrity. It had a tall oak chest of drawers with a record player on it. It even had an adjacent kitchenette. Nobody from the rest of the household needed to come up there. This was my cousin Petunia's room.

I called Bertrand Smye to ask him if he had a job for me. I explained my situation.

"Come in tomorrow and we'll talk about it."

The next day, he gave me a job right inside his private office where I addressed envelopes for hours and hours. I never talked to other people in the rest of the office. His private secretary installed me at a desk facing a wall. It had an IBM electric typewriter and boxes with hundreds of white unaddressed envelopes and a thick list of addresses. It was a promotional mailing for a real estate development on the island of Eleuthera.

His very handsome married son stopped by to say hello for very short periods of time. Bertrand Smye's new glamorous wife visited once in a while. I noticed his nose was very much like the nose I used to have. I never dared to ask him anything, but the suspicion has lingered. I didn't stay for more than a week. Soon, I got a Christmas season job selling ladies' underwear at Bonwit Teller.

It was at this time, staying at Tanti Lili's, working, going to school at night that I began to listen to Beethoven's Sixth Symphony over and over again, "The Pastorale"; it seemed to say just what I needed to hear: fields, open space, rolling gentle hills, grazing sheep, a big bluish purple sky, tall shady lacy trees, days that reach out far into the horizon attempting to catch the dreams we cast out into the ether.

I came across a copy of *The Art of Loving* by Erich Fromm. The more I read, the more I understood that love was an unconditional giving of oneself, that it was a much deeper communion of spirit than the attraction or repulsion I had experienced. It also is a skill that requires practice. If I could unconditionally embrace and nurture myself, then I might be able to deeply appreciate someone else.

Soon, I got my transcripts from the Lycée and was able to apply to the New School of Social Research, where I attended classes in American and Russian literature, political science, writing and playwriting, psychology and parapsychology. I thought I might want to become a psychologist or a writer. Mostly, I wanted to learn how to be the best mother I could be.

In the parapsychology class, the professor asked me to sit at the front of the class. Before he guided me into a light trance, he showed us a sealed envelope in his hand.

"There is a specific drawing on the page that is folded inside this envelope. Now once Lili is in her trance, she will know what is on the folded paper. Let's experiment."

Once my eyes were closed and I had entered into a relaxed state, the first image that came to mind was that of a simple vase with a stem in it. I drew it on the board as I imagined it. The professor then opened the envelope and showed us the drawing he had made. It was exactly the same shaped vase with one stem and a flower on the stem. I had omitted the flower; the rest was identical. Did I have X-ray vision?

I had so much energy. My life was all mine again. I jumped and skipped up a crowded Madison Avenue at midday. I worked, attended school, and went out dancing almost every night. Sometimes I got home from El Morocco at 2:00 am, wrote a paper until four, slept for three hours, and got myself to work by nine. I was a soaring baby eagle who has just begun to fly on her own.

I had to define my limits. There were no real limits. I was divorced. Sex was safe, as long as I had a contraceptive. Every man I went out with, wanted to have sex with me. A couple of times I allowed it to happen when the man was very attractive. The next day a slimy cloud of sadness would drag me down. If the man inspired me with enough confidence to be the father of my children, then I consented. Sometimes by the next morning, I changed my mind.

Soon I met a man who was my boyfriend for two-and-a-half years. He was an Italian from Verona, first secretary at the Consulate. He spoke French like a Frenchman and English like an Englishman. He had been educated at Oxford, was sensitive to art and music and loved to dance. With him, I learned to relax and enjoy sex. He allowed time and encouraged me to luxuriate in the subtle sensations. The affinity was close and intense for a long while. Marcelo was tall and thin with reddish curly hair and a strong aquiline nose. He walked with an elegant swagger and always dressed appropriately. He lived in the converted living room of a large townhouse. It had very elaborate mahogany wood paneling, a large fireplace, and majestic high ceilings. We often met there after work and took a Badedas bubble bath together while talking about music, philosophy, or simple events of the day.

One day, he asked me, "Why do you have such a sad look on your face?"

"Because everything good has to come to an end."

"Well, let's enjoy it while we have it." He turned the music louder. We danced naked around his vast bedroom, with a sumptuous crackling fire, and tumbled down on the bed with abandon.

I was grateful Marcelo helped me find a steady job at the Alberto Bufalini Marble Co. I was their "girl Friday." I learned to make delicious lasagna. They gave me a week off if I needed it for a sporadic modeling job. A lot of my girlfriends were models working through agencies. I never found an agency. I didn't look very hard. When my friends knew of extra jobs that they couldn't take because of other preferable commitments, they told me about them and I got hired. It saved the employer the agency fee.

The Italian company where I worked sold Italian marble and travertine to American builders and architects. It was on the top floor of a beautiful neo-baroque townhouse with wide skylights. It was on 56th Street near Fifth Avenue.

We served informal lunches for architect clients: lasagna, salad, fresh bread, and wine. I met I.M. Pei. I wish I remembered the others' names. I got to sit at the table with all of them and enjoy the lunch and the laughs. Leonetta was our boss's executive secretary and a good friend of mine. She and I made lunch and served it; someone else cleaned.

Marcelo also helped me find my first apartment on 72nd Street between Park and Lexington, on the ground floor.

The windows opened onto the sidewalk, only a few blocks away from his. We traveled a lot together and became very close. He asked me to marry him, after a lovely trip through the south of Portugal and a stay in Estoril with friends of my parents. I said no, because as time went by, it became obvious that he was also a philanderer.

We didn't go out every evening together. Sometimes I called his apartment and asked him if he had another woman there.

"Is she in your bed?"

"Yes, I'm sorry."

It was painful. I became disenchanted and slowly began detaching emotionally. When my mother came to visit and met him, she and aunt Lili called Marcelo "*Panfilo*." In their vocabulary it was a caricature name that depicted a pretentious fool.

It took time to sever all the invisible ribbons that bound us together, because of a strong physical attraction. Why had I placed myself in that situation? I deserved more consideration.

20

You are your thoughts. Don't let anyone else have dominion over them.
—Shad Helmstetter

Marcelo and I spent a weekend on Georgica Pond in Wainscott, near Bridgehampton, Long Island, with my friends Tim and Sabba Ostuve. Wainscott borders the South Shore beach. Only a post office and a general store edge potato fields speckled with houses; tall flowering privet hedges scent the properties. We arrived with the fiery sunset. It was a multileveled Victorian house with bay windows and creaking floors. The aroma of freshly cut lilac filled their living room. Indigo wavelets on the pond glistened. The Ostuves lived partly in Brazil, where Tim's family was established, and partly in New York.

A Brazilian architect friend of theirs, Emmanuel, showed slides of his work. They were homes made with painted concrete, yet with cozy open spaces within angular lines, high illuminated ceilings, surprisingly large glass windows.

His eyes were easy-going green and intense. He moved gracefully. The houses were unique. I had never seen anything like them. He and I flirted furtively, a couple of tentative glances, tiptoeing our gazes around the Swedish model he brought for the weekend and my Italian boyfriend. Emmanuel sat next to me and said: “Why didn’t we meet before?”

“Before what? Now is always good.”

“Yes, you are right. What about houses with many closed doors?”

“I like houses where doors can be opened easily and stay open,” I replied.

He smiled and said, “That is really good.” Then walked away. I had him hovering in my consciousness; so handsome, tall, with a black long mane of hair to his shoulders, and jungle eyes.

My boyfriend Marcelo and I hadn’t seen each other for a whole week. So in the middle of cocktail hour we slipped upstairs into a room and made love passionately. We were lying in the glow of pleasure and blissful communion, when suddenly Tim, our host, and Emmanuel, the architect, barged into our room carrying a large chest of drawers. We were lying naked. They said, “Hi, we’re putting this chest in its place.” They spoke in a very matter of fact tone, as if they were seeing us dressed, yet knowing very well that they had torn into our intimate moment. I suspect they thought it was funny and daring. I was baffled; nevertheless, I let it go. Now, I realize I had spoken of open doors. Maybe he took me literally.

Marcelo felt jealous and was more attentive than usual as a result. A week later, he told me he couldn’t see me. He had another social engagement without specifying what it was. When he asked me what I was doing, I bluffed, to bug him, "I'm going out with the Brazilian architect Emmanuel." We hung up. I knew he was worried. I was sitting in my office.

Suddenly the phone rang. It was Emmanuel. He invited me to join him for dinner in the Village. It was perfect. I had a class after work, and then we could meet.

The distant thunder and glistening sidewalks provided flashy pink and white reflections. I climbed up a badly lit rickety staircase. We met in the room where he was staying. It smelled of fried onions. Blue, yellow, and pink dresses hung as tapestries on the wall. Jasmine incense smoke wafted through the air. It was a tiny space with high ceilings on Eight Street across from Nathan's. We spoke Portuguese.

"*Tudo bom? Que maravilha que você veio!*"

"*Deu certo.*" (It worked out.)

The piercing seashore eyes, the curious intelligence, the boyishness, the pace of his language, the gentle timbre of his voice and the attentive way he listened to what I said, all held me.

"Let's seet down," he said, pointing to the makeshift table on the floor. His English was good with a charming Brazilian accent.

A picnic on the oak floor. There were two glasses of white wine on a green plaid cotton blanket. One single candle in a classic brass candlestick lit the space with a feeling of tropical adventure. Sitting cross-legged on the blanket, he handed me a goblet of wine.

"Would you like to taste the cheese?" he said, preparing a little bite for me before eating himself. He tore a piece from the baguette and covered it with brie. There were also some green seedless grapes and a bottle of wine.

I had just discovered that Dostoyevsky spent four years in forced labor in Siberia. The only book he had to read for all that time was a Bible. We talked about how it might feel to be epileptic and imprisoned for so long with only a Bible to read; all this for a political leaflet denouncing the czar's actions.

We felt privileged with only this blanket and a mattress. It was as if I were Cleopatra and he, Marc Anthony. Roberta Flack was singing, "The First Time Ever I Saw Your Face." The passion was a seismic event. There was more intensity than consideration, and there was a lot of that, too. I didn't quite know how to handle it. I was swept off my feet. In the morning, I went to work in the same clothes, and my work companion and my boss noticed.

What was it about that man that tantalized me for so long?

He had built many dramatic concrete houses with sacred spaces inside for rich people in Brazil. He was wondering what else he was meant to do. He listened to me, with reverence. He heard me and helped me so much to hear myself. He set himself up to do an experiment. He gave away all his money as soon as he arrived. He lived off the generosity of his friends.

"Of course, it's easy to become poor for a month, when you know your bank account is waiting for you somewhere," I pointed out to him.

"Yes, you're right," he responded and paused in silence. "There is no hopelessness," he continued. He sighed heavily, taking his time, and then added, "That must be devastating."

His pauses were punctuated with gazes of amused understanding. I savored his silences as much as his words. He seemed transparent to me.

From then on, I was smitten. He called me a couple of days later to invite me for the weekend out to Wainscott at Tim's house. With Tim as our captain, we sailed around Sag Harbor on a wavy sea and sang amid the spray. We had six foot swells and 40 knot winds. It was a challenge steering the boat safely back to port. Back at the house, we sat by the fire to mitigate the late September chill. We told stories and laughed and stared at the flames, in wonder at the bliss of being together.

In the city, Marcelo shouted over the phone: "What are you doing? Why did you spend the week-end with Emmanuel?"

He had the key to my apartment. On my bed lay a poster size paper.

"*Sei una putana!*"!" (You are a whore!) in large red lipstick letters.

Emmanuel came to see me, one last time. "I hope you'll come to visit," he said with an embracing smile.

"Yes, I'll come for Christmas; Tim has invited me to stay at their house."

Secretly, I hoped he wanted to make love again, right then and there. Yet, he was quick to say, "Great, I'll walk you over to where you need to go."

"I need to go over to Marcelo's."

“Okay.” We strolled. He kissed me good-bye, on the cheek, at Marcelo’s door.

Upstairs, Marcelo had seen us from his window and was very upset.

“What kind of behavior is that, coming to my house with him?”

“We just walked over here. He’s leaving tomorrow.”

“So when are you going to see him again?” he inquired with a haughty detached tone of voice. His pride was hurt. Fickle flickering flames.

21

That which fills the universe I regard as my body,
And that which directs the universe,
I see as my own nature.
—Chang–Tzu

In São Paulo I stayed at first with my cousin Margaret who was completing research for her dissertation in anthropology. Then, I called Emmanuel.

"Come over" he said. I brought him the Roberta Flack LP, "The First Time Ever I Saw Your Face." He had called me in New York just before I left, to make sure I was arriving.

What a thrill to see him when he opened the wood gate to his house. His eyes shone with warmth. He was happy to show me around. His little sports car was parked in his living room. His house was two juxtaposed pyramidal triangles. There were many levels to the two twin spaces. You could enter from one side to the other through small openings that forced you to lift your legs and bend your body. It was a workout to get through the house. In the back, there was a terrace overlooking a tropical forest with a small waterfall whispering its freshness. All the windows were triangular and felt more like skylights. I had never been in such a contemporary and yet so personal a space. That same afternoon, he took me down to the seaside where he showed me some of the other houses he had designed. After having seen a few, I said, "There was an evolution from cave to temple in the experience of the spaces."

"I'm glad you noticed that," he said with smiling eyes.

We spent the rest of that weekend together, sleeping together but never making love. One morning, when I attempted to snuggle a little closer, he pushed me away. I felt lost and confused, burst into tears, and sobbed right next to him in the bed. He comforted me with no explanation.

"It's okay, baby," he said, got out of bed, and brought me some fruit juice. When I was dressed, he dropped me off at my friend Tim's house. I was confused. I suspected he had another girl he needed to spend time with, plus the family gatherings around Christmas and New Year's. He didn't say. I didn't ask.

I spent most of that visit with Tim and Sabba. I wrote a short story celebrating the recent birth of their first baby. It was an allegory with ladybugs. I needed to keep myself active and interested so as not to miss Emmanuel so much. It was a blessing that Tim and Sabba organized many events at home, in town, and at an apt. in Guarujá, A beach town on the island of Santo Amaro. I asked Wesley, an artist friend,

"Would you read my story?" After he read it, he tidied his white mustache for a while. Then, said with an encouraging smile,

"First, live your life and gain experiences, then you'll be able to write."

The first drawing I ever bought was a Wesley. It was titled, "Anatomy of an Orgasm." I learned so much contemplating it, mostly how it is my responsibility to claim pleasure for myself. I spent most of the holiday with Tim and his group of friends. Emmanuel showed up only after the New Year.

"Happy New Year! How have you been?" He greeted me with a jolly tone, over the phone.

"You could have called sooner; it's taken you a while." I had come to see him, and he had hardly made himself available.

"Lili, calm down; I'm calling now. I'd like to come by and see you."

"Great."

He came over. We sat around the wrought iron table by the pool with Tim and Wesley. We discussed art and ideas and people. We were all barefoot. He grabbed my foot with his toes, under the table, and we held feet for a long while.

We went out to dinner and after ended up together in his house. It was late at night. When he was about to take me back to Tim's house, I remembered in time that I had no key and that I would have to wake up the whole household to get in. He invited me to stay. He seemed to imply in his tone of voice that I had set it up to have to stay. I was not sure that I had understood correctly though. However, as the night moved on, we slowly peeled each other's clothes off, and our bodies came closer and closer together. Exploring, touching, caressing. When I was so naked, he said, "*Eu gosto de voce.*" (I like you.) We spent more days going to the beach together.

The last day, he drove me to the airport.

"Let's stop by the river and have a picnic."

"No," he said. "It would be too romantic." I couldn't discern whether he did not feel romantic or whether he did and was afraid to admit it. I was afraid to ask.

On the way to the airport, we saw an enormous fluffy marshmallow man made of clouds waving to us with a big smile, a distinct cloud cartoon in the sky.

"Good-bye, for now, but we'll be seeing you," he seemed to be saying. Emmanuel also was amazed. The smiling giant accompanied us all the way. I was convinced it was a sign that Emmanuel and I were meant to be together.

I felt there were moments he was getting what I was thinking, as I understood what was going through his mind, and we burst into laughter together.

22

The mind is its own place, and in itself
can make a Heav'n of Hell, a Hell of Heav'n.
—John Milton

Back in New York, I didn't hear from Emmanuel. When I made some quick money modeling, I called him in March and asked him if he would meet me halfway, somewhere in the Bahamas.

"I'm sick," he said.

"Sick? What's the matter?" I asked dismayed.

"I've got hepatitis and have to stay in bed. Would you come here, *meu amor* [my love]?"

That was all I needed, to be called "*meu amor.*"

"I'll be there tomorrow," I vouched with certainty.

His brother was at the airport to pick me up. As soon as I arrived at his house, the doctor came. After checking Emmanuel, he said he needed more supervised care unless he could remain very calm.

"It'll be easy now; my nurse has arrived from New York," he said with a cheerful smile.

His level of bile was much too high. His sheets were turning yellow from his perspiration. The doctor said if he continued this way during this coming week, he'd have to hospitalize him.

"There have been so many people stopping by, to say hello, it's been a constant party. Now that you're here, maybe it will be quieter. Look what this girl made for me!" He showed me this enormous *papier maché* airplane sculpture. It was covered in blue, green, turquoise, and pink enamel paint with an oily sheen. He was surrounded by presents. I began placing them in other rooms and clearing out the space. That first night he arranged for me to go to a Chico Buarque concert with some of his friends.

The next morning, I filled his house with perky peonies, lilacs, hyacinths, and dancing daisies. There was a wispy spring scent in the air. His mother arrived the following day and said, "It smells of marriage here."

I massaged his feet every time I sat at the end of his bed. I prepared little dishes of vegetables, and his maid also cooked healthy food. We noticed the harmony in sounds, in the ideas we were discovering, in the placement of objects, and in the sequence of events. We observed how the progression of some shadows on the wall improved with richness of detail as time went by. We pointed it out to his mother.

"Yes," she said. "Everything in our experience becomes richer as we age."

We read and discussed *Animal Farm* together. We listened to Gal Costa and to piano performances of Richter's. The Brandenburg Concertos were also some of our favorites. Within the first week I was there, the doctor returned and tested his level of bile. He was amazed; it had gone down to almost normal.

Those days blended into lulling evenings and nights. We weren't supposed to touch, hepatitis is contagious. Sometimes we didn't, and sometimes we did. It was very gentle. There was no sex. It was the most idyllic caressing time I've ever spent with a man.

"Stay," he said one night.

I searched in his eyes to understand where he was coming from. Then I responded, "I still have to finish my courses. Then I'll come back." There was a long pregnant silence. We were both digesting the consequences of what we were beginning to affirm. This man was the one I most valued in my life. He encouraged my writing. He always wanted to read it; he understood nuances about me, I hadn't even discovered. I felt brilliant and beautiful and honored with him.

"But what if I have to force myself to make love to you?" he said suddenly.

"Force yourself?" I uttered in disbelief. "That last time we made love in December, did you have to force yourself?" I asked, dreading to hear the response.

"Yes."

"I don't want you to have to force yourself ever," I replied as fast as I could. I felt misled and betrayed. The magic spell of those ten days shattered. I definitely did not belong to this man. I packed as fast as I could. I felt as a flower must feel when it has been plucked out of the water and forgotten on a parched surface. As I was leaving, the next morning, he waved from the second floor.

"See you tomorrow," he cried, pretending it would make it easier to say good-bye.

When I got back to New York, I plunged into a great depression. I could not believe that the one person with whom I could communicate in this unique way did not want me. It was the end of my world as I knew it. I had no more desire to work or study or go out or anything. I just lay in bed in a daze. Thank God, I had another friend—Sandy, who kept calling and bringing me flowers.

One day he said: "You have to see a psychiatrist; you are in bad shape. You can't just keep lying here in bed all day every day."

"I don't know a psychiatrist."

"I do. I will ask him to talk to you and to recommend one for you. We can't have the same one if we're friends. I've been going to this one for years."

"Nobody out there that I know knows how to communicate the way I do with Emmanuel. I feel so alone. I just want to die."

"I have also felt like that, and the psychiatrist I've been going to has helped me feel better."

"All right; I'll talk to him. I do need some help."

A couple of days later, I went to see a psychiatrist who told me it would take two years of therapy, three times a week. I went for three months. I understood intellectually that because I had felt and believed to be abandoned, neglected, and abused by my father, mother, and stepfather, I kept recreating similar situations in my life. But what was the next step? The psychiatrist only said one phrase to me, in all that time, when I described to him how lifeless I felt when I got to Spain.

“Like a puppet without his puppeteer?” he chimed.

Shivers of icy separation scurried down my spine. It was an awakening. How much of my experience was still being shaped by those early years?

23

"The human body is made of electronic vibrations, with each atom and element of the body, each organ and organism, having its electronic unit of vibration necessary to the sustenance of an equilibrium in that particular organism."
—Edgar Cayce

At about this time my friend Amanda, the actress, attended a seminar called Silva Mind Control. She said, "Oh! Darling once you take the Silva course, you won't need your psychiatrist."

Amanda had been successful very early in life. She played Juliet for a Joseph Papp production in Central Park, and then the parts kept coming. From my point of view, her life seemed charmed. A tiny young woman with porcelain complexion, she was a Latin beauty with two dark brown eyes as big as Lake Titicaca. As I combed my fingers feverishly through my hair, I thought, *you don't know how complicated my problem is.*

Nevertheless, I was willing to experiment and try to understand what she meant by that statement. Before I attended the course, I let the psychiatrist know.

"Mind control! You better be careful! I want you to come early Monday morning and tell me what it is all about," he exclaimed, sincerely concerned that I might be getting into something dangerous, yet also wanting to keep me under his control.

"Of course, I will," I said, readying myself for this new adventure.

After one intense weekend, I felt so much better than I had after three months of therapy.

With the psychiatrist, I was able to understand intellectually how I had become the warped human being I was. With the first half of Silva, I began to feel inner peace. I didn't know how to explain it to the psychiatrist. The course had given me a technique to program a dream that would give me the solution to my problem. I would remember it and understand it.

I programmed as the course taught me. In a dream I had, it was the first time that I felt I was in my light, as if I were a light bulb but with no glass at the outer limits of the bulb, just darkness. In that darkness stood my mother, my aunt, and my grandmother all wagging their fingers at me and repeating, at old-movie speed and in sepia color with an old musty scent: "You're too fat, or you're too dumb, or you're not behaving as a young girl of good family should."

And, yet, for the first time, I was clearly aware that I could accept or reject anything they said. This was a revelation for me at the time. After hearing the dream, the psychiatrist said to me, "You have found yourself."

The following weekend, I completed the Silva course. In the last set of exercises, we were guided so deep within ourselves our experience became clairvoyant. I was given a name and a place. My companion in the exercise knew the person, but I didn't. We tuned in for the purpose of sending healing light and verifying our intuition. My companion confirmed my inner vision.

While helping someone else go through a psychic experience, I had a split second image of a vast chasm of wailing suffering voices; a vague scent of hospital wards, bursts of red flames of uncomfortable thoughts, accumulated over years, searing destruction, billions of people writhing in their own fear, shame, revenge, hate, and suffering. I felt dizzy. I heard my inner voice say, "This is hell, and we create it for ourselves."

I got up from my chair walked straight over to the instructor, Wingate Payne, and said, "I want to become an instructor of this course."

He smirked. He wasn't taking me seriously. I didn't care. I knew this was for me. He told me I had to attend as many courses I could and read many books. He gave me a long list and added, "You must practice every technique and be able to share a personal success story with each one."

I went to the psychiatrist for two more weeks and then announced: "I don't want to come back any more. With these techniques, I can take care of my problems and feel so much better."

"It's true; you are flying," he responded. "You may fall again," he added.

"If I fall, I'll come back."

My mother had a car accident in Brussels and cracked part of her knee. I went to see her for a few days. I wanted to share what I was discovering, about our mind power to heal ourselves. It did not interest her. She had moved into a big house and was going through a tough moment of her own. Everything was a challenge with pain in her knee. My sister, one of my brothers and I helped a little. I spent a lot of time with my brother Alex. I was amazed with his mind and his capacity to articulate so much, at seventeen.

When my mother and I were in the kitchen, I explained how I had been going to a psychiatrist and how that led me into being interested in the Silva Method. I also told her I felt Alex was brilliant. "Really?" she responded surprised. Alex was always rebellious and didn't have the best grades. She felt Samson was the brilliant one because he did very well at school. As the conversation evolved, I was able to finally ask what I wanted to know.

"How come you spanked me so much and Popi beat me with a belt?"

"We never put a hand on you; how can you say such a thing!"

What could I say? I was silenced by such a response. I realized how intransigent her position was in her mind. It would be hard to have an open healing conversation.

Back in the U.S., all I wanted was to have my brothers and sister, who lived in Europe, take this course. I wrote them and offered to buy a second-hand car and drive across the country with them after they had taken the course during the upcoming summer. They agreed, except for my middle brother, Samson, who planned to meet us in San Francisco; Alex and Ilona arrived and attended the course.

During the seminar, we met a very pleasant woman called Fate. She was heading to South Bend, Indiana, for the summer to visit her parents. She was tall and wiry with bobbed hair and very bright blue eyes. She laughed easily and had a very open gaze. I invited her to come along with us. She was the head mistress of the Montessori school in Brooklyn Heights.

We were all impressed, and I wanted to learn about the Montessori system. She accompanied us in the car to South Bend. After visiting with her parents for a day or two, she decided to continue on the trip with us. My brother Alex, who was in his last year of public school in England, was about eighteen, and Fate was twenty-six. They fell in love. When my brother went back to school in England, Fate followed him to stay in the village where the school was. My parents were outraged.

"How can this older woman stalk our son?"

When it came time for him to go to university, they said they would pay only if he stayed in Europe. So he moved to Chicago to live with Fate. He worked his way through school and got many scholarships.

When he expressed the desire to marry Fate, my parents cried, "Why do you have to marry her; just live with her."

Soon they planned their wedding. The greatest comment at the time was when my cousin Malcolm said cavalierly to my mother: "Tanti, don't see it as if you're losing a son. Rather appreciate that you're gaining a countess!"

My mother had *'en famille'* expressed her distaste for the Midwestern middle class blandness, a vague, misinformed description of Fate's family.

I actually found Fate exceptionally intelligent and sensitive to young people's needs and passages. Her mannerisms and the sing-song of her language had more of a cadence and a swing than I was used to. She had a turned-up nose, pale white skin, and a thrilling way of changing possible fearful situations into something to look forward to.

My sister and I commented on her meticulous cleanliness. When she got herself ready for a shower, it was with the same precision a surgeon might prepare himself for surgery, making sure every necessary instrument was present. I expected her to speak a different language, yet when I listened, her sentences were clear. I noticed how there were people with whom I felt stilted and paralyzed and others with whom I felt spacious, winged for a clear destination.

We became friends on that trip. She explained the Montessori system to me at length, during long drives and plenty of time to talk. What I understood is how the child learns to respect and explore his own desired pursuits, feeling supported by the group and the environment. Most of us in school are encouraged to do always what the teacher is telling us to do. How can we discover what truly excites us; what we are truly curious about? Schools must cultivate our individual curiosity. Each of us has a special talent and purpose. People without curiosity are much more easily manipulated into thinking one way or another without questioning authority.

One of the first nights on this trip, while lying in my sleeping bag, under the open sky, I had an unusual dream.

I saw myself traveling through my body and greeting and embracing personally every single cell of every single tissue in my body. Each of them was very pleased that I had remembered it, and every one smiled and thanked me profusely. I saw each of my cells, pink, translucent, and shiny, smiling at me. I knew I was healthy.

One night in New Orleans, we'd smoked some grass in a camping ground, enjoying the stars. Venus was so bright it seemed to beckon. As I was staring at it, I felt drawn up, as if I were beginning to levitate.

"The planet is pulling me!" My arms were raised way above my head, and I felt I was being stretched by a magnet-like sensation that emanated from Venus. I climbed on a box to see if I could get a little closer to it. The pull continued for a while. I was a helium balloon before it is allowed to float away. It lasted a few minutes and then subsided.

I wondered if the others thought I was being weird. I kept questioning myself, yet felt totally sincere. My brother and Fate did take me seriously and helped me validate my experience. That was what was so refreshing in Fate. She was always willing to acknowledge our experiences in a sincere way. There was not a spot of cynicism in her. She was so playful that I could laugh at the sight of myself preparing to be ascended into the heavens.

During this trip, I talked a lot about my Brazilian architect friend. I shared with my brother what I had understood architecture to be for him: a marriage of the client's needs and the dictates of the location or geography of the land. We had long talks and allowed ourselves to expand. We filled up those big skies with our ideas and absorbed into our minds the vast all-inclusive spaciousness.

We also talked a lot about the Silva Method. How was it changing our perception of what was possible? It will probably take a couple of hundred years for people, each and every one of them, to understand that their thoughts and beliefs create their reality. By realizing our inner power and choosing to focus it on a solution for all concerned, we will have less need to manipulate with exterior power.

It probably sounds naïve to many who cannot fathom a united humanity. It can only happen when enough of us imagine it as a real possibility.

24

"When we surround ourselves with negative emotions and do not allow love to penetrate, we are only hurting ourselves. We must learn to express our emotions properly so that we do not build up unreleased angers, tensions, and resentments."
—Richard Gerber, M.D.

I latched on to the Silva Method as a drowning swimmer grabs a rope thrown at him. I practiced all the techniques and meditations and wrote to myself a lot to understand what I was discovering and what I valued most. It was a time of self-examination and re-evaluation of my beliefs. Little by little, I got more confident in the recognition of my intuitive experience.

The greatest result was this almost constant feeling of having the power to choose my thoughts. At the time, I was battling with myself about my weight and my figure. It was a silent and relentless internal discussion. Since I had arrived in New York, I occasionally got a modeling job that provided a sudden handsome income. I was very strict with myself. I would go for a week or two not eating dinner, just a salad of greens and a hard-boiled egg with a raw carrot during the day. Unless, someone invited me to dinner; then I ate a fish filet. Yet, now after the Silva Method, I was beginning to allow myself to eat whatever my body longed for. It was a risky business because I was gaining weight. I had to start examining my beliefs about food. If someone was going to like me, it wasn't going to be only because of the shape of my body.

In San Francisco, we met up with Samson, my brother, who had been sailing on the Mediterranean. He is a tall handsome fellow with dark blond hair and greenish eyes. This was the brother who cried through my first wedding, the brother who sometimes opened the door to my room with one of his friends behind him and exclaimed with great enthusiasm, "The movie star!" There always was a feeling of tenderness between us.

He seemed rather distant throughout the trip, and I couldn't understand why. He didn't talk much. He kept to himself. He decided that he needed to lose weight, so he only ate fruit for the whole ten days.

One night, while we were all in our sleeping bags outside, it began to pour in the middle of the night. We scrambled to continue sleeping inside our station wagon. Samson and I ended up sharing the back seat. One of my knees snuggled in between his legs. Our arms entwined each other very closely. We were both startled out of our slumber when we realized our bodies were behaving more like lovers than siblings. We laughed at ourselves, turned over, and fell asleep.

Only decades later, he explained to me that while still in Europe, before the trip, he had expressed the desire to bring a friend on the trip. Alex had vetoed it, claiming there would not be enough space. He said it was supposed to be a family trip. Then, when Samson realized that we did have another person on the trip and that she was my brother Alex's new lover, he was angry. Furthermore, the whole picture got exacerbated by the end of that year because Samson's friend died suddenly in a car accident.

During this trip, I called Emmanuel several times. He didn't seem interested and tolerated my calls. Nevertheless, my enthusiasm for him did not wane. I was convinced that he was the only one who understood me at some unique level. When we got back to New York, I called him and insisted he must come up and attend the Silva Method. He arrived on October 12, Columbus Day. Sitting in the cab, going into Manhattan from the airport, he looked at me and said, "Your eyes have changed; you have a new expression." He stayed two weeks with me in my little apartment on 72nd Street, between Park and Lexington. We attended the course together. He said he enjoyed experiencing his psychic ability.

"I knew all that," he said afterward. Did he really not learn anything? We ate and slept together. We didn't make love.

"I've taken a chastity vow, for a while. This is hurting me more than it is hurting you," he declared after I attempted to seduce him. Once he pulled me down on the bed and hugged me and said, "Why are you so perfect?"

Statements like that confused me even more. I felt he liked me, loved me, but didn't want to surrender into it.

"I'd like to have a child with you," I said. He stood, contemplated me and smiled.

One day I returned from work, and he had left me a note. "Marcelo and I have gone out for a drink together." Marcelo was the Italian boyfriend I had broken up with to be with him. Why did they have to talk? When he returned, he had a big silly grin on his face.

"We've formed a pact," he declared. "It's between us; we can't tell you about it."

"How can you take off with one of my friends and invent some secret pact? I'm sure it has to do with me. I have the right to know. How dare you be here in my apartment and have secrets from me?"

"Do you want me to leave?"

"No, I want you to tell me what this is all about."

"I can't."

I went to sleep feeling angry and left out.

Within the next couple of days, Emmanuel said to me, "Come to Brazil, and stay with me; you can live with me as my sister."

"Your sister!" I exclaimed astonished, as I was pouring a cup of tea. I considered it for a while.

25

The Greek word for truth, aletha, *means not hidden.*
—Catherine Kober

One evening, a month before Emmanuel came to visit, I drew the curtain of my street level window when I heard the voice of a man outside talking to my black cat who was sitting on the sill, mesmerized by all the attention. The man stood tall on the sidewalk.

"Hello," he said. "I'm having a conversation with your cat."

"Yes, he is quite talkative; do you speak the same language?" I replied, wondering if the playful tone was too familiar for someone I had just met on the street. He had black eyes and black curly hair framing his pointy face. He wore jeans and a jean jacket and carried a shiny guitar and a black leather shoulder bag.

"What is the cat's name?" he inquired.

"Ripples," I said. "I wrote a poem the first day he arrived; that's how I found his name."

"It's a name full of movement," he added, nodding slowly.

"What is your name?" I asked. I better know his name since I am beginning this conversation, I thought.

"Emmanuel," he replied promptly. What an eerie feeling, to hear the same name.

"What's your name?"

"Lili," I answered reluctantly, wondering what I might be getting into.

He wore a black felt hat, almost a cowboy hat but not as tall. We talked a little. I said good-bye and retreated behind my heavy satin cotton royal-blue curtains. It was summer. I often opened the windows. He showed up a few more times. We talked through the window for a little while. He mentioned he knew Castaneda, the California anthropologist who was guiding a whole generation into *A Separate Reality*.

When Emmanuel from Brazil was there, with me, and the other one showed up, I dared invite him in for some tea. The two Emmanuels sized each other up. When the blue-jeaned one left, the Brazilian one said, "He's trying to get to know you because you're an attractive Upper East Side girl."

The Emmanuel with the guitar returned many times to chat at my window, after the Brazilian one left. When it began getting cold, I invited him to come in and have tea. We talked some more, and I explained about Silva. He told me that Castaneda and Silva knew of me even though I had never met them. It seemed too weird. I thought it was some kind of line. He told me: "They know who you are, and you are very strong." We talked more and more sitting on my Spanish-Arab blues and violet reds carpet. He asked me, "What do you want to become?"

"A healer," I said.

I sipped my mint tea. He did the same.

"You are a healer." He set his cup down on my pearly, oval marble top set on two milk bottle racks. "Let me show you a meditation." He drew a triangle on a piece of white paper and named each point respectively: *me, you, environment*. He asked me to experiment and meditate on those three words on the tips of the triangle.

"This triangle represents God," he said.

I closed my eyes and meditated on that concept of the triangle with those three focuses. I imagined being all three simultaneously. After about twenty minutes of silence while we were both meditating, I opened my eyes, and so did he. I looked into his eyes and could not find him. In wonder, I pinched myself to know I was there. All I saw in his eyes is what I might see through a very powerful telescope. I saw no pupil, no iris. I saw worlds spinning, exploding moons around large planets; I saw novas emerging in a flash of immeasurable energy; I saw the universe in his eyes, and when I exclaimed my amazement, he responded with more astonishment, saying that he saw the same in mine. We stared into each other's eyes in total awe. We were straight, no drugs, no alcohol. His almond-shaped eyes were the frames of two windows to look into the heavens.

From then on, every time he came by, he was dressed in a white rabbit fur coat and wore very dark black sunglasses; his hair was down to his shoulders and his presence undeniably intense. A scent of musk surrounded him. His guitar seemed pregnant with chords.

"Whenever anyone wants or needs a piece of information to solve any problem in the world, that person needs to ask the universal mind, who will seek out the right answer and make it manifest. Everything can be revealed," he said to me almost as a sing-song.

One afternoon, he arrived clad in his dramatic attire, stood in my little living room and announced he was leaving for the hills in Mexico. He was going to meet up with Castaneda and Don Juan, the sorcerer.

"You must come with me. You will have great experiences," he said in an indisputable tone.

"I can't. I'm doing this training, and I must complete it. Thank you for inviting me."

"You must come. This is a very important opportunity for you," he retorted, as he stood brilliantly white in his rabbit fur.

"I'm sorry, not now," I said. I sipped my tea, sitting on my carpet.

He turned, opened the front door, and was gone in a huff of cold icy steam.

26

Trust thyself: every heart vibrates to that iron string.
—Emerson

As soon as the Brazilian Emmanuel left, Marcelo began to call me and take me out.

"So how did you leave it with Emmanuel?" he asked, as we finished a meal in a neighborhood Italian restaurant.

"I'll be going down there as soon as my training is finished. He has offered to have me live with him as his sister." I patted my napkin reassuringly.

"As his sister? That doesn't sound very satisfying. What if he has another girlfriend, and you're there living with him? You wouldn't like that, would you? He told me how much he admires you and appreciates you, but he is not in love with you."

At first, I felt it was part of their pact; he was manipulating me. Then, after a little time, while we drank our coffee, allowing his perspective to sink in, I said, "You're right. I must not go live with him. It would put me in a very awkward situation."

The next morning at dawn, I penciled a note for him. There was an aching hollow in my heart.

> *Dear Emmanuel,*
>
> *Whatever you are, illusion or not, I let you go. I will not come in December to live with you.*
>
> *Big hug, Lili*

I dreamt that night that I went to his house, and his father received me at the door and told me Emmanuel was still sick and could not to see me at the door. I went in and saw him in his convalescent bed, his father sitting beside him. He lay there wrapped in a sallow complexion. I felt helpless.

27

"If you do not know your own identity, who is going to identify you?"
—Thomas Merton

My training to become a Silva instructor was partly self-designed and totally absorbing. My mother called it "your monastic period." I did a lot of reading, a lot of meditation, hatha yoga, journaling, self-searching, and redefining. The instructor who was guiding me, June Graham, suggested that I expose myself to as many other instructors as possible, so I could get a sense of the same material being presented in different ways. I traveled to Vermont, Boston, and Philadelphia and met and listened to these experienced lecturers present the concepts and techniques to show us how to create our own reality.

At the Silva convention in Boston that year, I met José Silva for the first time. I went up to him after a big conference. As soon as I got close to him and extended my hand and introduced myself in English, he said to me in Spanish, without knowing I spoke it, looking straight into my eyes: "*Dichosos son los ojos que te ven.*" (Lucky are the eyes that see you.)

It felt as if my father had recognized me. From that day on, whenever I had doubts about myself, I recalled that moment. Sometimes, I suspected that it was a very good recruiting technique. Then I brushed that possibility aside. I never heard he'd said that to anyone else.

During this time, I spent a lot of time meditating, reading, and hearing my inner voice. She was becoming more and more distinct. I could feel her ripple through my heart and feel so certain of what I heard. "Know thyself," "*Gnoti se auton,*" in Greek, is attributed to Socrates and was inscribed on the Sun God Apollo's Oracle of Delphi temple in Delphi, Greece.

GOD is the acronym for Grand Outrageous Diversity. In meditation, I experienced myself as a multitude of mirrors reflecting each other.

Near Burlington, Vermont, I was invited by one of the instructors to his beautiful house, modeled on a French chateau at the edge of a lake. I had come to hear and learn from him. This house was scented with rose incense and spicy tea. The instructor, Rob Fitchins, was tall, thin, with dark brown straight hair and a beaky nose and green eyes. I love those powerful noses. I felt charmed by him immediately. He showed me around the grounds after picking me up at the airport. When we stood on a promontory overlooking the lake around his house, he whispered to me, "Your eyes seem to come from the center of the world."

"They do, my world," I retorted.

Thirsty for all the Silva information to piece it together, apply it in my life, and share it with others. If every word and thought I have is creating my reality, how can I be as responsible as possible?

Still riddled with fears, I didn't always dare to express them. He was more forthcoming with his apprehensions. He got irritated when I only retorted in the most positive way I could think of.

"I don't think I gave a good intro. Probably not too many people will sign up," he said as he shuffled nervously through his desk to find a cigarette.

"Of course, they will. You gave a very engaging introduction. There were a lot of interesting questions and you gave clear responses."

"Don't give me the party line."

"Why not see the events from a positive point of view?"

"Who do you think you are, Polyanna or something?"

I didn't insist. He wasn't in the mood to hear.

That Thanksgiving I accompanied Rob to a hippie commune, where some friends of his lived, way up in Northern Vermont. Halfway there, he asked me to take over the wheel of his sleek Mercedes. I wasn't completely secure driving, but I didn't want to let on. I certainly did not know my way around and there was nobody on these poorly marked roads. All I know is that when he woke up again, I had driven us almost to the Canadian border, and that wasn't at all where we wanted to go. I was a fool not to dare wake him up to ask for directions! He was furious, of course. It took a lot of food and pot to smooth things out.

I stayed for two weeks during a class he gave to observe his style and learn. We got closer and closer. For a while, we talked of my moving up there with him. I came back for Christmas, laden with gifts and good cheer. Then, in the next class, he met a girl with long blond hair and a giant ass, and he was crazy about her. She was living in the woods with a poet. So I left and cried in my apartment for a week. A friend invited me to the country; I went on long walks, and talked to my invisible friend.

"You are attracted to men who are flamboyant but who have no staying power or no substance," I heard my inner voice say.

"Why? I don't want to be. I want to find a man who wants to be with me and whom I love and respect and vice-versa."

My girlfriend took me to a woman who read my hand and said, "You will get married when you are thirty-one."

"What! I don't want to have to wait so long!" I cried in dismay. I was twenty-five.

I worked on nurturing myself, on being kind to myself, dissipating the gnawing emptiness of being rejected and feeling unworthy of being loved. I needed to treasure myself more.

It took me two months to center myself. I still continued with my training and planned to go to Laredo, Texas, for the instructor training at the end of March.

Before I left, my friend Tim Ostuve came to see me after arriving from Brazil.

"Emmanuel had a girlfriend for these past months, but now it's over. She's moved to Rio. He says he loves you. You must come down to Brazil."

"If he loves me so much, why can't he say it to me himself?" I responded as I handed him a glass of fresh lemonade.

“Well, we just spoke yesterday, before I left. He wants to see you.”

“I’ve gone to Brazil several times to see him, and it has never amounted to anything. From now on, when I go to Brazil, it will be for me, after I complete my training, not for him.”

The training was fabulous. We covered with a fine-tooth comb every word, meaning, and intention in the method. José spent a lot of time with us answering questions and explaining how he came up with those techniques and most of all how he persevered self-educating himself. We were asked to present different parts of the course in front of a video camera. I did it, but I was so embarrassed, I didn’t even take a look at it to learn from it. I felt I was overweight, and I didn’t want to take a look at that. Somehow, if I didn’t see it, it didn’t exist.

José told us we were pioneers in this area of consciousness, developing the science of tomorrow, today. I wish he had talked more about defining our fears, and how they are linked to certain beliefs. He did show us how to place our fears into our blue-framed mirror and make them disappear, then into our white-framed mirror to allow ourselves to feel and be and envision 360 degrees all around us, just the way we want to feel, in the most satisfying way.

28

In each of us are places where we have never gone...
Only by pressing the limits do you ever find them.
—Dr. Joyce Brothers

When, I got back to New York, a message from Tim asked to let him and Emmanuel know by telex the date and time of my arrival in Brazil. So I did. I received a telex back, saying Emmanuel would be at the airport to pick me up. Maybe he had thought it over; maybe he was interested in exploring our relationship. If not, why would he bother coming to pick me up at the airport, so out of the way?

It was Easter Sunday, April 22, 1974. I arrived at Viracopos early in the morning. By the time I went through customs, it was already mid-morning. Chubbier than the last time he had seen me, I felt embarrassed. However, now I was ready to teach the Silva Method.

There he was, waiting, outside the customs' doors. Tall. His head hung slightly to one side. His eyes were faintly amused. The traditional two pecks on the cheeks were enough to say hello. He packed my bags into his sports car, and we took off.

I was asking myself, "Is this it? Are we going to be together from now on?" I certainly wanted it to be so. He sped in his camouflage painted convertible Volkswagen Porsche. When we passed under a bridge, I waved enthusiastically to some little boys who stared back. Emmanuel looked at me as if to say it was too much of a demonstration of emotion. I felt slightly mortified but did not say a word about it. He drove me to his cousins' colonial farm with lush flowering purple jasmine and manicured grounds around the main house. It was a farm we had visited before.

"Now, the surprise," he declared.

I climbed out of the car. He accompanied me into the farmhouse. There was a long polished dark jacarandá wood floor corridor and cathedral ceilings that led to all the main rooms of this spacious house. From the depths of this corridor emerged, in tight jeans and a T-shirt, the most beautiful girl I had ever seen. She was thin and tall with blond long streaky silky hair. She had powerful green eyes, an aquiline nose, and luscious lips. She wore a deadpan face. I know what she was thinking to herself, because she admitted it to me years later. "Who is this woman who's just arrived from New York? I thought we were having a honeymoon. I was expecting a chocolate bunny, not a "*ménage a trois*!"

As soon as she approached, I understood she was his girlfriend. I felt as if the floor had disappeared under me, and I was falling in shock, fright, pain, disappointment and humiliation. Paralyzed into silence, I put on a persona of, "Hey everything here is cool; I can handle anything; I'm a Silva instructor; this is just illusion; let me find the lesson." I was spinning.

The girl, Francesca, who managed to nourish herself with one lettuce leaf and maintain her frail feminine figure, kept making small talk that seemed so trivial to me; I could not believe this woman fulfilled Emmanuel. Yet, he seemed as totally engrossed in her as he was being polite with me.

By the evening, the three of us piled into his vehicle and drove into the city. When we were sitting in the living room of his modern concrete angled house, Francesca exploded and said, "Don't you think this man is crazy? He doesn't tell me you are coming; he doesn't tell you I am here. I don't even want to be here. Now I am pregnant, so he came to get me in Rio because he wants the child. He promised himself that the next girl he got pregnant, he would not ask her to abort. I don't know what your relationship is with him, or why you are here. What is this?"

"Francesca," admonished Emmanuel, implying she wasn't telling the whole truth about not knowing who I was in his life.

"Well, you want me to tell you about my relationship with him?" I said in my meagerly defiant voice.

"Yes, tell me," she replied.

"We met two years ago, and we have been on and off seeing each other since. I thought, because I got the message through Tim that Emmanuel loves me and wants me to return and then because he came to get me at the airport..." My voice trailed off and transformed itself into uncontrolled sobs. Now I was dying of shame, and yet I couldn't stop crying. Finally after a while it subsided.

"Come, I'll take you to stay at my brother's apartment," said Emmanuel as he got up. I followed meekly and totally quiet. During the drive, he said, "Let's have lunch soon. I'll call you."

It hurt he had misinformed me and set me up in such an awkward situation. I wish I had said that to him at the time. I was silent.

Francesca was Brazilian and lived in São Paulo. The connection he and I had was one of sharing ideas and discoveries. With Francesca he had a more lusty and passionate time.

He accompanied me into the apartment, gave me a peck on the cheek and left.

29

I am my world.
—Ludwig Wittgenstein

I stayed in his brother's apartment for about a month. I began teaching Silva at the existing center and started to weave my familiarity through São Paulo friends and new acquaintances. By the time he called for our lunch date, I was surer of myself in relation to my work.

"Why do you think I've ended up with her?" he asked, once we were relaxing after our meal.

"There must be something about her that you need," I said.

"Yes," he ponderously nodded. He had extended his legs out the length of his sofa, relaxing into the tone of my acceptance of the fact. Inside, I felt my heart smile. I noticed I was beginning to feel a little freer of him. I had to take care myself.

It was painful to be in São Paulo. I decided to move to Rio. I would start the Silva Method there.

I began staying with friends in Rio and gathering a small group who might be interested in Silva. After teaching a class, I got on a bus back to São Paulo, taught there, returned to Rio by bus, where a slightly larger class awaited me. My groups got larger and larger. That's all I did.

When I announced to my friends that what I wanted in Rio was a *cobertura*, an affordable penthouse apartment of a building with a terrace and a view to the ocean. They all laughed.

"That's what everyone wants in Rio. I don't think you're going to find it." Despite their doubts, I visualized myself just the way I wanted to be, hearing and seeing the ocean from my *cobertura*. Within days, a friend called me and said he thought he had found it for me. There it was, the most inviting terrace, with the beach and the waves. On the inside of the fuse box, in this apartment, I found this quote of George Bernard Shaw: "Those who teach don't know, those who know, just are."

I knew then, that was the right *cobertura* for me. It was on a street perpendicular to Leblón beach with an enormous terrace on the ocean. In meditation, I was practicing being empty like the Tibetan Bodhisattvas Avalokiteshvara. This means emptiness or "Lord of Compassion." Out of the emptiness comes the creation. With our intention we define it, envision it, taste it, smell it, hear it, feel we deserve it, and accept it.

One evening I was giving an introduction at someone's house, a man suddenly stood up and in a shaken voice cried out: "I'm a reporter from *O Globo* [Rio's biggest news paper]. I came here to expose this woman. I heard she was giving mind control classes around town. Yet now I see this woman is good! She is really good! She is good!"

I thanked the man for his vote of confidence, and continued the presentation. The next day there was an enthusiastically favorable article in the paper about the Silva Method. My classes got even bigger after that.

Because I didn't yet have a resident's visa in Brazil, I had to keep returning to the States every six months to renew my tourist visa. While we were all in Laredo for the next convention, the man who was the director of the center in São Paulo approached me and said: "I've talked to José and we've changed the percentages." The percentages were the way we calculated what percentage was assigned to the instructor from the money collected from each class and what percentage was sent to Laredo and what percentage was kept by the director of the center.

It sounded strange to me, but it didn't really register in my mind. I was a naïve fool. I never inquired how, or how come. I could have gone to talk to José.

I just trusted that in this organization, everyone would be as good and uplifting as they could possibly be. Of course, I was totally right. They took care of themselves, and I hadn't learned how to do that. When we got to São Paulo, he announced that now, instead of paying me 70 percent of the class, he would pay me 30 percent. Again, I didn't complain; I was too intimidated to speak of money, and I hated myself for it. I needed the courage to question "authority." That same man ended up being indicted for cheating José Silva out of many of his commissions.

30

"It came to me that having life itself, life being such a miraculous achievement, is like winning the grand prize. What we do after that is like frosting on the cake."
—Earl Nightingale

I met Geoffrey through the Ostuves out in Wainscott, L.I. He was an enthusiastic sculptor, preparing for a one-man show at City College. A new love interest had that quality of bubbliness where my body felt so light and naked. Savoring those magic moments and most of all filing them carefully so they can be pulled out in the moments of doubt, fear, and feeling undeserving of being intimate and accepted unconditionally.

We wrote to each other back and forth from Brazil. I had to go back to continue my work. He had to do his. Yet through the letters that came every week, he promised he would come to Brazil and visit me. I went back to New York, and we returned together. Because of him, I bought a fabulous Nikon. I had never owned such a good camera and relished taking pictures with it. When he was in a jolly mood, I could kiss him all over, and did in different ways. Sometimes he criticized so many things. He probably felt he showed his intelligence by discerning the problems. Intelligence is finding the solutions. He didn't search for ways to reformulate his interpretation of "reality." He didn't want to be happy. I see it now. I'd been attracted to men like that before. Then, I didn't notice it, until after the initial glow of romance began to fade. I kept expecting him to change or to be delighted with something.

Nevertheless, I spent three-and-a-half years with him, thinking I was going to marry him and have my children with him. Because of him, I moved back to the States. I started teaching Silva in Bridgehampton, Long Island. We lived in Wainscott.

I was tongue-tied in English, when I taught the Silva Method. In Portuguese it had been so easy. I was not able to teach. For six months I meditated and started planning to go to India to be with a spiritual teacher. Instead, I enrolled at Stella Adler's acting studio in Manhattan to loosen up. I needed to work on my ability to communicate true feelings in English. I spent the whole week in New York and came back to the country on the weekends.

The acting studio was on 56th Street, behind the New York City Ballet. The building was always teeming with dancers rehearsing in pink and black leotards. The New York City Ballet rehearsal halls were in the same building. So many beautiful bodies held with great reverence for their grace. I often observed how regally they held themselves. They practiced stretching and dancing the eight working hours of the day. They were very aware of a nutritious diet and yearned for greater and greater control of their movements. It was an inspiring context for an acting school.

The acting classes were large. Stella Adler was an impressive presence. She shook the middle-class niceties out of our repertoire, so we could get to our real emotions. We all had our share, yet we were terrified to express them.

"So here. What do you think of that?" she exclaimed. My eyes almost popped out of my sockets. She pulled out one of her breasts and let it hang there naked out of her décolleté, completely shameless and present. She became my new mother, even though I was frightened by her criticism. I thirsted for the freedom she was allowing me to express.

Trembling like an overgrown blade of grass in all the workshops, especially when it was my turn to go on stage and perform my piece, I was giving myself permission to express my true feelings even if it was through a fictitious character.

Her best class was the script interpretation class, which guided us to study a character from the day it was born to the moment where it had its lines to say in the play. Those lines had to be wrapped in the tapestry of that one life. The tone, the manner, the movement, the choice of words, and the accent gave away a whole invisible history.

"The talent is in the choice," she repeated throughout her commentaries of scenes.

The Shakespeare class and teacher opened a whole new world of depth, knowledge, rhyme, and rhythm. I felt so rich I was rolling in jasmine-perfumed silks, satins, and crimson velvets. Every word became a visionary tunnel. I became stronger and was cast as "Desire" in the Kenneth

Koch play, *The Red Robins* at Guild Hall, in East Hampton. *The Red Robins* is an allegory about the interplay of human emotions and ethical principles.

While living with Geoffrey, I discovered Bob Dylan. Amanda, my famous actress childhood friend, turned me on to him. Amanda spent a lot of time staying with us out on the island, when she was between parts. Now she had left for Los Angeles, and I was longing to join her.

I could listen to Dylan's songs day in and day out; I felt he was giving me the clues I needed—the ones about myself and the ones about the world in which I lived. He was showing me the colors of the local soul and I reveled in his poetry. The song "Just like a Woman" became my anthem, and all the other stories he told nourished me in unspoken ways. Amanda and I laughed as we figured out his meaning or ours. She said, "He is our great American poet."

Geoffrey and I were living in his beautiful glass and cedar house that his grandmother had financed, with a large studio attached to it, a few hundred yards from the Wainscott beach. At the theater during rehearsals for *The Red Robins*, we were asked if we could put up an actor who was coming from New York. I asked Geoffrey if we could let him sleep in the studio for a couple of weeks. He said, "Absolutely not." He strutted around the house with his favorite toy, the vacuum cleaner. "I'm going to start working, this week, and I need the space."

"He's going to be busy at the play, during the day; he won't be in your way."

"I don't want the interruptions."

"You can put a cot in a corner. He'll get up early and leave."

"I don't want to talk about it anymore. That's the last word I have to say about it, no!"

"Why are you being so closed minded?"

This was an excuse. He hadn't used the studio in months. Now that this actor was around, he decided he would. And even if he did, why couldn't this man sleep there at night? It didn't make any sense.

"Why don't you care about what I would like and need?" I asked.

"This is my place, and I decide what happens here."

"If I live here with you, why don't I have a say, too?"

"It's my studio you're asking me to share."

"I know. You were lucky enough to have your grandmother finance the building for you. Why can't we share a little and let this actor have a place to sleep for a few weeks while we work on this play?"

"I have the last word, and I'm not budging."

Why stay in a place where I felt like screaming because I wasn't being heard.

I was busy calling him names. Selfish, self-centered, arrogant. He became more defensive. Not a winning strategy.

Had I shared how I felt about his indifference to my needs—sad, neglected, unappreciated, unimportant—maybe he would have heard me better.

I was so furious, it gave me the energy to pack some boxes with my belongings and take off in my black Volkswagen Bug, called Isadora.

The next week, I moved into the Ostuves's attic.

31

"It is only with the heart that one can see rightly. What is essential is invisible to the eye."
—Antoine de St. Exupery, *The Little Prince*

A French video artist, Francis, who had been videotaping the play, took me to Neil Williams's studio in Bridgehampton.

"I'm going to introduce you to a great painter. He is not very well-known, but he is respected by many artists."

We stepped into a converted potato barn next to the train tracks. From here, they used to load the potatoes picked in the fields all around onto the trains. This building was Neil's studio. It was so big he shared it with Frank Stella who wasn't always there. Neil looked like a Cyclops to me. His nose was so small for his enormous head, and his eyes were two vast sky-blue ponds of awareness.

It was the painting that hung on the wall behind him that mesmerized me. Shaped as a rocket, it was hung pointing up diagonally. As I stared at it more and more, the energy of the paint seemed to be moving. There were many visible depths of blue and white with whiffs of metallic copper.

The space smelled of stale cigar and paint. I was glad when we were on our way. Nevertheless, this pyrotechnic vehicle stuck in my mind.

Francis and I spent time together in my new "little attic home." He introduced me to his friends and acquaintances and invited me to move in with him in town. I accepted. While living with Francis and watching a lot of his videos, I discovered that I was still quite tongue-tied, compared to his first wife Diva. Diva had been one of Andy Warhol's wonderfully outrageous actresses.

Bob Smith, shared the loft in New York City with Francis, the "frog," as we called him. Bob and I had an instant connection of understanding. The first moment we were together alone, he confided that he desperately needed $100 to pay his electric bill. I believed him and wrote him a check. He was a wonderful artist. At the time, he was obsessed with Egypt and the pharaohs, the desert of North Africa. He had lived in Spain and Morocco for a while. He looked a bit like a young Jack Nicholson with a kinder demeanor. He was gay, yet had no obvious mannerisms.

I missed Amanda in California. I thought I still had some of my father's inheritance. So I went ahead and planned the trip very loosely across the country. Little by little, I got the courage to drive off into the horizon and go west in my little black "Isadora." I was taking dance classes and moving my body quite dramatically at times; Isadora became my heroine. I drove without a radio, singing the wildest sounds like Native American calls, hooting with owls. In fields of corn, I laid down my sleeping bag and slept under the stars.

I got to Chicago, where my brother, Alex, the one studying architecture, was living with his new wife. It was reassuring to see them together, each one so focused on his or her own work, yet also so willing to enter into the most detailed and profound discussions of whatever they needed to discuss. They included me in a lot of it. I was even invited to give my input.

While I was there, my stepmother, who had been deteriorating with bone cancer for years, died. I flew to Florida for the funeral. We had grown to appreciate each other. She had been very helpful and supportive, especially on the transition when I left my first husband. Our talks were doused with love and respect. She had been ill for so long, it was a relief to know she was free of her pain. I had suggested when she first found out that we go to the healers in the Philippines. It did not interest her. Nothing "complementary" seemed to have any value for her, even though she could feel the chemotherapy debilitating her. She became more moody and awkward, and shrank to half her size. I don't know if she was fifty yet.

A few months later, I inherited some more money from my father. It was very good timing because I had run out of money and didn't even realize it.

Then, I returned to Chicago for the continuation of the "embracing of my land." It was my sky and my land and my water and rivers; everything was mine. I appropriated it all. It wasn't so much that I owned it; it was more that I belonged to it. As opposed to feeling alienated from it, I was part of it.

After my return to Chicago, I moved on to Boulder and crossed over vast plains, mountains, and desert, always finding a little road that led to a field or to desolate and barren land. Tucked in my sleeping bag, in good company with the universe, I was in the desert at the foot of the Rockies. A clanking against a hard metal surface rang all night as the wind blew. It was so dark I couldn't see where it was. The dry sand cooling off scented my imagination. I invented a vagrant making rhythms with a spoon and a tin can, alone at night. Finally, I dozed off and woke up to an orange sky and a purple-yellow horizon. I drove up into the mountains ensconced in fiery heavens.

After some days in Boulder with my stepsister's friends, we all went to camp in a sacred camping ground covered in pine trees piercing the air with their clean scent. A crystalline lake up in the mountains was where the Native American chiefs of tribes of the mountains and the chiefs of the plains met in the summer. They swam, ate, hunted, and smoked the pipe together. They discussed and agreed on what policies would rule for their tribes for the coming year. This way they lived peacefully side-by-side, dividing the hunting grounds and the agricultural land in an equitable way. They didn't have a concept of ownership; they shared the land that provided the food. Imagine if the Israelis and Palestinians could do the same. I took off on my own and had a profound meditation and then swam naked in the icy cobalt blue lake.

Driving through these territories, deserts, and golden mountains, I kept recalling Neil Williams' paintings. His canvases were immense and felt as if pure life was flowing through them. They came to mind as I drove for hours and hours. I determined that when I'd be back in Long Island, I would call him and go look at his paintings again.

I was amazed at their effect on me at such a distance. The man was half Navajo, half Mormon. His colors reflected the purple-blue skies I was living with now and the red glistening earth that was peeping up in the horizon.

When I arrived in Los Angeles, I was elated. To be and play with my friend Amanda was always magical. She saw every experience as a metaphor for life, and we had constant revelations by being together and sharing a similar perspective. She had a boyfriend, she said, a Canadian filmmaker who had won a prize at the Montreal Film Festival for his first film, *Eliza's Horoscope*. I was thrilled with the film when I saw it. It was a Fellini-esque story about a girl who is out to look for a rich husband but only looks at the material riches and not for the ease to relate to others and the fullness of solid integrity. In the film, Eliza meets and befriends a Native American fellow. He is strong and helpful, whereas the rich friends only seem to use her for their own agendas. By the time she finally realizes who loves her, it is too late; he is killed. The Canadian filmmaker, Gordon Sheppard, was well-built. He had a powerfully chiseled chin, sensual lips, and penetrating gray eyes. He had the beginning of a monk's bald spot on the crown of his head. I knew how much Amanda liked him.

Whenever he could, he stared at me in a piercing and suggestive way, through the rear-view mirror of my car. He was driving us around. I wanted to be closer to him, but felt uncomfortable because Amanda was expecting his attention. He expressed the need for financial backing to distribute his film in the United States. I decided I would take that on, go back to New York, work on calling people to show it, and see if I could help him find a backer. I had no experience in this field; I told myself I was being courageous in spite of my inexperience. I wanted more contact with him.

One evening before I went back to New York, the three of us sat in his house and listened to some music he admired. He said, "I'm not sure what this music means." So I surprised myself by saying, "I'll show you," and got up and began to dance my interpretation of the music. I became wild in a single moment. I didn't know I had that in me. They both were silent, and eventually, I stopped, satisfied. Sheppard stood and reached for the wine bottle. As he poured us each a small goblet, he asked, nimbly changing the subject, "Where shall we have dinner tonight?" We were all confounded, I suspect. And that was fine. Nothing was ever said about that moment. It was treated as if it wasn't real. They probably didn't like it and didn't want to take the risk of hurting my feelings by telling me. Better to be silent. I flew back to New York and lent them my car. There, I planned and prepared the screening of *Eliza's Horoscope*.

When he and Amanda arrived from Los Angeles, I was happy to see them. She took me aside and confided that she did not like Sheppard anymore. She was going back to her previous boyfriend. She mentioned that she thought the Canadian had a little crush on me, giving me the green light.

The next time I saw him, I hugged him, and instead of maintaining an appropriate distance of colleague and friend, I pressed the tips of my fingers in a suggestive massaging way into the sides of his back and remained close to him an extra second. He got it immediately. What was thrilling about him was that he got me instantly. My intonations spoke volumes to him, and he responded with laughter and mirth in his eyes. He seemed to understand more about me than I did. He didn't do small talk. He was to the point. He permitted himself to be quite incisive about what he perceived were his own or someone else's shortcomings, always with a twist of lighthearted verve.

"A flabby ass comes from a flabby mind," he often said.

He kept me motivated to exercise. He had been the boyfriend of a famous actress for several years. "Then," he muttered under his breath, "she betrayed me." I felt he always had a longing for her. I began to imagine I looked like her. People stopped me on the street asking me if I was her sister.

While looking for a new home, Amanda and I were staying at the Gramercy Park Hotel, a quaint hotel full of musicians. Sheppard and I conveniently took another room in the same hotel. Initially I sneaked from room to room before we dared let Amanda know what was going on. When I told her, she seemed to be fine with it, but I wasn't sure.

"But of course, darling, you are much more his type. So beautiful and so efficient."

When she gave me messages from him, I sensed something twisting the corners of her smiles or keeping her eyelids closed for a little too long when she talked to me. She had difficulty looking me in the eyes. When I asked her to introduce me to her theater agent, she said she couldn't. She was not getting any work. She was depending on me to take care of her, and I did. I could at that point in time, and I enjoyed her company. Some people thought we were lesbians. We laughed at the possibility they took it seriously.

32

'It is more important for a child to have a good nervous system than to try to "force" it along the line of book knowledge at the expense of its spontaneity, its play. A child should learn through a medium of pleasure, not of pain. Most of the things that are really useful in later life come to children through play and through association with nature."
—Luther Burbank

We moved out of the Gramercy Park Hotel. Amanda went to stay with another friend. The Canadian went back to Canada. I found a charming loft in Chinatown, at 179 Canal Street. It had been a Chinese theater. It had a stage in it and enough space to put mirrors up to dance. There was only one sink in the whole place, the kitchen sink. But the view made up for it. There was the Seamen's Association Pagoda on Canal Street, the Woolworth building, the Trade Towers. It was an impressive, mostly phallic view that gave me potency.

At first, I slept on the stage; then, it got too noisy. Eventually, I placed a mattress in a small alcove in the back. Another little room had closets and space for a desk. Around the kitchen was a counter with fixed stools and caramel plastic upholstered seats like in the old drugstores.

Outside the kitchen windows, there was a tiny landing onto the fire escape and across the alley a few feet away, you could see and hear the Chinese sweatshops where Chinese girls were sewing day and night, like amplified zippers opening and closing frantically. They never stopped. I think they made fifty cents per piece of clothing. The whiny Chinese music constantly accompanied the zigzags of the sewing machines. Eventually, when I put the fans on, the wafting of the circles and more circles of breeze seemed to frame every moment with a deeper cooler rhythm. I had some planters out there, with marijuana stalks that grew very well.

The noisy street kept me company. Trucks emerging off the Manhattan Bridge rattled the buildings. I preferred coming home at night with people on Canal Street at all times, rather than on an empty street. I could order hot watercress soup at any time of day or night. I lived on top of four Chinese gambling houses. These gamblers were very serious. Sometimes there were violent brawls that shook the building to attention. Once, they threw one guy out a window for cheating. We heard him crying at the bottom of the alley.

The man who owned the building was a bald Cuban jeweler with a square white-bread face and bright, sharp sea-blue eyes. He had his storefront on the ground floor. He kept showing up at the oddest hours at my door, hoping that I would cuddle with him or something. I couldn't even imagine it. He implied I could get my rent reduced if

I wanted to. I said, “Senor Crespo, you are a married man. Enjoy it, and let me be on my own.”

There was a Chinese market around the corner on Mott Street where we could buy large round red plaid painted tins of shortbread. The streets smelled of raw fish and sweet Shanghai hanging duck. There were so many fresh greens and vegetables on the stands: mountains of watercress, Chinese cabbage, dusty dark green kale, red and white cabbage, long Chinese parsley, and short Italian parsley, rich wine-colored beets, and freshly washed carrots. Cobblestone streets, it felt more like the countryside. These were the freshest vegetables in town.

The first night in the loft, I slept alone and cried in the night: a desperate baby who feels abandoned and neglected. The sound came from so deep. It was a wailing bigger than the whole building. The sorrow was so complete. As the sobbing subsided, I heard a voice. On the far wall, I saw the outline of a shadow of a young woman swaying gently towards the window with her arms open.

“I know it’s scary to be on your own; you are on your way to becoming ‘independent of the good opinion of others.’”

“Who is talking like this?” I asked, looking around attempting to understand from where was the shadow.

“It’s me, Joan. You have neglected me for so long. I’ve been waiting to be called upon. You are so busy all the time.”

“Is that you who was sobbing like that?”

“*No*, that was you feeling lost and abandoned, a part of you.”

"A part of me that I have not heard? What do I need to hear?"

"You can enjoy being alone."

"You are very kind to acknowledge me this way. I feel stronger already, and I don't know who you are, or if you are a figment of my imagination."

"I'm right here, with you to wipe your tears and remind you of the privileges you do have."

"I know, I'm feeling sorry for myself. I'm allowed a little bit. Not for long I promise. I need to claim the assertive part of me. Yes, yes, yes, I want and need to write."

Perched up on top of these Chinese smells and sounds, dragons dancing in the street on New Year's day, drums keeping the sacred beat of live red satin and black flowing ribbons, making eternity symbols on the slushy thick snow.

"You have a lot of power only in the now. What do you value?"

"Thank you for showing up just when I need you. This way I feel I am in good company."

"Well, you were calling. Your cries are magnified in heaven, and no one can sleep when a baby cries; all the angels are on alert."

"I had no idea you were all watching so closely." I finally slept like a baby.

The next afternoon, while waiting to cross Canal Street, I talked with some young men from the Netherlands who needed an inexpensive hotel.

"Well, if you don't mind sleeping on your sleeping bags, I'll be glad to lend you part of my floor to sleep on." They were thrilled. I was glad to have some extra souls around even if only for a few days.

By the time they left, I was able to enjoy my solitude. Soon, though, Amanda moved in with me and brought a tiny little Siamese kitten. She named it "Persephone."

She hadn't had a part in a long time. Her agent called her for a part on a TV program.

"I can't be in a soap opera. My grandfather was president of Chile."

She needed a job. What did one thing have to do with the other? I thought to myself.

When Sheppard arrived in town, Amanda moved out and stayed with some other friend so that we could have the space to ourselves.

One time, she announced right after he had arrived that she was taking a bus to Canada. As she left through the threshold of the door, she said, "Remember, Jesus at Gethsemane."

All I remembered was that it was there that Judas kissed and betrayed Jesus to point him out to the Roman soldiers. It was at this pivotal moment that he, Jesus, admitted to God to feeling terrified for what lay ahead. Yet somehow, he gathered the courage to go on with the purpose of his life. I didn't understand who of us was getting betrayed.

After Amanda left for Canada, I took off to a rehearsal of a mime group I was performing in. The Canadian stayed in my loft relaxing. When I returned, Amanda was sprawled in her gauzy long dress on the stage bed, the smell of sex in the air. I knew they had made love. Shocked, numb, and silent, I didn't say a word. Sheppard was in the back on my bed in the alcove. Nobody said anything, no one suggested dinner, and the evening kept turning into night. Finally, I got up, sat next to Amanda on the bed on the stage, and asked her giggling, even though I was seething inside, "Are we like the Chinese wives?"

She nodded. I thought to myself "I am the queen of this place, I could send them out now, but it would be hard for them to find a hotel. I'll wait until the morning." Then out loud, in a slightly imperious tone, I ordered Amanda: "Go and sleep with him." She stared at me startled and rose immediately to join him on my bed.

They spent the night together, and I couldn't sleep all night. Anxious, confused and hurt, I didn't know what to do. Persephone, the cat, kept tiptoeing in and out of my office over and over again until I got it. She was giving me the message to write. As soon as I got a notebook and scribbled as fast as I could all the torrent of intensity that was flushing through me, she sat and made herself comfortable next to my legs on the handmade woven blanket. All I could do was write everything I was feeling and cuddle with my Persephone. In the morning, I went over to the bed in the alcove, sat on it and said, "You better leave, guys."

And they did. I never lived with Amanda again. She overstayed her welcome with other friends. Then after a few months, an ex-boyfriend of hers called to ask for her mother's phone number in Spain. He said he had found Amanda sleeping on park benches, unwashed, and a mess. He took her into his apartment. She needed help. Her mother finally came and put her in a hospital where she was treated for drug and alcohol abuse. She was diagnosed as a psychotic schizophrenic. I have heard recently, twenty-five years later, that she has improved, that she is living in a special community in Chile. Her mother is nearby.

I saw Sheppard one more time to talk things over.

He said that once the film was distributed, he'd give me a percentage of his profit. I never pushed to know what percentage nor how it would be calculated. I trusted that because I was helping him, he would want to be fair with me. I must say in his favor that he has paid back the whole debt. I claimed it back bit by bit through the years and have not spoken to him in years.

33

Estrangement permeates our educational system.
—Star Hawk

During that time in Chinatown, I developed a routine for myself. I had enough income to live on from the inheritance. I got up at seven and ran to the Carmine Street Pool in the West Village. There I swam for half an hour in the steaming chlorine smell. Ran back to my loft, by 8:00 a.m., made breakfast and worked. I was writing a play about the dangers of nuclear power, especially the waste from the power plants. All this was enmeshed in a story of a woman married to a nuclear engineer and pregnant with her third child. The woman wanted to write, but it was hard for her to find the time. An old boyfriend of hers, an environmentalist, shows up and cannot believe she has married such a narrow-minded engineer. There is a terrible, destructive explosion in the civilized world as we know it. The last scene is a guide taking a group of mutant humans through the remains of a typical home of the twentieth century. These are the survivors of the atomic devastation. They are in amused awe at the way we used to live.

I was creating a radio program for children in Spanish and attending a couple of courses at the New School, and the fabulous script interpretation class with Stella Adler at her acting studio. My life was busy and structured. For a while, I even worked at a health-food store part time, to experience what went on behind the scenes. Were they so sincere and wholesome as they depicted themselves to be? No, not really. The carrot juice wasn't fresh every day, as they claimed.

I called the Navajo-Mormon painter who lived out in Bridgehampton. We met again in the city. He invited me to an opening for his friend Chamberlain, a sculptor. At the end of the evening, Chamberlain and his girlfriend invited us to go up to their loft. Chamberlain looked straight at me and blustered,

"Is it a yes or a no?" I wavered. I knew if I went up, I'd end up sleeping with Neil.

"It's a yes," I said. We started seeing each other every weekend. He was intense and fascinating to me. He spoke few words. I bought three of his paintings for my loft. But his violent moods when he drank made me want to slip away. I eventually did. He loved to speed in an old car of his through the woods and crash the car against a tree. That was fun for him.

These are pieces of what I wrote in his studio:

> *"This pen makes me feel like writing. Yesterday, I arrived from the city, and Neil got his Mont Blanc pen. He had always wanted one. We had dinner here. I danced for him. We went to bed, made love, and fell asleep.*
>
> *"This morning, it got a little heavier for a while only because I asked Neil why Chamberlain said*

that theater like dance was becoming the lowest form of art. I wanted to understand. He said because it was only the body. I answered quoting the poet Robert Creeley, one of his dearest friends, 'The plan is the body.' Everything is in the make-up of the body. He said, it was classically thought that way. I answered, 'Why did I have to stand by that?' He replied, 'You sound like an art student.' I said, 'I am.' Then, after a pause, 'aren't you an art student?' He said he was. I said if you truly agree with the classical point of view, it must be because it is part of your experience. He said he didn't like how I asked questions and then I said 'fuck you' to anything he answered. I said I had to challenge him, so he would share his experience. He said, 'Why share?' I said, 'Because that's what life is about.' He said in a definitive tone, 'Know thyself.' And then I said, 'You are so pompous; I don't believe it.' After long silence, I concluded, 'It's both.'

He said to me, 'You're a writer, just write.'"

I thank him for that. After the end of those two love stories, Sheppard and Neil, I promised myself that with the next one, I would get married and have children. I was thirty. I decided that I would not make love to any one until this wonderful person showed up. Six months went by.

One night I had a dinner party and invited a friend who had married a very pretty girl, England Boulted. She was a famous model and actress. We were estranged because I had not kept an appointment I had made with them to come over one evening. I couldn't find their number to call them. It took me days to finally call and apologize. My friend,

England's husband, was upset with me. I decided that I would only invite them when my life was more organized. About a year later, I invited them for dinner. She called and asked if she could bring her younger brother, Edward, and their mother. Her very good looking younger brother seemed to be floating a foot above the ground.

A few months later, she called and asked if I could teach Edward some French because he had accepted a job at a record company. He had claimed he knew more French than he actually did. I agreed to do it. The second time I saw him in my kitchen, while looking at his very handsome face of twenty-six years, I saw an arch of his faces, an aura of holographic heads, from very young until very old, and was silently stunned.

"What is going on here? Can you hear me?" I beckoned to my invisible friend.

"He is an important person in your life. You'll soon find out how. You will learn a lot through him."

"Can't you give me more information than that?"

"No, you have to experience it. You've been forewarned."

This whole dialogue happened silently in my mind as I went about my usual hospitable gestures and developed a conversation with my new French pupil.

At first, he came for a lesson once a week. Very soon, he asked to come three times a week.

In conversational French, we got to know each other a little better. He was a saxophone player. He arrived from England with four saxophones. He had sold the fifth one to buy his ticket to New York after he found out his girlfriend in London was cheating on him. He shared his favorite music with me, the Sex Pistols, the Pretenders, John Coltrane. I revealed a little of my story. He gave me his perspective, I elaborated on it in French, of course, for him. After the lesson, I often ran back to the Carmine pool.

Three months later, one afternoon, he asked me please, not to go swimming. He pulled out a bottle of Beaujolais and offered we drink it together. We did. I excused myself because I had to get dressed to go to a dinner party for the staff of the *New Yorker.* A friend who worked there invited me. I took my shower and came out wrapped in a towel only to find that my pupil-turned-guest was leaving. He had put his Burberry trench coat back on and was almost at the door. We met in the hallway to say good-bye. Did I know what I was doing? I leaned over to kiss him good-bye; I must have stayed in place a little longer. I touched the skin on his chest between the buttons with the tips of my fingers. That must have been the signal for him to pull my chin up with his fingers and kiss my lips and slowly push me in a gentle dance step toward my bed. I allowed all this to happen without hesitation. When my back touched the mattress that was placed on a high platform, my towel slipped. I was in another world. I wondered how lightning feels when it penetrates the ground. And how does the earth feel being invaded by so much intensity?

34

The bird a nest, the spider a web, man friendship.
—William Blake

My date was about to arrive. I had to beg forgiveness and take leave. Edward understood and disappeared down the stairs. I arrived dressed in a topaz, satin-silk *chemisier*. At the party, I danced and felt slightly suspended over the ground. I hadn't made love with anyone in so long, my body felt transparent.

A famous writer approached me and told me he had never seen anyone dance with such charisma except Marilyn Monroe. I was flattered, yet wondered if it was a line.

A few days later, the writer took me to lunch in Little Italy. He seemed so protective. I burst into tears without knowing why. I sobbed through most of the meal. My tissue-thin veneer of worldly sophistication was tearing. Then he left for the Playboy mansion because Hugh Heffner was his friend, and he wrote me a letter from there asking me to see him again. By then, I was too involved with Edward.

When Edward showed up again, he said: "I can't stop thinking about you."

"You're too young and un-established. I want to get married and have children and you're too young!"

"I'm not! Lots of people have children young and without a lot of money, and they do fine. I want to have my children young, so I can be a young father."

"You don't understand. It entails a lot to be a father, to provide for a solid household and education. You're not able to do that."

"Not right now, but eventually I will be. I'm writing some songs, and I will sell them or produce them. A lot of people have children without money. I'm your man, Lili. I'm your man. Let me be your man. I'm your man, Lili."

"I don't know. We'll see."

"I'm your man, Lili."

I began to believe it. I wanted to believe it.

When I read him some of my poems, he told me they were good. "How do you know they're good?"

"I know; I've read a lot." He gave me the courage to keep writing.

I loved his English accent and his command of the language. I loved that he was tall and thin and so good-looking. "I've never had such good sex," he told me. He was open about the money he was making and how he wanted to contribute for half of the expenses. He was a good man. He moved in with me. We stayed up talking until our place on earth turned toward the sun. I had so many questions for him. We had so many stories to recount. On the Chinese stage we watched the Chinese Seamen's Pagoda glisten with the copper-colored sunrays of the dawn, then fell asleep in each other's arms after making love. For our late breakfasts, we had tea and tons of delicious toast and marmalade. The more I ate, the thinner I got.

Months went by, and we longed for each other more and more. He played the saxophone for hours and worked five nights a week, as the maitre d', at Harper's on Third Avenue.

He was very conscientious with sharing the expenses. It took me a while to get used to the constant saxophone and piano. I learned a lot about music and started to take piano and saxophone lessons myself. I told him one day: "I want to get pregnant, so I'm not using any contraceptive."

He nodded to signal he understood.

After a couple of months my period didn't come. So I said: "I'm afraid I might be pregnant."

We were lying in bed; it was very early in the morning. He said, "Go have yourself cleaned out, as soon as possible."

"What? What are you talking about? You're the one who said you wanted your children young!"

"Yes, but I'm not ready for the responsibility. And you are busy with this radio show, how can you manage both?"

"But we're never really ready. I want to have this child. You said you wanted children, and I told you I wasn't going to use any contraceptive."

"Well, I've changed my mind. I don't want it now. Go have an abortion."

I was reeling in confused disappointment. At that time, I wrote this poem:

There is a tremor in my stomach
A funny pain
That seems to be connecting
strange tubes and pink twists

at times it rises, at others
it shoots down my legs.
Sometimes I want to get it out
Sometimes, I'm thankful
It is kneading in my womb
Maybe it's imagination
I feel it more as conjugation
How can one ever know for sure?

Through a gynecologist friend of mine, I found an abortion clinic. I wanted the baby, but I didn't want a baby whose father didn't want it. That would have been too much pain. I knew that pain intimately.

I set it up. The morning of the abortion, I expected Edward to come with me. He was not able to come. His tooth fell out. He had to rush to the dentist. He didn't have the teeth to bite into life, and I took on the responsibility.

Sheppard called that morning to ask how I was doing. I updated him about the crossroads I was on. He warned me. An abortion for me might be traumatic; I brushed him off.

"I know a lot of girls who have had them, and they have been fine."

"Yes, but you had a Catholic upbringing, and for you it may have much deeper implications."

I didn't believe him. I was sad and scared, but I couldn't have a child unwanted by its father.

When I woke up from the anesthesia, I was sobbing, heaving. I had never felt this way. I was totally disoriented with an unfathomable desperation. I came home and rested as the clinic had suggested, expecting this sadness to disappear slowly. My mother called as if intuitively sensing the imbalance. I told her.

"It's very sad, very sad." She said, "Good-bye."

As the days went by, it seemed to grow larger. The guilt that went with it was unbearable, and I poured it onto Edward. I was furious with him. I screamed and yelled and cried and sobbed. I couldn't control myself. I didn't want to. I wanted him to feel guilty to the very edges of his soul; I wanted him to suffer my anguish. I felt as if I had betrayed the sweetest part of myself, the essence of my being. I had torn it out to please him. Now, I hated him with a passion. I was out of control. I would call him at the restaurant and start shouting, menacing to show up and break every single bottle in their bar. He felt so guilty, he would humor me and try to calm me down, but he couldn't. I slammed my typewriter and broke it. I was a living, moving rage, like a hurricane or a tornado. I didn't care anymore. I was so angry with myself. I had been weak in not insisting on having the child. I was a wimp. I hated myself. It was a death for me. I was eating guilt, blood, and gore for every meal.

Edward developed sores oozing with confusion and guilt all over his neck, back, and chest from his constant scratching. I screamed so much, made such a fool of myself, shouted at the top of my lungs, so that he would pick up and leave me. I thought consciously, *I'm going to be so horrible that he will have to leave.* But he didn't. He stayed. He empathized with my pain. He felt it himself, day in and day out. I just wanted to get pregnant again. Of course, I was so tense I couldn't. I started insisting that we must get married, so that when I did become pregnant again, we would be married. More than once, he jokingly set a date and then broke it. That drove me crazy. Part of me wanted him to leave me, and the other part was so needy of him that I clung to him for dear life.

The winding Chinese nasal tone from across the alley repeated its circular melody and ground in the pain and the search for relief. Yet, next to those women who worked so relentlessly in the sweatshop, my desperation seemed self-indulgent.

"Cup of rosie?" said Edward. That was the English solution to any problem. Take a break and have a cup of tea, with milk and honey.

I gathered a lot of old photographs and caressed them as fallen leaves of my life, moments that gave me a smile. It was the height of summer. Ninety degrees. The fans were whizzing in an embracing whisper. In this place, in this moment, I had just gone through this abortion I didn't want but did not have the guts to keep the baby even though the father said he didn't want it. I felt I had killed the very life I longed for and could not forgive myself for being such a coward. But my father had never seemed to care about me, and I didn't have the courage to repeat that story either. There I was, feeling completely worthless. Yet, at a dinner the night before with a girlfriend of many years, I was able to open up and give her a glimpse of my desperation. She truly understood and said, "Maybe it wasn't the right time."

For her, I made a collage of snapshots of my life, trimmed the edges of a profile or of an architectural detail or maybe of a flamboyant tree. In the center was a cutout of Marilyn Monroe dressed in a tight white dress with her seemingly innocent gaze and her intended puckered lusty lips. She tragically molded herself to be the ultimate seducer. Is that what I had done? There she was in the middle of my collage of the puzzle of the images of my life like lingering snippets of different shades of blond hair.

A homeopath recommended some drops for me and said in a very matter of fact tone, "You know, Lili, the spirits today in this twentieth century have to understand that we don't live anymore in the olden days where people had children very easily and large quantities of them. Now, in this hectic life, we can't do it sometimes. We need not beat ourselves up for this; we need to understand that we didn't kill anybody. We didn't provide the physical vehicle for the soul. Maybe its purpose was to experience abortion. There are all kinds of learning experiences for souls."

I took the drops he gave me faithfully and began to calm down. After my typewriter was repaired, I wrote a one-act play about this saga. Getting it onto paper freed me of my turmoil. I was beginning to let it go. I went to England and Ireland with a theater group led by Harold Clurman, the famous theater critic and Stella Adler's ex-husband. Harold Clurman was the first man who told me I was intelligent. I did it to get away for a while and to see how I felt about Edward. Every play that we saw in England and in Dublin was about adultery. It was the big message. Adultery exists in abundance, through all levels of society.

While I was away, "by coincidence," Edward's ex-girlfriend came to visit in New York City from London. She was a popular English singer who had had one big hit. I kept dreaming that they were making love in my loft.

He had asked me over the phone, when I called, "Can I let her stay here?"

"Only if there is no more romance."

"Of course not."

Yet, when I called and when I dreamt, I knew there still was attraction. These perceptions were driving me into a constant panic. There seemed to be a bomb ticking inside of me.

When I arrived back in New York and questioned him about that, he swore to me that nothing had happened. Yet I kept dreaming that they had had sex. I felt confused not knowing whether to trust myself.

Finally, we set a date for the marriage. He left me a postcard inviting me to get married on the thirty-first of March. He didn't want a family get-together.

"Let's just go downtown and find a judge."

It had a Bonnie and Clyde flavor. My brother Samson came as the best man. So on March 31, a regular rainy Monday afternoon, we went down to the courthouse.

John Wayne had just died. There was a makeshift altar for him on the windowsill and an 8 x 10 inch color portrait of him with lit candles on either side. The scent of burning wax gave it the liturgical feeling. The music was the shuffling of feet and the chatter of pedestrian voices echoing in the hollow high ceilinged rooms.

We stood in line for our turn. Then, we were called in front of the judge, who repeated the words in a rushed mechanical way. I wanted to give meaning and presence to the "I do." It was skimmed over like a brush stroke on a painting that is so light it barely gives the tone. I was dressed in a green lamb's wool sweater set and a plaid skirt with high chocolate brown leather boots and a raincoat.

Afterward, we had coffee at the closest diner to celebrate. After a little kiss on the cheek, he went off to work. I was married. Just like that. Terribly English, very minimalist, so succinct.

35

Life has meaning only in the struggle.
Triumph or defeat is in the hands of the
gods...so let us celebrate the struggle.
—Swahili Warrior Song

The next morning, the phone call that woke me up early was a voice that I recognized immediately.

"I've arrived," he said.

I wasn't sure if I was dreaming. Five years had gone by since we last spoke, so I asked hesitantly, "Emmanuel?"

"Yes," he insisted, in disbelief that I would even have any doubt.

"You're in New York?"

"Yes, I just got off the plane, and you are the first person I call. I want to see you. Francesca and I have separated. It's over. When can I see you?"

"Today."

"Let's meet at our favorite little park with the waterfall on 53rd Street at twelve."

"Okay. I'll be there."

I hung the receiver back on its stand and stared at Edward to see if he even suspected who had just called. He was impervious. He did say, in a nonchalant way, "Who are you meeting?"

"An old Brazilian friend who's just arrived," I said in a quiet tone. Yet, I dressed with great care. I chose a new T-shirt with a silkscreen drawing of a broken heart opening only to find a new star within. Green corduroys and my new sexy high chocolate brown leather boots, a never-ending hand-knit beige scarf, and a mysterious raincoat.

As I climbed the steps onto the indented park on 53rd, I saw him, his hair curly and slightly graying. He had a boyish grin. My heart started beating faster. I could barely believe he was there, right in front of me, this love of mine. We chatted, giggled, and had some tea and muffins.

The waterfall kept rushing with its cascades of whispers. I wondered about this irony of timing. Then we went up to his hotel room and smoked a joint. The afternoon sun streamed in gold. He asked, "So what about this guy you're living with? He wants his papers, huh?"

How did he know? He must have heard about Edward through our mutual friend who kept him up to date about my life.

"Yes, he needs papers to stay here."

"And the best way to get them is to get married to an American?"

"Yes, so we did."

"You did what?"

"Get married."

"When?"

"Yesterday afternoon."

"I can't believe it," he stammered. "I was going to leave a day later, and something told me to change it. So I did. To a day earlier and you are already married."

His green eyes pierced me, questioning me. I did not want to let on how thrilled I was to see him. I wondered whether he wanted me so badly.

A friend of his came by. We walked all the way down to the Village to try to get into a James Brown gig. No luck. We left his friend behind and walked to my loft in Chinatown. I told him the whole story with Edward, and he told me the whole story with Francesca. When we arrived, we sat in the front, on the stage, admiring the view. I lent him a copy of my play to read. He took off. We agreed to meet the next day. We invited Edward to meet him.

The next morning, when he called, I decided to meet him at five later that day at the apartment where he was staying. He showed me around. We smoked a joint. And then he sat across a desk looking at me. My bones were shaking. I was thinking to myself, *here I am sitting in front of the great love of my life, and I'm married to someone else.*

He stood up and said: "Who is this guy? A restaurant manager? Who is he? Just tell him I'm here. I've arrived." He was pacing in front of the desk.

"It's very intense. What can I do? It's very intense," I replied, sitting in the chair, almost paralyzed. I could not speak anymore. I was trembling. He must have noticed because he placed his blue blazer carefully over my shoulders as we stepped out into the hallway and down the elevator.

"What are you thinking?" he asked impatiently. I suppose he could feel my desolate tone, my disappointment at not being available. But I had nothing to say. Yet I was hurt and angry after his rejection.

"What are you thinking?" he insisted again.

I could only be silent because if I spoke it could be a volcano. I had to distill it into its essence to be so succinct like the Englishman was teaching me. How to condense a volcano into a civilized phrase that contained the whole message of my being at that moment?

By now, we were sitting in a cab rushing through Central Park to go to the West Side to meet Edward at a movie.

I reached over to his cheek with my bare hand and patted him gently, whispering in the softest tone I could muster, while the moss-covered stone rushed by, outside the cab window. "It's very safe and easy to want someone when they are not available," I said.

As soon as he heard me, his face tightened in a pursing lip look. He avoided my eyes. He never said a word. I'm certain he understood. When I was crazy about him, he pushed me away. It doesn't make any sense.

After dinner, he invited me to come the next day with him to Washington, D.C. He wanted to go meet a boat builder. He wanted to familiarize himself with the technique so to maybe apply it to his "ball," as we called it. He had designed and built a contemporary family dwelling in a three-leveled sphere. Now he was about to build another one for his parents, bigger and more sophisticated. He had been my "Roarke." Edward didn't seem to mind. So we went by train.

After the investigation of the boat builder, we strolled through the National Gallery and under the blossoming cherry trees. Emmanuel finally left and I was glad. Life went back to the real story I was living. This experience had been a gift. I was able to concentrate on the creation of my family.

36

The duty to be alive is the same as the duty to become oneself, to develop into the individual one potentially is.
—Erich Fromm

I was cast as the architect in *The Killer* by Ionesco, produced by a small company in the Village. It was fun and challenging. Edward's comments about actors were always derogatory. "They are people who will do anything to get attention."

I remained in silent disappointment.

At the corner of Broadway and Grand, I raised my voice. "I want to be treated as a beautiful woman."

He stared at me in dismay, completely at a loss. Suddenly from the other side of the street an old boyfriend of mine suddenly showed up, chiming joyously: "Lili, it's so great to see you. You look great." He said with a warm smile of appreciation. "It's been years."

I introduced him to Edward. Talk about instant manifestation. He hugged me, we talked for a bit, and then he went on his way. Gratification!

One morning we went to the biggest Picasso show ever at the MOMA. The line went around the block. We waited almost an hour. When we were almost at the entrance, I collapsed to the ground and lost consciousness. They carried me into the museum and brought me back to life. I suspected I was pregnant. We saw the colorful show and went home.

Within the next few days, it was confirmed. I knew her name was Michaela, for the archangel. Edward thought it was too florid a name. If it were to be a boy, we would have called him Rupert after his brother. We both wanted this baby.

"I'm pregnant," I confided to my husband's ex-girlfriend. She was in New York for a gig. It was 1980.

"Anyone can have a child," she replied flippantly.

Did she think I was a knocked-up third-world Latina? I wasn't. I longed for a child; knew it was right.

Every massive fear in myself that could be traced to my upbringing, strengthened my determination to parent my children differently. My mother's commanding voice echoed: "This is what you'll wear to the party," or "Do what I say, not what I do." My children would choose for themselves as soon as they could.

"Being a parent is an opportunity for rebirth," a spiritual teacher said. I gathered information to be the best mother I could be. Their deep sense of self was my priority. Yes, anyone with an able body could have a child. Not everyone questions personal beliefs and values. This is sometimes painful. It's hard to ask the question, "Why am I in this rut? What do I need to change in myself?" It takes determined concentration to confront myself. This cavernous murmur, this intuitive voice from my heart grounds me.

I highlight my self-destructive beliefs when I am willing to acknowledge my responsibility. "What belief am I holding to create this reality?" Acknowledging, experiencing and embracing the underlying pain that created the destructive belief will allow me to integrate it. Only then, can I choose the most empowering and uplifting vision to live by. I often repeated to myself and later to my children:

"Mean what you say and say what you mean. The truth works."

The priority of my values was redefined by my children's needs. I was blessed by their existence. The continued study of meditation, psychology, hypnosis, healing and integration allowed me to recognize and revere the spirit within us all. I counted on my intuition. My mother gave me precious guidance when she said, "Above all else, trust your instinct as a mother." Aside from their health and wellbeing, I wanted them to recognize their passion and purpose on the planet as soon as possible.

José Silva had often said we could program our children before conception and during gestation. I sang to my Michaela, "You're healthy, beautiful, and brilliant," over and over again with many different melodies. I also took piano lessons, hoping that she would get used to the sound of the piano and long for it later, up close. Her father played the saxophone with the mouthpiece touching the belly. We were excited.

When we got the first recording of her heartbeat at the hospital, we recorded it on a small tape recorder and then played it so proudly to the taxi driver who took us home. This was the new heart that was coming into our world. We felt so privileged to be its parents. I got a nesting fever and began to look for a new place to live. I wanted a solid place with a real bathroom in a building that would stay in place when the trucks went by.

Soon I found and bought a "raw loft" in the West Village. I designed the interior, and became the contractor as my belly grew bigger. The workmen teased me, but I pressed them with the deadline, we had to be out of the Chinatown loft by the end of Feb. We kept as much of the space wide open. It was a historical building built in the early 1800s. You could see the outline of the old arched windows in the fourteen-foot-high brick walls. It had the great advantage of having an outside space in the back, over the post office's ground floor garden. They used it for their massive air conditioner. It purred shamelessly in the summer. We had a deck with planters built over it, secured on steel beams. Red and yellow tulips sprouted to announce spring. Everything was baby-proofed and geared for Michaela's development. There was one room that we had lead-lined, so Edward could practice the saxophone without concern for the neighbors.

In looking for clothes to fit this belly, I felt totally discouraged window-shopping in pregnancy shops. Very self-conscious about my body, I silently thanked all the mothers in the world who had preceded me for preparing the world for this enormous tummy I was about to have. When I mentioned my confusion to Bob, my artist friend, he said, "Why don't you go see Toma, the girl who is making big colorful shirts and sells them on the sidewalk on Canal?"

"You're right; I'm going."

As soon as I held one of the shirts to my chest, this beautiful tall African American girl with a milk-chocolate complexion came over to me. She wore her hair in several long braids hanging as graceful vines. Her voice felt like an effervescent spring.

"I'm expecting my first baby, and I need something for my belly. I'm in my fifth month."

"Oh come here, sweetie, let me show you how you have to exercise and open your hips as much as possible."

We climbed the stairs to her second floor apartment where she sat and invited me to join her. She placed her legs folded and knees wide apart, holding the soles of her feet together with her hands and opening her hips. I followed suit. She continued, "I've had two girls, and they are in college in the top 95 percent of the country."

I watched her in awe. There she was with her own business putting her two girls through college. "How did you do it?" I asked amazed.

"Honey, all I did was giv'em the 'titty' all they want, just giv'em the 'titty', and they will blossom." Her voice flew up an octave in a sing-song lullaby. "Just giv'em the 'titty', honey. That's all they're crying for. That's all they want; just giv'em the 'titty', honey. Now let's choose some pants and tops for you. It's very important you feel wonderful and happy while you are pregnant."

We picked out a royal blue and a pink pair of pants and soft cotton, enormous T-shirts that flowed all around me as flags of the promise of new life. It was the beginning of a new friendship that still lasts. I found my live "Nanny Preta."

As I was getting ready to have Michaela completely naturally with the help of midwives, I encouraged Edward to participate and help me get ready for this unfamiliar experience. Of course, I read all the books I could get my hands on. Still, it doesn't replace experience itself. The Lamaze teacher made it sound easy. I told Edward, "Make sure you'll be there with me."

"I can't stand the sight of blood," he said.

"You have to figure it out because I'm going to need you there right next to me. I'm not going to take any drugs. I've read that one of the reasons why our generation is so hooked on drugs of one kind or another is because they were born out of an anesthetized mother. So that's what the child learns: when there is a difficult situation, just take a drug to get through it. In fact, the child develops its intelligence by going through the birth canal conscious and finding out that no matter how difficult the situation may be, there is always light at the end of the tunnel, and more than light, there are also hugs and food and kisses and cuddliness."

So he went to the butcher on Mott Street to get used to the sight of blood and was a great support during the eighteen hours of contractions that Michaela favored me with. There never was such a wanted child. Michaela was the announcement of our salvation. We had been forgiven. Now we were blessed with this perfect being. We were both in profound awe.

Edward left a message on our answering machine that sounded like a prayer. He said in a whisper with great respect and wonder, "Michaela, our daughter has arrived. She is truly perfect and beautiful."

On my way back to Chinatown from the hospital, as I rode down in a cab with my new baby in my arms, I understood why it was so intense to give birth. I realized that I was much stronger and resilient than I ever imagined.

When I lay her down on the kitchen counter, all rolled up in her blankets of flannel and hand-knitted, pale-yellow wool, she was smaller than the cat. Persephone tiptoed over to smell her black hair. I had a flash of so much vulnerability. She looked like a little loaf of bread that I could easily slice. I was horrified with myself that I could even think that way, and then I cuddled her even more protectively. I was put to the test with the whining and crying at night.

I remember one night vividly. I had picked up Michaela several times already to breastfeed her and change her diaper and placed her back in her tiny crib, and after a short while, she began quibbling and whimpering again. I picked her up and looked her straight in the eye and said to her in an annoyed tone of voice, "Please be quiet. I can't stand it anymore. I need to sleep. Here is your dad."

She opened her eyes so wide, astonished and shocked that I was irked with her cries, it was clear she understood. Then, she just melted into her father's embrace. They bonded so closely. He was so patient with her at night.

When I arrived back in Chinatown after giving birth, there was a message from a director announcing a casting for dancers and actors for a play called *Sappho*, the Greek poetess, 620-570 B.C., who lived on the Island of Lesbos with only women poets; hence the word *lesbian*. I was cast as one of the dancers. It was rehearsals every day, and my figure benefitted immensely. Michaela was a little bundle backstage. Sometimes if she cried, I danced with her in my arms and then breastfed her until she fell back to sleep.

Life was idyllic. We moved into our new loft with our new baby.

Edward decided to dedicate himself to his music. The radio stations were happy to air my program and the advertisers were delighted to promote their products but would not pay me to produce it. I felt discouraged and didn't ask enough questions to find out how to get what I wanted. Years later, I discovered the possibility of grants.

37

If you think you can do a thing or think you can't do a thing, you're right.
—Henry Ford

Because I was breastfeeding, everything I ate became of magnified importance.

I felt stronger when I tried Shaklee food supplements made of organically grown vegetables and needed less caffeine and sweets. A nutrition business from home was something I could blend part time with mothering. I learned about vitamins, minerals and enzymes, and how they get absorbed more easily into the blood stream if they come from whole foods. I wrote stories late at night. My baby was my main concern.

It was at about this time that Edward's ex-girlfriend, the English pop singer, came to visit. She often came to New York to meet with other musicians or producers or even for a gig. She wanted to see our new life, our new baby girl, and loft. We chatted. She was duly impressed with the beauty of it all.

I wondered privately why she needed to keep visiting Edward. Was there some unfinished tie between them? Those dreams I'd had while I was in England and Ireland of the two of them making love in our Chinatown loft, all the multiple times he denied this having happened, my uneasiness with his response, came rushing into my awareness. Could I confront her now?

We were all standing in the kitchen. Edward was standing behind me facing her. She was facing me on the other side of the counter, when I asked her, "Did you and Edward make love that time when you stayed in Chinatown, and I was in England and kept calling him from there?"

She stared at me, stunned that I would ask the question, right into her big black eyes and with her henna-colored hair. Somewhere within a pregnant silence, she said, "Yes."

I turned to look at Edward behind me and saw him gesturing to her with his finger perpendicular to his lips, wagging his head frantically, begging her not say anything. I stared at him.

"You lied!" It seemed an eternity between each word. I was so disgusted and disappointed he had married me with this lie. So revolted.

"Get out," I said. "Pack up and leave; I can't stand this anymore. Leave." I stormed into my room and shut the door. That was it. Let him go. I'll make my life with my baby. He did not leave. Hours went by in silence. I felt as if I'd been falling off a cliff. Where was the bottom? Not only had he lied before we got married, he couldn't come clean in that moment. Where was his conscience, his essence? How could he live with his divided self? No wonder he was scratching his neck and head all the time.

But then I also had felt divided when Emmanuel showed up. I didn't make love with him. Had I shared honestly all my feelings with Edward? Why is it so hard to admit the truth when there is something to lose?

Finally, Frit, the ex-girlfriend, knocked on my bedroom door and asked if we could talk. I wondered why she was still there. Had they been talking while I was watching the baby? Why didn't he come to me? Maybe he was making her feel guilty for "having spoiled everything," and she wanted to fix it.

I nodded. She stepped a little closer to where I was sitting on the bed playing with the baby.

"Listen," she whispered, "you have a beautiful new family. What happened between Edward and me over a year ago was nothing. There was nothing there anymore, and that's when we found that out. It was empty. How can you destroy this beautiful budding family for a meaningless act that was hidden from you so not to interfere with your new life?"

"He lied to me before we got married. Our marriage is based on lies. Where is the trust? Where is the real communication? What is this about? I'm fed up of lies."

"He hasn't lied about loving you. He lied to protect you from a closing act."

"I deserve to know what's going on."

"Of course you do." There was a pause. The baby gurgled. She sat on the bed next to the baby. "Can you forgive him? He is distraught; can you forgive him this one time?"

Silence. What to do? I thought: *I love this little family, too. Shall I destroy, or shall I build? Shall I be intransigent or forgiving? Shall I stick to my standards, or shall*

I compromise them? Shall I give more importance to the past or to the present? It was a pivotal moment. After all, they had made love before we were married. I was still overwhelmed that he couldn't own up to it now. He had to send her as his spokeswoman. But I also had not owned up to my feelings with Emmanuel. If I could forgive myself and live with myself, I could also forgive him.

"All right," I said after more silence. "I'll forgive him."

"That's great. I'll leave for now, so you can talk. I offer you each a massage. I know this great massage therapist who lives around the corner."

"Okay," I mumbled, feeling uneasy and lost. She left. Edward and I didn't speak for twenty-four hours.

I moved with silent awkward steps, socks on my feet. My favorite socks were hand painted with serpentine colors all the way to below the knees. We went to the massage and returned more relaxed, still mute. The next day I sat next to him on the sofa holding the baby. The first thing he said was, "I want to become a physician."

Astonished and eager to be supportive, now that I had forgiven him, I offered, "That's great; do it." I didn't question how could he make that happen. I didn't wonder if it would affect us in any way. I can't figure out if I was dumb or just mesmerized in a trance of total acceptance. I had faith it would all work out. I looked around at the Kilim carpet in pinks and blues we had chosen together and how well it worked with the Marimekko blue and white cotton slipcovers for the sofa. This was our nest. We placed so much care in building it.

A few nights later, I had this vivid dream. It had a title: *The Baby Train. We had moved to the country. I remembered asking for firewood from a chubby woman neighbor. She owned a bakery. I remember walking along a dirt road with odd-sized stones on it. I remember the silence and the country air.*

Then we were at the train station running to catch the baby train. We called it the baby train because it was the shortest way across the river, the most comfortable one for our baby, who could nurse herself to sleep and arrive home for unfathomable dreams in her crib; a crib surrounded by two luscious ficus trees, some flying Thai fish painted in twinkles of green, red, yellow, blue, and pink with dots of gold, and the mobile of all the Beatrix Potter characters.

This time Edward was way ahead of me, in the crowd, running with the baby in his arms, and I cried, over the heads of the crowd, "I'll meet you in the baby train."

He kept signaling "no" with his head, and once I heard him say he would take the boat. This boat was a ferry that took a little more time. It arrived on the same quay as the baby train and would link up with another train to get to our town. I saw him once more in the crowd and shouted this time, "The baby train."

Again he signaled he would take the boat. So I thought that would be a fun ride for them both, and we would race each other home this way. At the same time, I wasn't sure whether he might change his mind.

Now I was on the train, and it was very full of people; I had to stand. I knew I was on the right train because I met the chubby woman the one who had a bakery, and she was reminding me of what I had to do to get home. Pick up the key next door. Then I turned around to see as the other aisle of people lined up with their backs to the windows, like a seat on the subway. From the corner of my eyes, I noticed a man all dressed in black like a priest or a minister trying to catch my attention. But I didn't remember knowing him, so I ignored him even though he was smiling and twitching his hands around his face attempting to keep his spectacles in place.

I decided to speak to a fat man who looked like Robert Morley, the actor. I didn't know him from before, yet I asked him if he had seen my husband, a very tall thin man carrying a baby. I wasn't sure whether he had taken the baby train or not. I called it the "baby train" even for him, and he understood.

Then, I looked over in the direction of the minister. He smiled at me as if he expected to be recognized, and I went along with the smile of being recognized although I still did not remember him. And we shook hands and I kissed him on the forehead, as I do to Uncle Ogilvy. Then, when I raised my head, I could see our tracks speeding by under us. When the train arrived, I stepped out. There was a great quiet emptiness on the quay. I looked all around to see if I could find him. I heard a cry and then saw a large empty 1940 Ford station wagon very clean with lots of glass windows. It was moving very slowly at a ceremonial pace, and I followed it on foot. The quay was completely empty. The station wagon stopped, as if surprised, and I passed it. I was trotting by then. At the very far end at the left, I saw a wheelchair being lowered and wheeled out from the train. It was my Edward, dressed in a red satin dressing gown, completely keeled over, face down and stiff. No sight of the baby.

I knelt on the cold concrete, and cried out, "Oh, no, my Lord."

Then I woke up and felt Edward there and called his name. He woke up. "I just had a very sad dream."

"What was it?" he asked, as he slid me over to nestle in his arms.

I was so glad to touch him, caress his back, cuddle with him, and hear him breathe that I could not answer.

Michaela, let out little sputtering cries and began sucking her fingers noisily to let us know she was hungry. What a relief to be awake. What a joy to be alive together. He picked her out of the crib and brought her to me to nurse. A cool rain after a blistering hot day.

I wonder sometimes if I had paid attention and had gone into meditation and changed the images and the outcome of the dream, if the reality would have changed as well. I know of a few cases where it has.

38

No one can make you feel inferior without your consent.
—Eleanor Roosevelt

When Michaela was two, I knew I didn't want her to be an only child.

"I want to get pregnant again soon," I whispered to Edward, early in the pink dawn light, as Michaela suckled noisily.

"Tanking up! One boot full now for the next one." He commented on Michaela's rhythmic determination at getting a good dose of nourishment.

As the day swanned in and we were all cuddled in the same bed, it seemed it was the best time to talk. "I've been reading how primitive cultures keep the breastfeeding going for at least three years so there is less of a possibility of getting pregnant again. They are aware of the strong jealousy that can arise. A lot of the literature mentions how the child has to get beyond the terrible twos when it is going through moments of panic at realizing that it truly is separate from the mother. To introduce a sibling within that period would be allowing for a high probability of jealousy of the intruder and the taker-away of mommy's attention. Even if I got pregnant right away, it would still be born when Michaela was two and three quarters."

"Are you sure? It's going to be double the work."

"Yes, they will have each other. They will be friends."

Two months later, I was pregnant. It was hard to imagine being able to love another human being at least as much as I loved Michaela. Yet, as soon as Stephanie was born, I fell in love so deeply once again. Being a mother has brought on feelings as enormous as the deepest oceans. I have never felt for a man, the immensity of devotion, energy, and love I discovered in myself through and for these children. I never wanted my girls to cry themselves to sleep alone. I wanted them to deeply believe someone would respond if they expressed a need. If Stephanie was whimpering at night when Edward came home, he held her in his arms and walked, sometimes in the street, until she fell asleep. I was influenced by "*Touching, the Human Significance of the Skin*" by Ashley Montagu.

Edward kept studying, preparing for the MCATs. We saw less and less of him. He and I talked less and less. We did all meet sometimes on Washington Square Park. I felt pressured for money because now we were spending capital to buy groceries, and that was dangerous. I often wondered how I got myself into this situation: two kids and a husband who was mostly absent.

Even though money was tight, I found a very inexpensive way to fly and stay in Puerto Rico. One winter, I took off for ten days with the babies to stay at Rajneesh's ashram in the mountains above Luquillo beach. A *sanyasin* (devotee) took care of us, cooking and cleaning. A clear stream rushed by the rainforest flanking the hill around us. We arrived in San Juan at a modest rooming house with a vegetarian restaurant on the ground floor that smelled of curried lentils. The first thing Michaela said to me when we woke up there was, "My daddy held you in his arms when you were a baby."

Instantly, the picture in my mind was one where my grandfather held me in his arms when I was a baby. It was a year before he died, and I was one-year-old. Maybe Edward had to practice as a physician in this life because as my grandfather, he hadn't. After medical school, he married my rich grandmother who wanted to entertain and travel, although she did go on suffragette marches.

This calmed me and allowed me to accept the whole picture of my marriage in much vaster terms. Edward resembled my grandfather physically, with the same strong aquiline nose. My grandfather was also a musician. He played the violin and made objects in wood. Edward's identical twin does the same. Recently, I found a photo. In it, I am sitting on Edward's lap in a white linen slip-like dress and the top part of his head on the picture has yellowed and faded and looks like my grandfather. Coincidence? He is four years younger than I am.

Every year we went to visit Edward's mother in Coconut Grove, Miami, Florida, and whenever we returned, I wondered what we were doing in New York City. We finally decided to move. I went down with the girls while Edward stayed behind to pass his MCATS. I searched for a house.

39

Like the one who lives in a valley and then crosses the mountains and sees the plain, he knows from experience that the sign saying, "Do not go beyond this point," like the high mountains, does not signify a barrier.
—Alice Miller

When the moving men were there, Michaela played with the magnetic letters on the fridge and wrote two words, *uncircle* and then *nucircle.*

We stayed at first with my cousin in West Coconut Grove in a modest little house with five other tenants. The girls and I shared a double-bed mattress on the floor of the screened-in back porch.

I found a house adjacent to the park where I wanted to live, the Merrie Christmas Park, a magical place. It was sunken in an old coral quarry that had become a construction dump. When the mayor of Coral Gables, Mr. Christmas, lost his little girl to a station wagon backing-up in a driveway, he made the construction dump into a park, so the rest of the children in the neighborhood could play safely.

Immense banyan trees hang their ambitious roots from their branches, claiming more territory. Some of the trees have caverns within their trunks. The owners allowed me to rent until we got our mortgage approved. Our new nest was beginning to take shape. After a week in this new house, Michaela, 3 years old, ran in from the garden and said to me:" Mom, I've just seen Jesus in the garden and he told me not to worry. Everything is going to be alright."

"That's wonderful to know, thank you. Where did you see him?"

"Over by the gardenia bushes."

"How did you know it was him?"

"He told me his name."

What puzzled me was that I didn't remember ever talking about Jesus to her.

All I repeated at different times was "do to others what you would want others to do to you."

The girls and I moved in and waited for Edward to return from New York having passed his MCATS. With those results, he could apply to medical schools. At first, we were all inseparable: excited, we accompanied Edward in the car when he inquired about his first job at Baptist Hospital as a technician in the emergency room. All he knew how to do was draw blood, which he had done over and over again at St. Vincent's Hospital in the West Village in New York. The girls and I played by the ponds full of ducks and ducklings on the hospital grounds.

It became a fun ritual to take grain or boxes of stale cereal to the ducks. We watched them mate in the water. The male jumped the female and pushed her neck and beak into the water while he fertilized her with his foot-long corkscrew rubbery penis. Then, he dragged it on the earth nonchalantly until it shrunk again. There were so many sweet fuzzy ducklings faithfully following the mother ducks. Lots of blackbirds waited for the appropriate moment to steal one and eat it.

We had one car, a wine-red Tempo. I drove Edward to work in the afternoon and picked him up around midnight, piling the girls in again, completely asleep by now. Many times I waited outside the emergency room witnessing either people rushing in frantically or others waiting endlessly. Bits of words or conversations wafted through the moist dark night. The entrance was a lit-up stage. Once I saw a couple hugging and sobbing, defeated. I became serious about my seatbelt after Edward, in his bloodstained scrubs, told me about the young son they had just lost because he didn't have his seatbelt on.

Edward had nightmares after a seventeen-year-old girl had a car accident. They were doing everything to sew her up as fast as they could to see if she could keep her fluids. They were wading in them. Most of her mouth and teeth had been knocked out. He felt so guilty because he noticed her lifting her hand ever so slightly making a gesture that she wanted to write something. He was the only one who noticed it, but because everyone was in such a frenzy trying to sew her up, he thought he better do the same rather than take down her message. He even told me that for comic relief of the high stress level one of the doctors came in and said: "Her mother told me she has a dentist appointment tomorrow, and did I think she would make it. I told her I wasn't sure." Everyone laughed because she didn't have any teeth in what was left of her mouth. Then she died. He couldn't sleep for days, waking up to the repeat image of her wanting to write a last message. He said, "I was playing God."

We had rented the loft in New York and were living off the rent. The second time he applied to medical school, again he was rejected.

I visualized over and over again that one day I would walk into our house with shopping bags in my arms, and he would hang up the phone and say, "Guess what, I was accepted into medical school today, just now."

The third year in a row he applied, and that's exactly how it happened. I was amazed. The doctors at Baptist Hospital got to know him and recommended him as a student to the University of Miami.

The next day, while he was at Baptist Hospital, I sobbed uncontrollably because now everything was going to change. I didn't know how or why, but my sadness was very deep. He came home and tried to console me and understand what I was crying about, but I myself could not explain it, except that I knew somewhere there was a big shift about to happen. I mostly felt that it was a change in my status in relation to him, but could not define it. With hindsight, I see it as a clear emotional premonition of what lay ahead. Or did I create it by feeling it?

40

There is only one corner of the universe you can be certain of improving, and that's your own self.
—Aldous Huxley

Before Edward began the first year of medical school, we were invited to a gathering by a professor for the freshmen and their families. They sat us around the living room in bent bamboo chairs with bright red hibiscus upholstery, a glass of wine or a beer for each, and a large table full of crisp raw vegetables served with dips and cold cuts. It felt like a party.

"Medical school is going to be hard, and if anyone, whether you the students or you their families, need any counseling along the way, there is some available at no cost to you, within the university." He extended his arm and hand and allowed his fingers to open up like the wedges of a fan, to point to us in two separate gestures. He seemed sincerely concerned.

Edward felt the gathering was a mere formality. He was excited with the prospect of having a cadaver to study in intimate detail. Several times I asked Edward to show me around the school, but he always found a reason not to. Sometimes he called from the library to say how lonely he felt, and I rushed over to spend a few moments with him, bringing a snack and cup of coffee we could share in the outside patio of the law library where he studied. He admitted to me that his Ph.D. professors were telling students to ignore their relationships and their families, their primary concern must be only their studies. I felt indignant in hearing this and begged him please not to follow those instructions to the letter.

He said: "I must because I am at a disadvantage. I am older than the rest of the students, and I have to work extra to keep up with them."

When we disagreed, he stopped talking to me.

"Please, let's arrange for us to go to the counselors," I said.

"I can't go because then I will be black-balled as someone who is unstable and who needs counseling."

We never went, and everything between us got more constricted. He often hung out at Baptist Hospital where a nurse was flirting with him since he first started working there. I often found cards with very friendly messages. She was still married at the time. Eventually, she got a divorce. He could talk to her in "hospital language." Even when he had free time, he ended up at Baptist instead of coming home to help me with the girls and with the house. And when he did, I'd lash out.

"Why can't you come home and help me with the girls or the paperwork? I feel like a widow without the benefits."

I became aware of how I had to rein myself in when frustrated, so as not to lose control. Years ago after receiving my first paychecks from the Shaklee business, I bought two hand painted ceramic lamps for our bedside tables. I treasured them because they came from money I had earned myself. Often I had to admonish Michaela to restrain her rambunctiousness when she was near them.

There was an undertone of panic in my voice when I said: "be careful with the lamp." One day, while jumping on and off the bed, she knocked one of the lamps over. It fell and cracked into many pieces. I felt an internal short circuit. I grabbed her put her face down on my knees and spanked her hard. I was furious. Edward looked at me horrified. I felt totally justified. Michaela cried "I want my Mommy, I want my Mommy".

"I am your Mommy!" I answered back to no avail.

If I wasn't being sweet to her, I wasn't her mommy. What a lesson. The next day, soaked in guilt, I apologized to Michaela. Eventually I glued the lamp back together and Michaela forgave me. I told the girls that when I was angry with them, it really meant I was angry at myself. Several times if I began to get upset or angry, they would say:

"What are you angry at yourself for, Mom?"

It worked with the girls most of the time, but with Edward, I couldn't control my anger. I yelled and was frustrated with his distance. I wish I had thought of going to therapy on my own. It didn't even occur to me. In my mind, I was right, and he was wrong. My friends in New York were saying, "If you're so unhappy, have an affair." It sounded appealing.

I had to go back to teaching the Silva Method of Mind Development and Stress Control. Looking back on my life, when I was teaching and practicing those techniques, my life seemed to flow much more harmoniously. With a little savings, I took off to Laredo two summers in a row. My mother took the children one summer, and Edward took care of them the next. I updated myself with a lot of reading, took the training again in English and in Spanish, and returned to teach in Miami and Ft. Lauderdale.

During that year, it was more and more difficult to accept the neglect and the lack of interest on Edward's part. I could explain it that he was busy studying, yet I felt abandoned and hurt.

One night I dreamt he had a girlfriend dressed in white. She was influencing him to kill me and was inflicting him with wounds. I tried to kill her even though I felt terrible doing that around the children. Then, I heard he had another girlfriend. I ran far away through parties and secret bicycle paths and then bumped into the children who told me they missed me but were beginning to look like the girlfriend and were covered with spots of fresh blood. I remember I saw them wrapped up in a white sheet, hiding under it. Then I had to run away again. I think the girlfriend was trying to catch me through this apartment. I was trying to run, but the rugs were sliding. Then I arrived and Edward's uncle told me he was fine, on the way to recovery. I felt optimistic. I walked in. He was lying on the floor almost passed out, with three pools of grayish yellow liquid dug out in his body. He was lying on the ground trying to get some rest. She was cutting open all his limbs and allowing all the juices to flow from him. Through his esophagus, then his stomach was a round pool of dark liquid. His new girlfriend was drawing with the blood coming out of his genitals. She seemed to savor her job and was bathing herself in it. I was so furious I began to attack her with pointed tools. Edward, in a very weak voice, kept saying, "You shouldn't do that in front of the children." She was dark-haired, and I could pierce her skin. She said she was itching because of all the fluids from Edward's body on her skin. I woke up as I was trying to kill her but couldn't.

One morning, Michaela said, "Daddy, I dreamt you had a girlfriend." He ignored the statement and went on with making coffee. I heard it very clearly, especially after the dream I had just had.

Another time, *I had a dream where I saw a woman dressed in white with a little white cap trying to get into his white car.*

Sometimes I was so lonely and distraught, I would be crying when he got home. He looked at me annoyed and walked away.

For Christmas, I wanted to place my disappointments behind me. The girls and I found a small Christmas tree on sale and decorated it with little wooden toys we'd been collecting for a few years. Gifts in shiny colored, bright paper were placed on the white sheet surrounding the base of the tree. I was determined to invent a sweet family reunion, with the aroma of warm sweet coffee cake and happy Christmas carols playing. The girls woke up early, excited about opening their presents.

Edward gave me a present in a big box. I didn't want to open it until everyone had opened their gifts. When I opened it, it was one of those floating chairs to put in the pool and relax in with a hole in the arm for a drink. I was triggered by the style of this chair. It was framed in aluminum tubing and had wide plastic navy blue ribbons braided for the seat and the back. The whole chair was balanced on pale-blue Styrofoam floaters. The arms were also covered in the same blue Styrofoam with a hole to hold the drink.

"I hate it. I find it horrible. How can you spend your money on such a disgusting middle-class contraption?" I was furious and uncontrollably vociferous. Edward, of course, was at a loss for words, probably upset and very hurt that I wasn't able to appreciate his gift. On the contrary, I insulted him with my fury and abhorrence of the whole thing. I was never able to apologize for that horrible behavior. I was out of my mind. Through the years, I have tried to understand what happened. Was he implying I should just relax when I felt that I had all the weight of the family on my shoulders?

Of course, it had nothing to do with him. I associated that kind of chair with my father, the lounging on the pool aspect of it. I remember my father for hours sitting by his pool in Ft. Lauderdale. He had enormous thirty-pound bags of dimes, nickels, and pennies. Could he find one that was minted much earlier and, therefore, would have a much greater value? He sat at a card table for hours doing this. I was visiting him for a short while, and he ignored me. I was happy with the pool and a lounge chair. I felt awkward with his emotional absence. I played in my imagination continuously. If there ever was a slight reprimand, I ran out into the lush tropical garden and hid under a gargantuan avocado tree. My stepmother's little gray toy poodle, Sweetie, followed me around. When I was totally out of everyone's sight, I planned how I could run away, but never did.

It was the morning of my fortieth birthday, a turning point for any woman. *Life is slipping by. What have I done with it? Have I contributed? Also, and mainly, is this the beginning of the aging curve? Am I still sexy? What do I look like to the world? Am I happy with myself? Is this the way I want to live? Am I being true to my heart?* These questions were stopping me in my tracks and shaking me up. What to do next was always on my mind. As Edward shuffled out of the house in a hurry repeating, "interruption disruption", I caught up with him at the door and said, "It's my birthday today; I'm having a few people for dinner, will you come?"

"I'm in a panic; I'm in a panic; I'm in a panic." His voice trailed away drowned by the crocodile coughing motor of the VW I got for him as a birthday present. He never showed up until very late; I was ready to go to sleep. Nothing was said.

A dear Brazilian friend, staying with me, asked me the next day: "Don't you think it's strange that it's your fortieth birthday and your husband doesn't show up with anything for you? Not even a hug. Don't you think there is something wrong there?"

"Well, he's so overwhelmed with his studies, but I guess you're right. It would have been sweet of him to acknowledge it in some way."

Like a shard of glass, this ground into my heart. I mentioned it to him and cried as I admitted that I felt so unimportant in his life. He hugged me, kissed me, and made love to me but did not speak.

Years later, one day, after Edward left, I was irritated with Stephanie who was ten at the time. I couldn't get her to calm down and listen to me. I don't remember the details. She was teasing me. I commanded her to lie on the bed. I got my belt out and began belting the walls so loud I could hear the snapping of the leather and the hissing of the swept air. I knew that people who have been abused often have the automatic reaction of abusing their own children as I had done that onetime with Michaela. This time the walls got it. I felt relieved and Stephanie, out of fear no doubt, quieted down. We were able to talk again. I needed to find more inner calm.

41

"Every autobiography is concerned with two characters, A Don Quixote, the Ego, and a Sancho Panza, the Self."
—W.H. Auden

After the Silva training in Laredo, I was told I could either teach in Miami or have my own territory in Ft. Lauderdale. I chose Ft. Lauderdale. I was excited to develop my own territory.

I began to teach Silva in Ft. Lauderdale. I gathered groups from previous mailing lists and met in some of their houses. They got a discount for offering their home as a meeting place.

I said to several friends over the phone, "I'm very excited, but I don't have any money for advertising."

I tried different loans, that didn't work. After hearing myself say again and again, "I don't have any money for advertising," I realized I was programming myself into a corner I didn't want to be in. I canceled the thought in my mind whenever it would appear.

If I thought of money for advertising, I declared out loud: “I have plenty of money for advertising. Advertising. I have all the money I need for advertising.”

A week later, a man called me: “My name is Ed. I’m an agoraphobic. My psychologist told me to find myself a Silva instructor. I called Laredo to find out who was the Silva instructor in Ft. Lauderdale. They gave me your name. When can I find out more about it?”

“I’m giving a free introduction next week. You can attend.”

I gave him the address. He got there, and explained to me he had been housebound for ten years. He lived with his wife and two small boys, but that he was too afraid to have a panic attack in the middle of traffic. He only dared to venture out to go to his Agoraphobics Anonymous meeting or to his psychologist. This situation caused great difficulties in his life. He was eager to free himself. He signed up for my next class.

After the class, he was so excited that he repeated it a few weeks later and again a third time. After that, he began to go out and to feel more and more confident on his own. He was applying the techniques and getting results.

His parents were so delighted, they came to meet me and thank me for having helped their son recover mobility in his life. His father, an oncologist in Ft. Lauderdale, owned a large medical building that housed several different practices. He offered me a room to teach the Silva Method at no cost. He sent me some of his patients. His son, the recovered agoraphobic, said to me one day, “Lili, you teach, I’ll take care of the advertising.”

We became business partners for several years, until our lives changed.

Ironically, Edward also got assigned to follow the progress of an agoraphobic diagnosed by the teaching hospital. He met with him twice a week to talk and follow his possible improvement. He told me the man was not changing.

Sometimes, when my partner organized a weekend class, he would book a suite in a hotel in Ft. Lauderdale, right on the beach, and the girls and I and a babysitter spent the weekend there. Sometimes the girls stayed with me in the class while I shared the material. They made pictures sitting on the floor in a corner of the room. I was learning again that I did have something to contribute to the world.

42

There is overwhelming evidence that the higher the level of self-esteem, the more likely one will treat others with respect, kindness, and generosity. People who do not experience self-love have little or no capacity to love others.
—Nathaniel Branden

An ear, nose, and throat surgeon who trained as a plastic surgeon and was also a sculptor attended one of my classes. He was recently divorced with three children and was very interested in the Silva Method. As a rabbi he was learning a lot about the Kabbalah.

The Kabbalah is the oldest Jewish mystic wisdom that creates order out of chaos. Its ultimate source is the Zohar, an ancient manuscript of twenty-three volumes. It is not about the power of religion; it is about the power of light. It is about who we are and why we are here.

He shared with us the points of convergence between the two schools of thought, the Kabbalah and the Silva Method. He attended half of the class and said he would finish the second half at another time. He mentioned he was living on a houseboat.

"You must all come and check it out and have one of the meetings there."

The houseboat was floating on a big wide canal. It was spacious, with two floors and wide glass windows overlooking the glistening moving blue water and the silhouettes of other boats bobbing and clanking against the docks. There was a flavor of adventure. He had massive pink, white, and purple quartz crystals and many of his bronze sculptures rhythmically placed around his living room. He was talented, and we talked and laughed effortlessly. His eyes were wide set and clear blue. He was tall and strong. We began talking more and more over the phone.

I invited him for dinner to meet Edward. Edward was not too happy after the surgeon left. He helped me clean up and said he didn't like him. I had made some tortellini with ground meat inside and a cream cheesy sauce. The surgeon could not eat it, because, he said, "Jews are not allowed to mix meat and cheese in the same meal." So all he could eat was the salad and the dessert. I felt so ignorant.

We talked a lot over the phone. He was lonely and so was I. He understood what Edward was going through, but seemed also to understand how abandoned I felt. I called so much, he told me to call him collect so it would not cost me. It was a very protective gesture, and I welcomed it. Nobody had protected me in a very long time. Finally, after months of talking and laughing on the phone, I invited him to an event about nutrition. I picked him up in Ft. Lauderdale; the meeting was in Boca Raton. We had fun. I asked him if he thought he would get married again and he said yes. What I admired about him was how he cared for his children, always making time for them and respecting them so profoundly.

He gave a big party on his houseboat and invited me. I asked if I could invite a girlfriend. She never came. I knew I was playing with fire. I was attracted to him. I caught him watching me from the corner of his eyes when he was not talking to me.

We were living on very little money. What I was paid from Silva covered the groceries. Going to a party represented an opportunity for me to network and find new clients.

Jennifer, the friend who didn't come to the party, was my confidante. Her family was from Miami. She was a pretty Vassar graduate and a publicist for people in the film industry. Edward's family name was familiar to her. "The Boulted brothers, in England, were as important as the Selznicks in Hollywood," she used to say.

She admired in me the strength it took to keep everything together. I shared with her how lonely I felt within my marriage with Edward. I admired her lightheartedness and her quick intelligence. Many times she called and ask me to come over to her apartment, when she felt too sullen to go out.

When she got a job to head the Arts Council of Miami Beach, she often came over after work to share with us how her day had unfolded. We knew a lot about each other's lives.

She couldn't understand why she didn't have a boyfriend. I couldn't either. I suggested that she imagine and feel as if she already had one. Then an ex-boyfriend from

France came to visit. She brought him over, so we could meet him. He was articulate and attractive. He went back to France without any follow-up. To help her feel better, the girls and I took her for walks on the beach.

She got closer to me and to Edward. He could be sensitive. Yet, with me, he was becoming so distant.

Once he said to me, “In one week I learn more than you will ever know in your whole life.” I was dazed into silence. Thank God, a few minutes later, he said, “That’s bullshit.”

Several months went by. The plastic surgeon made several loaves of challah bread on Fridays for the Shabbat. He dropped one off at my house almost every week. Then one day he called and said he wanted to come and finish the Silva Method course. He came over to speak to me privately at the break.

“I’ve checked with two of my astrologers, and they both say that you are my soulmate.”

He took me to lunch and asked me to be patient with him because he still had to figure some things out. He said he definitely wanted us to be together and eventually get married. He invited me to come over to his houseboat after the class was over.

“Are you sure I am your soulmate?”

“Yes, I’m certain.”

“I don’t want to risk my marriage, if you are not sure.”

“I understand. I am sure.”

After the class, we went back to his houseboat. There was part of me that felt very attracted to him and yearned to be closer to him. There was another part of me that wanted my marriage to be as it was in the beginning, yet I felt powerless. And if there was nothing more to do, then, why not start another love story? If he was so convinced that I was his soulmate, maybe I was. I needed to know him better. Did I feel he was my soulmate?

We spent the afternoon together. He liked Bach. The elegance of the Brandenburg Concertos gave the whole afternoon a sense of order and harmony. He lit many candles in different shaped glass containers. He served us a Bordeaux wine in medieval goblets. The bathtub in his bedroom was a magnificent size. He filled it with warm sudsy water. We smoked a joint. He said, "Let's take a bath together."

I knew we both wanted to make love. I knew he was preparing me in that direction, and I knew I was surrendering. We talked about his children and mine. We discussed that we could not really be together until my divorce would be final. He said he didn't mind because he had a few things to finalize with his ex-wife.

We got closer and closer with tenderness. We made love and rested, taking it all in.

As I was getting dressed, I asked, "I wonder if Edward will want me back once he knows you also want me and have made love to me?"

"He won't," he replied very fast. I felt a shiver of fear run through my body. I was living a double life, and I hated it. I hoped that if Edward found out about this afternoon affair, he would realize he was losing me and want me again. Should I tell him? How foolish!

Years later my Brazilian friend came back and shared:

"That time when I was staying in your guest room, it was late one night, you had gone to bed with the girls, and your girlfriend Jennifer stayed up with Edward. They were there talking until about three or four in the morning, and then I heard them leave. So I got out of my room, and on the living room floor, I saw her bra. I kept it. At the time, I didn't want to say anything to you because I felt it would upset you. But I still have the bra because it was very nice, and it fits me. I'll show it to you some day if you like."

I was stunned. Jennifer posed as my best friend. I repeated my mother's pattern. My mother's best friend had an affair with my stepfather. I want to be free of all patterns. I don't know if that's possible. The gurus say it is. It sounds as if I have a long way to go.

43

He that respects himself is safe from others:
he wears a coat of mail that none can pierce.
—Longfellow

The next day, the plastic surgeon called me to let me know that he now knew I was not his soulmate.

A duped idiot, my body shook. I cried and cried on the floor and cried some more. Finally I admitted to Edward why all the tears. He was struck. He couldn't believe that I had been unfaithful to him. I couldn't believe it myself. Although there was a part of me that wanted to klonk him over the head so he would notice I was alive and that I mattered. I announced that I was leaving to see Emmanuel. Edward got worried and said that he wasn't going to school any more. He had decided to stay home so we could talk.

"So, what do you want to talk about?" said Edward.

He was fuming, pacing around the house or doing dishes and cleaning counters as if he wanted to wring them all by the neck.

"How come you dropped out of your last class in the year, when you only have one week to go?" I retorted impatiently. "You won't have a free summer. Why didn't you discuss it with me first? Your summer is ruined because of me. I don't want to be the guilty one, again and again."

"You wanted to talk, didn't you? Well, let's talk. What do you want to talk about?"

I felt totally blank when he said that with such a defying tone. I didn't know where to begin, or what he was sincerely willing to hear. He was mouthing the words, yet his tone was saying, "I dare you to come up with anything of any importance or of more value than my challenges at medical school."

We were able to talk in spurts and came to the conclusion that we were going to work on our marriage. Then, he left for New York to visit his older brother and his mother. While he was there, I called and asked him, "Are you my man, Edward?" He knew very well that when he tried to move in with me in Chinatown, years ago, he used to repeat that to me over and over again: "I'm your man, Lili. I'm your man."

On the phone, he replied dryly, "I don't know."

I was devastated. I couldn't even muster the energy to complain and say, "What's the matter with you? How come you don't know?"

When he got back to our house in Miami, he asked me: "Do you think it would better for me to move out?"

"I would respect you more if you would pay your own rent."

So he packed his belongings and left; he moved one block away.

I realize now that I didn't say what I meant. Also, I had mixed feelings and that's why I wasn't clear. It is so important to talk and in the talking, distill the essence of our intention and need. I meant, “I would respect you more if you could contribute your share of the expenses in this household.” He understood me to mean he could move out and pay his own rent. Our communication was always so clipped we never got a chance to clear it up. There were so many hurt feelings, it was impossible to focus and deepen the understanding. When I bicycled over to his place, I found him in bed with another woman.

A few weeks later, I left for training in Laredo. For two weeks, he stayed with the children in the house. Every time I called, he said: “I know what you are doing out there; just fucking around. Just go for it, Lili. Just let yourself go.” He said all this in an angry, cynical tone.

“You’re wrong,” I kept saying. “All I’m doing is going to classes and having meals with my colleagues. Edward, I thought we were rebuilding our marriage.”

“You can’t kid me. I know what you’re doing out there. Just go for it, Lili. Just let yourself go.”

I didn’t understand why he could only talk to me in such a bitter and sarcastic tone. I tried to bring him to his senses.

“Edward, you are the handsomest man I know. You are the man I love.”

“Yeah, yeah, that’s easy to say over the phone.”

“Why don’t you believe me?”

“Why should I?”

I was at a loss and said, “I love you” and hung up. He had no desire to connect. I was not skilled enough to allow him to acknowledge his pain and his fear. Or maybe he wanted me to go ahead and let it all go. To this day, I don’t know.

What I do know is that as the days went by I got closer and closer to an instructor who had become my friend in a previous year when I had been there and who was very experienced in the business. We were talking a lot and spending a lot of the free time together. We attended a workshop together and then had dinner. The rest of the evening, we wrote poems with a couple of other friends. Then I called Edward. Once again, all I could hear was his cynical encouragement to go ahead and just go for it and let it all go. He meant sex. No matter how much I would say that he had the wrong picture in mind, he kept insisting that he knew what was going on there. I was so confused. Why was he pushing me away? I knew I had betrayed him once. Yet, I was truthful. Why didn't he believe me? Why was he only expecting the worst from me? Why didn't I dare or know how to confront him on the way he was treating me?

By the time we hung up, I was alone in the room with my instructor friend and feeling quite desolate. I asked him to please make love to me, and he did.

44

Go to your bosom; knock there; and ask your heart, what it doth know.
—Shakespeare

When Edward moved out, he said, "It feels like I'm severing a limb."

It was devastating to me. He came over often. He also disappeared a lot.

He came one day and said, "I'm lonely." We made love, but it was like making love to a gray skeleton. He said, "Even the love-making, I took for granted."

"Come back," I said.

He walked around like a ghost, gathering his belongings, and then disappeared.

I wrote him a letter.

> *Dear Edward,*
>
> *You didn't do anything wrong, and I didn't do anything wrong. Could we claim that our innocence was never lost? Could we allow ourselves to be healed? Could we let go of the past and just*

be here now? Could we see ourselves as children ineptly going through changes? Could we accept ourselves, and each other? Could we claim our power of choice in the here and now and create the family we want? Could we start a new understanding through peace? Could we be in love again with a deeper understanding and respect for each other's needs?

I love you, Lili

Soon after that, he moved in with the nurse.

I dreamt of trying to get it back together, but it all felt like melting and disappearing threads in my hands. Once, I dreamt I was an old rag doll discarded on a garbage pile.

It was a dreadful time for me and for the children. I cried at any mention of anything that would remind me of family, marriage, or husband. I started going to therapy, attending classes of A Course in Miracles, anything I could find to alleviate the pain. Nevertheless, while the children were at school, I often found myself sobbing on the floor in a corner of the corridor. I felt more like a river than a person.

I called my mother. "Mummy, you need to come. Maybe you can come with Ilona. Please, I need somebody."

My mother and sister did come and spent a week with me.

My sister planted colorful impatiens around my tree in the front of the house. She gave a coat of paint to my rusty refrigerator. Ilona is always so energetic and witty, wanting to keep everybody happy and laughing. She is a tall, strong, high-cheek-boned beauty with straight auburn hair. We didn't talk about the separation. Sitting in my car with my mother, about to go pick up the children from school, my mother said to me:

"At age forty, I looked much younger than you do now."

I was silent.

The day before they left, I said:

"Mummy, I promised to take the girls to the Dade County amusement fair. Today is the last day. Would you and Ilona want to come with us? It could be fun."

"No, we'll be here and have a quiet evening."

"Ok. We'll back a little later, after dinner."

They were both asleep, when we returned. In the morning, Mummy said:

"How could you go out with just your girls the last evening we are here? What a lack of sensitivity!"

There was a falling out as they left. It took me back to my internal "drawing board."

My friend Bob Smith from New York called and let me know he had discovered he had the HIV virus. His doctor had put him on AZT, and since he had been taking it, his legs got too weak to climb the five flights of stairs to get to his loft in Tribeca. Bob was a great visual artist. One of the curators of the Metropolitan Museum of Art had bought and displayed in his home a large piece of Bob's, a series of eight canvases depicting camels and their riders galloping through the Moroccan desert.

I owned a couple of his pieces. He had many other collectors. He was Michaela's godfather. He was gay, but he hardly had any boyfriends; once in a while, a handsome

Norwegian or Dane. I was sure he didn't have the virus. I encouraged him to have himself checked out, and then it turned out that he did. When I heard how the AZT debilitated him so rapidly, I offered he stay with us, in Florida, until he found his way around. I'd met Bob because he shared a loft with the French video artist I lived with for a while. When the "frog," as we called him, wouldn't show up, Bob and I would hang out and sometimes even cuddle together. He felt like a brother.

Once, after I moved to Chinatown, I was alone one night, and some men came banging on my big metal door hollering, "Open up, we are the police!"

"I don't care who you are, I'm not opening up to anybody."

"Open right now!" they yelled.

"I'm going to call the police," I retorted.

"Let's go. She's got the right attitude. "They tambourined themselves down the steps. I called the police as soon as they left.

"Did you send some police officers to one seventy-nine Canal Street?"

"Let me ask," the guy who answered the phone said. "Yeah, we did. There was an anonymous report that there was a dead body on the fifth floor."

"Well, I'm on the fifth floor and there is no dead body here."

"Okay, thanks for calling." And he hung up.

I was scared after that. I called Bob, and he came over immediately to keep me company. We did a lot of projects together. He designed and painted several sets for abstract mime shows I was in. They were directed by an Italian mime, Luciano. We performed mostly at NYU.

Bob and I strolled through museums getting ideas. He was a great buddy and also a driven artist. He woke up at five in the morning to rummage through the discards in the streets and find the materials for his art. He often used to say, "I live from miracle to miracle."

This is why when it got so difficult for him to climb steps in New York, I couldn't think of anyone I'd rather be with. When we were together, I felt free as a child with my thoughts and imagination. He enjoyed my ideas. I felt nourished by his uncanny associations. His presence was soothing.

Right away, I began to inform myself as thoroughly as possible about the dangers and the parameters of living with someone with the HIV virus. The Health Crisis Network was my resource. I found out very soon that it is very difficult to catch the virus unless you take in some infected blood into your own blood stream. Soap and water for the dishes is fine. We did have an eye out for the dishes he used and we always gave him the same ones. He stayed in our garage, which had been converted into a room, and he used the children's bathroom. The children only used my bathroom. Sometimes Michaela and Stephanie were turned off by the disheveled way he looked or by his swollen legs or his bleeding lips or ears. They kept their distance.

He became incontinent many times in the pool. No one wanted to use it anymore except him. I cleaned it and had it cleaned. The Health Crisis Network people assured me that chlorine killed the virus. He set up his studio on my front porch. We had slabs of coral rock piled in different groups of sizes. We heard the sandblasting whine of the saw he used from early in the morning until late in the after-noon, as he sliced blocks of coral rock into manageable pieces.

"Since I can't have my own house, I'll build the model one I want." He built many houses of different proportions with this porous pinkish-gray colored rock. They looked more like European medieval castles or little houses from tucked away villages.

Once when he came back from a brain scan at the University of Miami, he sat outside on a chair and began to sob.

"My brain is deteriorating. It showed up in the scan."

"Oh sweetie, we've known that for years, it's been happening to all of us, all those drugs."

We laughed it away. Yet inside, I was scared: first, to see him weaken and second, to see him dead. I had never seen a dead person in my life. When my father died, I arrived for the funeral. He had already been cremated. I knew I had to prepare. I enrolled in a training for people who want to help people with AIDS at the Health Crisis Network. Then I volunteered to go see the ones in the nursing homes. They were all in their twenties; they were all on IVs. They were covered in sores and complained that the nurses didn't care about them. One week they could talk with difficulty, because they had sores also in their mouths. Then the next week, some had white foam in their mouths, others were in a coma, or some had gone to a hospital.

Because I speak French, they guided me to talk with a Haitian, Jerome. I made friends with him. He often said, "Heh, Lili, *j'ai beaucoup de problèmes*." A few weeks later, he was foaming at the mouth. The following week, I was ushered into his room. There he lay naked with no more IVs. Immobile, and quietly dead. He was the first person I ever saw so completely lifeless. Black as bitter chocolate, he had the whitest teeth when he laughed.

For a while after that, I could smell him and another guy I had met at the nursing home in my car. It was a mixture of medicine, disinfectant, and gnawing rotten sickness. When I mentioned this in therapy, the therapist suggested I might have their spirits attached to me. So we worked on spirit release. He helped me guide them into the light. I never smelled their scent again in my car.

This therapist also taught A Course in Miracles. Written in the early 1970s by two psychologists who taught and did research at Columbia Medical School, it was translated into many languages. They were agnostics. In spite of all their skills and knowledge, they still felt angry and resentful, back-biting each other and their friends. There must be something more, they supposed. Something they were not getting. They proposed to write together. They met several times a week. Soon it became evident the woman, Dr. Helen Schucman, was writing more. When she changed one word, the following day, she tortured herself about it and by the evening put back the original word. Soon she said this was not her writing; it was a voice within her dictating. The voice identified itself as Jesus Christ. It said it wasn't only the historical Jesus Christ, but the energy from where all avatars on the planet have come.

It is an enormous book of knowledge, a comprehensive and profound message. It corroborated what I learned through the Silva Method, in terms of personal empowerment. Yet it also underscores the divine presence so ubiquitous and willing to help at all times. There are constant reminders that the only reality is love and love is God. Anything that isn't love is illusion and of the ego. The ego's only desire is to gain control and separate us from love. Gerald Jampolsky, the first psychiatrist to embrace A Course in Miracles, always posed the question, "Do you want to be right, or do you want to be happy?" I recommend it.

My younger brother came to visit. He was married to a Venezuelan woman, had children, and lived in Caracas. I explained Bob was living with us temporarily and that he was living with this challenge. My brother was shocked that I would put my children at risk in such a way.

"I've researched it thoroughly. We are all aware of what not to do. He is very good company for me."

"You do what you want, but I can't bring my children here." He stormed out of the house. I understood where he was coming from. He had not come across anyone he knew with AIDS. It's much easier to be scared when all you know is what you read in the press.

Then a miracle happened for Bob. He won a Guggenheim grant, which gave him some money, and also, through a cousin, he found an organization that funded practicing artists with AIDS. He got his own apartment on South Beach with a maid, physical therapist, food, and medical care. With all this good news, his T-cell count went way up; he seemed rejuvenated before my very eyes. It's amazing what good news can do for you. He bought a second-hand car. We went to Key West to visit his friend, Peter, a fine carpenter and a great soul. We had fabulous times.

One afternoon Bob called to say he had heard on TV that early that evening the park officials at 75th Street and

Miami Beach were going to return to the ocean the little turtles that had hatched recently. In early spring, the mama sea turtles climb onto the beach and dig holes for all their eggs. The park officials used to circle them with wood and rope them off. The eggs were not sufficiently protected. The new method was to dig up the eggs, have them hatch in incubators in the park buildings, and then bring out the determined green turtles to find their fate among the waves.

Bob alerted me so I could take the girls. What a thrill for them to see tray after tray of teeming, climbing over each other, squirming tiny mossy green turtles.

The children were allowed to take one by one, place it carefully on the damp sand pointing it in the right direction. Sometimes it veered and then adjusted its course. Marching to the call of the ocean, it advanced into the gigantic warm waves. Only one percent reaches adulthood.

45

Let go of grasping for love from
others and give it to yourself.
Let go of grasping for nurturing from
others and take care of yourself.
—Barbara Brennan

About this time, I read that we are drawn to have relationships with people whose issues are similar to the ones we experienced with our parents. I decided to call my stepfather Victor to see if now we could have a more mature dialogue.

"Well, you know you caused a big problem for your mother. I don't know what we would talk about," was his reply.

He was still stuck twenty years in the past. I gave up that possibility pretty fast. I didn't want to challenge his position and get entangled in any kind of argument. I experimented with other therapies: banging on the mattress and screaming out all my anger and frustration, rebirthing, vivation, intense breathing, "the art of being," "radical forgiveness," and probably a few others. They provided relief, and every time I got another piece of the puzzle.

I followed what I had learned with the Silva Method, namely the importance of every word we say to ourselves and to our children, who up to a certain age don't know they can reject what we say to them. We are hypnotizing our children with everything we say to them. I decided that instead of saying to the children, when they were exploring or experimenting with their skills, "Be careful, you are going to fall, or you're going to get hurt," I made a point of saying to them: "Make sure you are safe. Climb the tree, swim in the pool, ride the bike, cut the cheese, and make sure you are safe." Over and over and over again, they heard, "Make sure you are safe."

One day, I had an appointment in North Miami. I asked the teenager next door, Lang, to watch the girls for a couple of hours. When I returned, Stephanie was visibly shaken, and her right leg had a long and blood red wide scrape.

"What happened? I asked. "How did you fall?"

She sniffled compulsively at the edge of tears and could not speak. Soon my mother-in-law, who was visiting Miami, arrived and invited us all for dinner at a Chinese restaurant. There, Stephanie spilled the tea and the soup. So I said, "Stephanie and I are going home. You all can catch up with us later."

At home, just the two of us, I inquired again, "What happened this afternoon while I was gone?"

"Mom, I was riding my bike up the street to meet Lang, who was walking her dog. Then the green station wagon was backing up, and my bike skidded and fell, and the station wagon was coming at me. Mom, I thought I was going to die, but then, Mom, I made sure I was safe, and I yelled to Jenny, who was right there in the front, 'Jeeeeeeenny, tell your mom to stop the car.' And her mom stopped."

"Darling, that was great, you made sure you were safe. You did the right thing. Congratulations!"

I thanked José Silva from the depths of my being for having shown me this.

46

"So emptiness isn't like the empty space within a container, but the very nature of the container and whatever it contains. ...Emptiness isn't something distinct from phenomena, it's the very nature of phenomena."
—Matthieu Ricard

Two more years went by. Bob and I talked every day.

"I got this great big frozen turkey on sale, such a great price, two dollars. I'm going to keep it in my freezer for a special occasion."

"That's wonderful, Bob. We'll have a party!"

A couple of days later, his physical therapist, a lovely English lady who lived nearby my house, stopped by in the middle of the afternoon. I opened the front door, and she walked straight into the kitchen.

"He's in my car. I think he had a stroke because half of his mouth has dropped and he can't move his right leg or arm. Do you want to go and take a look at him? I don't know whether to take him to the hospital. He wants to go to the Park at Matheson. I don't know what to do. Can you help me?

I went out to the car.

"Hi, Bob, how are you doing?"

He slurred, "I can't move this leg or arm, and my mouth feels funny. But I'm all right. I just want to go to Matheson Park."

"Are you in pain?"

"No."

"Would you like to go to the hospital to find out what's happened to you?" I said, trying to be encouraging, but at a loss.

"No. I just want to go to Matheson Hammock Park."

"I understand."

I went back in the house to speak to Christine, the therapist. She said, "I think I should take him to the hospital."

"He wants to go to the park. But what if they can help him if you can get there in time?"

"I know," she said. She marched out to the car. I heard her say to him: "I think it's better if I take you to the hospital, in case it's better for them to help you sooner rather than later. They can help you."

"I guess," he agreed.

I asked her to call me when he got in. They took off. A couple of hours later, she called. "He's still waiting in the emergency area. I had to leave. Maybe you want to go and join him.

I found a babysitter for the children and took off. I found him in a tiny, icy-cold tiled room with a sink. He was on a cot covered with a sheet. It was freezing in there. His mouth was bleeding. I found some cotton. He was thirsty. I drenched the cotton in fresh water and dripped into his mouth and also wiped the blood off his lips. His eyes were wide-awake, but he couldn't talk. His eyes were saying: "This is it, right? Right? This is it."

I nodded ever so slightly and smiled. I knew he meant the end. I didn't know for sure it was the end, but I did have a strong feeling. I said, "I spoke to Peter, from Key West. He went into meditation on the rocks, at sunset, and is sending you rays of sun through his body and mind and heart."

He beamed so gladly, so sweetly, so full of understanding, as an old man smiles to a child. It was the last time I saw him smile. I spent a little more time with him. Then, I had to get back to the children.

"I'll be back later to make sure you're okay for the night."

He nodded in understanding. I kissed him on the cheek and left.

When I got home, the baked potatoes I had left cooking were ready. I sat with the children at the table telling them about Bob. Suddenly our Springer Spaniel Spot began barking at an empty corner on the sofa, the place where Bob always sat when he got to our house. I said to the children, "I think Spot is barking at Bob. Bob is sitting there on the sofa. Here Bob, do you want a potato?"

To this day, my children remember that moment. After dinner, I rushed back to the hospital. He had his own room. He was in a coma and on an IV. We never spoke again. The nurse said, "The people from hospice have come by. They are ready to take him tomorrow."

I wished we had let him go to Matheson Park.

Edward had suggested to him months ago that he sign a living will. The next day he was moved to hospice. In the following two days, all his friends came from different parts of the country: a video artist (gorgeous girl with silver rings in her nose and on the full outline of her outer ears); a female attorney from Brooklyn Heights with a determined gait and a sonorous laugh; a chubby gay caterer with curlicue gestures; another painter with fire-red hair blazing from his scalp; a nurse, a kind man who had overdosed on acid in the 1960s (when he started talking, he couldn't stop); his roommate, a black psychic woman called Mama with colorful turbans. She was letting us know all the spirits she could see and where they were sitting in the room.

Only one of them was missing: Robert. He was a younger version of our gifted artist. They had been very close for years. After he arrived, all his friends discussed whether they should feed him intravenously again, and yet, within minutes, Bob left his body and stopped breathing. I wasn't there at that very moment. They called me. My neighbor stayed with the girls, and I came running. We all covered him with flowers. He looked so regal, like a pharaoh. It impressed me because he went through a period where he was only painting pharaohs. A minister came and spoke of the body going, but the love we feel lasting forever. That night, we all gathered at this apartment and cooked the turkey that was in his freezer for a great party.

This is the poem Michaela wrote after that party.
All his friends in the garden
of his
Michigan Avenue apartment,
Eating roasted turkey,
feeling really broken.
Silences were not enough,

thoughts, memories. and feelings
needed to be spoken.
October sky, Miami Beach,
anticipation out of reach.

We all felt deeply bonded by having known him in life and in death. We stayed together for the next few days until everyone slowly returned to their private lives. At the service, when I got up to speak about Bob and how dedicated he was to his art and to his friends, especially to me and the children, I sobbed. The loss of his constant sweetness left a big gaping vacuum.

47

Our creativity does not consist in being right all the time; but in making of all our experiences, including the apparently mistaken and imperfect ones, a holy whole.
—Matthew Fox

I needed to make a living at home. It was rewarding to go to school again. Hypnosis and hypnotherapy became the most important tools I had to learn. I signed up at Omni Hypnosis in Ft. Lauderdale. Jerry Kein, now in Deland, Florida, is one of the best teachers I've ever had. I became a hypnotherapist and slowly and tentatively began a private practice. For a year, I practiced for free.

Then, the doctor who had told me I wasn't his soul mate after all, asked me to hypnotize him to reduce weight and insisted on paying me. He called me to let me know that he was losing weight and was grateful. From then on, I charged. My practice was steadily growing. I could work from my house and keep an eye on my children.

When I began to examine more carefully what was happening, the children were getting more quality time with their father than they ever had, and I was getting a tiny bit of child support, the first since we'd had the children. I never got any alimony.

At a yoga class, I became acquainted with Siddha Yoga and their guru Gurumayi Chidvilasananda. She was Baba Muktananda's translator into English for years. Then, after he died, she took on the leadership of the spiritual community. I started frequenting their center more and more and feeling tremendous peace and friendly support. After attending my first intensive, I had a constant inner experience of feeling in love.

An intensive is a long three-day experience where by viewing storytelling videos, chanting, and meditating, one has the chance to re-examine one's life, marriage, choices, mistakes, confusions, and children. What are my values, my priorities, my motivations, and my intentions? I was lost, and now I was looking and retracing bits and pieces of myself scattered around like gold dust at the edge of a river. I had to grab a lot of sand and then sift it out to extract the gold I wanted to claim as myself. In that first intensive, during a very deep meditation, I felt myself on the ocean floor with the seaweed swaying with the tides. Suddenly, I was in a clean white sphere. Gurumayi brought me a red candle and lit it to keep burning at the center of this sanctuary. I woke up with the distinct impression I had been ignited. In Siddha Yoga, they call it receiving Shaktipat, awakening the Kundalini force or the spiritual awareness within. It unfurls at the base of the spine and rises spiraling.

The center moved to a new address and became larger. They asked me to participate, and I volunteered to help with the children's program. It was fun and an easy way to get my daughters involved. We were a family of fellow devotees. I wanted to meet Gurumayi. In a dream, my hand went up and up her leg. When I almost reached her crotch she sat up and told me, "It's time to go and see your beloved."

I took the message to heart. At the ashram in South Fallsburg, I stayed in a room with two bunk beds. At first, I walked around, attended meditations, and slowly got acquainted with the village community. Some people there were smiley. Others were introspective. Some stayed alone. Others sat in pairs and spoke softly. Some were with their families, including children. Some were only working, or rather volunteering. When I told a monk dressed in orange robes, I had just arrived, he said, "Welcome home." In all the meditations or gatherings, we were encouraged to do *seva*. This is volunteer work. It is meant to be spiritual inner work as well. It took me a few days to decide to sign up. Finally I did. I woke up at four a.m. to be in the kitchen by five to cut tomatoes. It made me feel great to be helpful. I wouldn't be surprised if all the jobs there were done on a volunteer basis. I know some people get room and board free in exchange for their work.

I went up to the guru during a program called Darshan. She was beautiful and regal in her saffron robes. I asked Gurumayi to allow for Edward's spiritual awakening. I attributed his lack of it as the cause for his not being able to understand and forgive and love me anymore. Even though we were separated, he hadn't gone forward with the divorce papers. Sometimes I wished for a resurrection of our love for each other. She gave me a look full of certainty, a definite "yes." Then she splashed the peacock feathers on my head and went on to bless the thousands of other people in line. I went back slowly to my spot and sobbed. I trusted her so much.

I embraced more of my own own power to make myself happy without depending on him. Before, I thought that he was the one who was supposed to make me happy, and if he didn't for X, Y, or Z reasons, I suffered and felt victimized and powerless.

New Year's Eve, we all chanted of "*Om Bhagawan Muktanada*". Dressed in our finer silks and rich evening colors, everyone sang slowly and softly at first, then, gradually louder and faster; thousands of lips open wide, necks arched, and opening hearts peeking through the open mouths. Everyone, sitting cross-legged on individual blankets placed on the highly polished heated marble floor, swayed to the rhythm. The incense made wider and wider spirals to curl around the sounds and scent the room with mysterious perfumes. In the midst of the snow, we were in a glass and steel building that allowed us to see out. "*Om*" is the primordial sound from which all forms and sounds rise and subside. "*Bhagawan*" means "great holiness," and "*Muktananda*" is the "bliss of freedom."

As the pulse of the chant gained momentum, some of the swamis got up to dance. From all corners of the room, the diaphanous incense was swirling its way gracefully toward the ceiling, spreading its winged scent of sandalwood. Gurumayi sat and chanted on her "throne," facing all three thousand of us. The children got up in clusters and also began to dance. I wanted to dance. I stood and swung my arms and body, expecting other devotees to follow suit.

They didn't. I was standing, swaying, praying, and hailing Muktananda. Self-conscious at times, I also allowed myself to melt into the feeling of reverence and thankfulness, either lost in prayer, or wondering how I could get down onto the floor again. When an attendant approached me and inquired whether I wished to sit, I acquiesced gratefully. Then, I felt a great silence, as if I didn't exist anymore. There only was the communal chant and each one of those souls was a cell in my body. My body was the whole world, and my heart was Gurumayi's voice leading the chant. I was suspended for about an hour and a half. I was not there. I had no limits. The stillness and peace were beyond words or measure.

The next day at Darshan, someone introduced me, and Gurumayi gave me such a stern look. I wondered whether I had been wrong in maybe showing off the night before. As I was putting on my shoes to leave, a girl from the center in Miami said she wanted to say how I had inspired her devotion by seeing me dance. I thanked her. I knew Gurumayi was setting my heart to rest. I still have been wondering what the stern look meant. Maybe it meant, "Get serious. Get your act together." That's what I've been working on.

I attended more hypnotherapy schools. The school that gave me the most clarity was Evelyn Shiff's. She taught me how to find out a lot more about the client and how to work with his or her inner child and transform their uncomfortable feelings into supportive feelings. Her work was detailed and worked with the body responses. I met her at a hypnosis convention.

At that workshop, she asked if anyone was having any problems with anger. I raised my hand. Just before

I had left Miami, I lost it with my girls when I felt they were being too demanding. When I looked back on it, they were being normal children, and it was pushing some of my buttons. I've learned through the years that when there is a sudden burst of uncontrollable emotion, it's coming from the subconscious: some unresolved emotional festering wound issue that is carrying a strong electrical charge. That's what needs to be investigated and transformed, so that it doesn't keep erupting unexpectedly.

I went to the front of her class and explained that I had over reacted in anger towards my daughters. She asked me if I wanted to work on that anger in myself. Of course, I said yes. She guided me into a relaxed state in front of everybody. Then asked me to go to the time when I was about the same age as my daughters, between eight and twelve years old. "What was happening to you at that time?"

"Nothing much," I said. "Just school and home, a couple of friends."

"So what happened when you got home?" she asked.

"I always asked the maid, 'Is my mother home?' That was my first question; I had a thirst for her. She was never home, and I was always disappointed."

"And your father?" she asked.

"My father was definitely not there. It was my stepfather, a friendly distant relationship. He wasn't interested in what I was doing at school or anywhere else. He played the piano, and I sang with him. He brought a chocolate bar once in a while. He beat me a couple of times."

"So how does this little girl feel about all this?"

"Okay, I guess." There was a silence with question marks floating through the room. Everybody knew there was more to it. "Neglected. Sad. Angry."

"Angry? How angry?" She held out her arm. "Hold my arm, and shake it as hard as you want and show me. Get out all the anger you feel from the way you were treated at that time."

I shook that little old lady, almost throwing her down to the floor. The whole room gasped. I was surprised how much anger and force I had accumulated inside of me, so hidden. That was the anger that reared its ugly head at the most inappropriate moments. Once I had expressed a lot of it, she guided me to meet that little girl, rescue her out of this place, and take her to my new field of possibilities. Once I was there with her, I hugged her, loved her, and appreciated her. I let her know the doors to the past were closed; she never had to return there anymore, and brought her home. At that moment, my body was filled with warmth and comfort. It was so pervasive. I was amazed with this work. When I found myself with my daughters again, I had gained a new calm way of understanding and enjoying their needs.

As soon as I got to Miami, I called her. "Hello, Ms. Shiff, I'd like to come and take a workshop with you."

"What do you want to learn?" she asked.

"Everything you know about the inner child and how to work with it. Everything you know about hypnosis. Everything you know about trauma release and about transformation of feelings."

I designed my own workshop, and there were two of us taking it. It changed my life.

Evelyn Schiff was a woman in her sixties who had been doing this for more than twenty years. She had her own clinic, and she taught at Las Vegas University. She was writing a book about all the techniques she was using. She is a huggable lady with great insight.

She gave me a structure to follow: get to know the client initially, hear the client, find the essence of the issue. Then, guide the client to tune into his or her body responses. The body responses are maps to reach the emotional key moments that are the roots of the issues. These uncomfortable feelings then are transformed into supportive ones. By the end of the work, the body feels relaxed at any mention of the issue. The body is a refined feedback mechanism. After working with these techniques for more than ten years, I have gained more and more precision with my work. I expect to develop with more learning and practice techniques that are more and more effective for specific purposes.

The past life regressions still amaze me. I explain to clients that the process in itself seems to be therapeutic whether one believes in actual past lives or not. I worked with a woman who wanted to understand why her father irritated her so profoundly. She had difficulty being in the same room with him for more than an hour at a time. She recognized that her reaction was too drastic in spite of the fact that she was separated from her father at a very young age and then pulled back and forth between her mother and her father. In the previous sessions, we had worked on rescuing that young inner child and embracing her in the present with love and acknowledgment. So she asked if this time we could do a past-life regression and we did.

She saw herself as a young man living in a sumptuous house. Also, on a hill nearby was an old man, a shepherd. When she took a good look at the old shepherd's face, it was her father. She was shocked, and tears welled in her eyes. At home, this young man had a wife and a boy and a father whom she recognized as her present husband. As the session unfolded, she saw the daughter of the shepherd having a child in a cavern. It was the young man's child. The young man could not marry and did not take care of this girl and her child. The next scene was before the young man's death. Suddenly she knew: The shepherd came to murder the young man in his bed because his daughter drowned herself with the baby in the river when she felt rejected by the young man; she tied a stone to her legs. My client began to sob. When she realized the tragedy, she kept saying the young man wanted to take care of the girl but didn't dare because of his wife and child. That is the way he died, murdered by the shepherd, her father in this life. No wonder she can't stand to be near him. Maybe now, after understanding all this, it may change.

48

Your own words are the bricks and mortar of the dreams you want to realize. Your words are the greatest power you have. The words you choose and use establish the life you experience.
—Sonia Choquette

As much as it ached to break up my marriage, after a while, I was able to glean the good in it for us. I still always hoped that Edward would come home and say, "I've thought it over. Let's keep our family together."

Every time he came to the door, I had that expectation. And every time, I was disappointed. He barely nodded, didn't look me in the eye, hardly said a word unless it was absolutely necessary. I realized I was always setting myself up for disappointment. I had to stop torturing myself this way.

It was a long separation. I found a lawyer because Edward insisted. We tried to come to an agreement between us, and nothing happened. All he did was scratch his head and say he could not talk to me. There, sitting on the sofa right next to me, he could not bring himself to utter all the terrible thoughts he must have had in his mind about me.

I said, "What I absolutely need, besides the child support and the commitment to pay for their college, is a stipend for a housekeeper, once a week. I can't handle everything by myself." That's when he got into a scratching frenzy.

I said, "I can't believe you're going to Europe with her." We had talked so often about taking the slow boat to China, when his struggle was over. I burst into sobs. I cried burrowing my cheeks into the pillows of the sofa. He scratched his head some more and then got up annoyed, at a loss, in a huff, and left the house.

Several times at different intervals during these months of torturous separation, I pleaded with him to reconsider. Couldn't we forgive each other and start fresh? "Please forgive me for my mistakes."

"It's not your mistakes; it's my mistakes," he replied, but never explained.

We never did get together and talk again in the direction of reconciliation. I longed for it, but did not know how to make it happen. When I finally found a lawyer I could trust, I asked him please to ask Edward's lawyer if there was any possibility of reconciliation. The reply was always negative. So then, I requested to get everything settled as soon as possible. It was all too painful. I was crying too often.

I had to find my talents and develop them. Sondra Ray's book *Loving Relationships* suggested a way. It conveyed that relationships have a life of their own and that sometimes they are over in spite of us; they turn a corner. The loss is devastating. She said relationships don't end; they change formats. The custody of the girls pushed me to redefine myself as strong and able. I needed to provide them with enough emotional support and avenues of expression so they adapted to the new way of life as unscathed as possible. I said, "Girls, please forgive me for not having been able to keep our family together." I often felt guilt and remorse.

Stephanie and Michaela said, "We like it better this way because now we have two houses to go to."

At ages five and eight, they were included in group therapy for children of divorced parents at their magnet school. They were both in the French program. They reported stories from other kids where moms or dads would leave the family and wouldn't come back to live with them. We were all new at this. It was a shock for me to be alone. Yet, I had been dealing with the parenting responsibilities on my own all along.

What scared me the most was when five years later, Edward moved to Key West. The girls were entering their teenage years.

Stephanie was beginning in a photography magnet program. Michaela was enrolled in a science magnet high school. Michaela's work was demanding. Once she blurted out to me: "Why do I have to study so much? I feel society has me as a prisoner. I have to follow its rules; if not I can't belong to it." She sobbed at feeling obliged to follow the path the school curriculum was forcing her to do.

"We don't have to stay here. We could rent this house and with the income live elsewhere. I can practice hypnosis wherever I go. We could go to an island with beaches. I can homeschool you. We can write children's stories; you and Stephanie could illustrate them."

"No, because then, if I want to get back into society, it will be that much harder."

"In that you are right."

She continued studying.

When she was three, the pediatrician had alerted me. "We all knew Michaela was smart; now I want to tell you," he said. "You really need to pay attention to her schooling. Out of thousands of children that I have tested with these video games, she is one out of ten who has gotten every answer correct."

A friend from Brazil gave me some passion fruit seeds. I planted them by our wire fence along the park. They became a vine that covered the whole fence and flowered constantly. The blossoms are exotic with deep purples and greens and many pistils arranged in a circle of magic wands. Year after year, they never gave fruit. One day, I saw one fruit hanging from the vine. I called Michaela to come and see. Standing next to me, she said in her quiet tone: "Yes, I took the pollen, with a q-tip, from one flower and fertilized another. I guess in Florida there aren't the same bees as in Brazil."

Before Stephanie entered into middle school, she decided to shave off her long blond locks. She dyed her hair black except for one longer strand that grew by her forehead down to below her cheek. Every day she dyed it a different color. Sometimes pink, sometimes purple, and sometimes green.

"Mom," she said, on her way home from school, "someone asked me if I was a lesbian, and I answered, 'No, and so what if I were.'"

Stephanie had shown since very young a definite style of her own in the way she dressed. Both Michaela and I often asked her for her opinion on how we were dressed before we left the house. By age thirteen, she had her first sewing machine and modified her clothes or invented something new.

Michaela once, lying on my bed with her legs up leaning on the wall asked me:

"Mom, Is it true, I could meet someone one day, talk to them, get to know them a little, say good bye and then, never ever see them again?"

"Yes, it's true."

"Amazing."

We sometimes played games where I hid a tiny object in one of my hands behind my back. When I showed them my clenched fingers, I challenged

"Guess which hand is holding the object",

Sometimes they got it right, sometimes they didn't.

"You have an invisible eye in the middle of your forehead, if you look through it, you will always get it right."

"Oh, but Mom, isn't that cheating?" Stephanie said.

"No, if you have it, it's because you are meant to use it."

After an intense weekend of teaching the Silva Method, I woke up one morning and felt a lump inside my left breast the size of an egg. My first impulse was to call a doctor who said I needed a biopsy immediately. Scared, I got images of knives and a surgeon wanting to practice his skill.

Both my daughters trusted their inner third eye more and more. I asked Michaela to visualize and imagine what was inside the lump. I did the same. She said she saw white gooey stuff. I also had perceived a white substance. "Let's both imagine piercing the egg in our imagination and letting all the white stuff out," I suggested. After we did exactly that, within minutes, I felt the length of my spine burning hot and my whole body trembled as a reed. For twenty-four hours, I was in bed recovering from a fever; drinking fluids. Two days later the lump had completely disappeared. Within a few weeks I went to get a mammogram, there was nothing there.

49

Perhaps loving something is the only starting place there is for making your life your own.
—Alice Koller

The excited TV weather announcers seemed younger than usual.

"This hurricane is really coming our way. It is at 165 M.P.H. Miami Beach and Coconut Grove are under evacuation orders. You must leave the area before six p.m. tonight. This is serious, guys. You must prepare. Get anything that is loose out of your garden: potted plants, garden furniture. Everything has to be inside. Close your hurricane shutters or board up your windows, and tape the windowpanes, so, if they crack, the glass won't fly in every direction. We know we have had hurricane warnings before, and in twenty years, not one has hit. But this one, called Andrew, is coming straight at us."

It was August 23, 1992. I lived in Coconut Grove.

My mother was calling from Budapest, Hungary, where they lived.

"Darling, get into your car and drive out of there."

"The girls are in Long Island, visiting their grandmother. I have three dogs and three cats. Where can I go with them? No motel is going to want them."

"But it's your life."

"I'll be fine; don't worry."

We hung up, and I hurried to get groceries and water. The market shelves were almost empty. There were long lines at the gas stations. There was an eerie calm, with hot humid air blanketing the city. I swam a few last laps. Then I dropped all the garden furniture into the pool. This way the strong winds could not sweep or crash a chair against the French doors.

The young boys across the street helped me pick up all the potted plants and place them inside the house. I had neither hurricane shutters nor boards. With wide tape, I made crosses stuck to every windowpane.

My neighbor down the street called. "I'm staying in my house with Violette, the dog. Come, if you want to sit out the storm with us."

"Thank you," I said. "I don't want to leave my animals alone."

Daylight dimmed earlier than usual on a summer night. Clouds moved fast. The evening engulfed my little house with six pets.

Soon after midnight, I lost the TV connection. As I fell asleep, I imagined white light protecting the houses in my neighborhood. I woke up around 1:00 a.m. with the snapping explosive sound of a tree branch colliding against my window. The wind seemed to be rising in waves. Trees and branches thrashed into windows, doors, and roof. Never had I heard such unstoppable terrifying uproar. The animals were all on my bed. I sat up, crossed my legs, took a deep breath, and began to chant.

"*Om Namah Shivaya.*" (I bow to the divinity within me.) I sang this over and over and over again, as we did at the yoga center.

I pretended the rumble of the wind and the twisting, cracking, and toppling of the trees were all part of an enormous orchestra. The more deafening it was, the more my voice boomed. I didn't dare move from my meditation place. The animals formed a circle around me flattened on the bed covers. Were they asleep? I closed my eyes and continued chanting with the whole flame of my being.

Then, with my eyelids closed, I saw a stormy sky with many cobalt blue and gray clouds soaring by. In the center of my vision floated a luminous triangle of brilliant and diaphanous white light.

As the clouds continued to drift by, the triangle hovered intact even when slightly obscured by a momentary passing darkness.

I chanted and chanted, focused on the triangle, no matter how loud or how terrifying the sounds.

Eventually, I must have fallen asleep.

I woke up about 6:00 a.m. All quiet. Pieces of tree trunks blocked the French doors of my bedroom. The pool was filled with green leaves and branches of all sizes. Two of our coconut palms had fallen in too.

I was able to call my daughters who were away with their grandmother. When I heard myself saying to them on the phone, "The house is fine," I noticed the enormous Indian Rosewood in our front garden had toppled over and crushed our car.

I had to go out the kitchen door to get outside. The front door was jammed. There were a few neighbors out on the street.

“Are you all right?” one of them called out when she saw me.

“Yes, I’m fine. How about you?”

“Yes, I’m fine. There is no water nor power.”

“Oh!” I exclaimed, assuming it was the same for me.

As I walked around the house to the adjacent park, I saw only devastation. Unruly giant mounds of tangles of broken-off trees littered the space completely.

In the days that followed, I was amazed at how people reached out. There was a man who drove around in his pick–up truck giving away bags of ice. At street crossings from one car to another, people asked:” Are you OK? Do you need anything? Many went down to Homestead, the most hard hit area, to help.

When the girls returned to Miami, we drove to the stable where they rode. The instructor told us: “After the hurricane, they found a horse alive and stuck up in the branches of a tree. They had to get him down with a crane.”

The fury of nature left me feeling quite vulnerable physically, even though there were people who got hit much harder than I did.

About that same time, Michaela wrote this story for school. She must have been sensing my fears.

Lili

About three years ago, in Maine, there lived a beautiful girl named Maria Theresa, but everyone called her Lili. She and her boyfriend settled in a large, old shabby house she had inherited from a local judge whom she had never met. No one understood why the judge gave the house to an unknown neighbor. On the first night, she had a dream. An aged woman came to her in her sleep and said, "It is time to say good-bye." She took Lili's hand and walked her down the main endless corridor. The woman said, "I have been waiting for you." She was about to show Lili something when a rooster let out his cry of dawn and Lili awoke.

During the day, Lili couldn't quell the urge of looking for something unknown and lost. This personal search continued for a week, until she decided it must have been her imagination and the pressure of moving into a mysterious house looming over her.

Then, she had another cryptic dream. This time, the old woman looked younger and a little bit familiar. Lili could not remember who the old woman reminded her of. Again, the woman took her into the interminable main corridor and again said, "I have been waiting for you." Then she revealed a small black velvet handbag. At that moment, the rooster let out his morning wail, and Lili arose from her disturbing dream.

She felt she was carrying two invisible weights on her shoulders. When Joseph asked what was wrong, she replied, "I didn't get much sleep last night; that's all. I'll take a little nap."

That very night, she had the strange dream again. The woman came to her bedside as in all the previous dreams. This time, the woman looked much younger and very familiar. Lili could not pinpoint who she was! Again, the woman led Lili into the main corridor, and again she said that she had been waiting for her. The woman withdrew the small black handbag and opened it in slow motion. She reached inside to take something out, when the rooster cockadoodledoed again, and Lili woke up. This time Lili was disturbed because she had a gut-grabbing feeling that something bizarre was about to happen. She rose from the bed and went to look in the mirror; as she studied herself she noticed that she looked older. The worst part was that she felt it, too. Lili locked herself in her room and kept on making up elaborate excuses for Joseph to go away.

That night, as she suspected, the woman came to her in her sleep, but this time, the woman was Lili! Of course, she was Lili as an old woman. With every dream, she became younger, Lili thought. The woman took Lili down the hall, which now had an end. The woman took the black handbag out and opened it. She pulled out a small mirror with Lili's initials on the back. She handed the mirror to Lili. The mirror had an elaborate silver frame. Lili gazed into the mirror and to her horror saw not the young smooth complexion of weeks before, but instead an old wrinkled face with bloodshot eyes and thin white lips. Lili threw down the mirror and looked at the young woman, and the woman laughed—not a happy gay laugh, but a vain loud laugh—and she laughed and laughed, and laughed.

This eerie story showed me how Michaela was picking up on my unspoken fears of growing older and losing the youthful, life- promising glow.

50

We do not learn by experience, but by
our capacity for experience.
—Buddha

A couple of years later, I sold the loft in New York and invested the money in the stock market. When I began to feel confident that it was making money, I decided to take the girls, ages eight and eleven, during the summer for the first time to France and to Budapest. First, I showed them Paris. We stayed in the apartment of a friend of a friend of Bob's. It was freshly decorated with new peach silk wall-paper. Everything was so beautifully done with antiques. It belonged to a bachelor. He came one day to greet us. Then, left for the country.

"Please girls, let's keep everything tidy." I had to keep reminding them.

We arrived July 14th, Bastille Day. There were so many fireworks on the Champs Elysees it seemed dangerous. We visited the Eiffel Tower and an amusement park in the Tuileries. We roamed through the Louvre, saw the Mona Lisa, gaped at the stained glass windows of the Sainte

Chapelle, and ate at little restaurants along the Seine. The girls discovered *crème brulée.*

We took the Orient Express all the way to Hungary from Paris. It was a good opportunity to see my parents and be imbued by a country that had freed itself from the Iron Curtain. My stepfather, being Hungarian, was asked to open an office for the multinational company he worked for. Communism, the threatening evil monster of my childhood, had disintegrated like the Wicked Witch of the West. There were remnants, of course, including the attitudes in people who had been trained to give the least of themselves possible since there was no payoff in extending oneself at all. At the government-run cafes, we waited half an hour for service, and the place was empty.

My parents lived in a large, old building with a massive swirling stone staircase running up the middle. The wrought-iron railings were topped with a waxed, rounded mahogany banister on each floor. Each apartment had been divided during the communist years into multiple dwellings. More recently, some of them had been reunified. I still felt that furtive spirit among the people I passed on the stairs, an ogling, suspiciously wide, glazed look, and a thin horizontal line running through their lips. Although happy to see us, after the first few days of excitement, it was hard for my parents to be with young children. Michaela said to me, "Why is it that when I'm around Grandmaman, I always feel like crying?"

"I don't know, darling. Maybe because she is very critical on the inside or maybe because the little girl inside of her feels like crying." The girls had stayed with her, years before, and Stephanie was angry and hurt. My mother had blamed her for something she didn't do. She resented the fact that my mother got furious when she found her sewing basket strewn on the floor. Stephanie says it was her cousin Ifigenia who did it and did not admit to it. Michaela witnessed it all. She spoke up for her sister but was not believed.

I brought my stepfather a set of motivational tapes by Anthony Robbins, thinking he might be able to hear a few useful clues. He was opening a new office and had to motivate and train a lot of people. Before I even got a chance to give them to him, my mother intercepted, "How can you even imagine that such a young man has anything to teach Victor, a man with so much experience in his business? How ridiculous." She had never heard of Anthony Robbins.

"He is a well-known motivator, and he helps many businessmen and heads of state."

She never gave them to him, and I felt too constrained to override her decision.

Victor, my stepfather, did appreciate a relaxation tape that I had produced and meditated with it. My mother, on the other hand, tried it and said, "All this forced breathing makes me nervous. I can't relax with it. Nobody has to tell me how to breathe; I inhale perfectly well on my own!"

We stayed about ten days with my parents. They were probably glad we were leaving, and so were we. We did have interesting excursions, and got to know a bit of Budapest. There was time to cherish each other in spite of our irritating quirks: Victor, roaming like a Frankestein; my mother, tidying up and talking about history. My girls kept saying, "She must have been a history teacher in a past life."

We returned to Paris on the Orient Express going west. I remember saying to the girls as the train stopped over the Rhine, "On one side it's Germany and on the other, France." I wondered if they would remember later being there as they familiarized themselves with the strife and wars between those two sides of the river.

In Paris, we rented a car and drove down into the Anjou to meet up with another friend of Bob's who had a little farmhouse she had transformed into a country inn, "La Petite Ferme." A magical place. She attracted so many artists that the two towns around there are being redone in charming ways.

It was during that trip to France that I met a sculptor, Michael Margan. He was staying at the same farm. In the dining room, a converted chicken coop and stable, dark beams held the ceiling. The mangers at the edge of the wall were filled with cushions to sit and enjoy the meals. A Peruvian Indian band with flutes from the Andes was playing. When I glanced in the direction of his table, he winked at me. We bumped into each other at the only village café. Their specialty was a great plate of 'frites' to munch on with a glass of wine. He took us out to dinner, accompanied us to the horses, and seemed very interested in us. The girls called him the "red hot dog." He did have fiery red hair and beard and sparkling blue eyes. He had been reading a lot of literature to help recovering alcoholics. I was familiar with some of it. We talked about it. He declared himself a recovering alcoholic. I was amazed at his sincerity.

The girls and I were staying in the barn full of hay. The partition of our space in the barn was a wall of prickly bales of hay; there was a mattress on another horizontal set of bales and a scent of dry gold straw. On the surrounding walls was a full-length mural that Bob, my dear friend, had painted. It was a rendition of the local countryside with a surreal pie in the sky and musical notes flying indiscriminately. We felt embraced by Bob. There were murmuring sheep and outspoken geese calling for attention before becoming *foie gras*. My girls set up a whole dancing show with skits and invited all the artists in the village, who paid a couple of francs to see it.

One night Michael surprised me at the door of the barn and called me to come out for a walk with him. It was a starry night.

"Let's get married. Please marry me. I love you. Please," he said.

"Let me think about it." Of course, I was touched, but I barely knew him; it had been a week at most.

It is true he was eager to please me. He was ready to help me with the girls. The girls were happy with him and with me. Those summer days were wonderful. We spent many afternoons by the enormous lake, where the cows also bathed. When I took the girls riding, he insisted on paying for the classes. He seemed to want to embrace us. So about a week later, I said yes. We began to plan it for the next spring. He would come to Miami in the winter, and I would go visit Colorado Springs. He accompanied us to Paris by car. He insisted on driving us up there. Then he said he would return by train to join his son and continue on their exploration of Spain and Portugal. In Fontainebleau at a little restaurant, Stephanie, eight years old, said, "We eat, you pay."

He remained silent, his lips tightened, and he squinted his eyes in suspicion. When we got to Versailles, we had to wait in a long line to get in, and that wore our patience thin. It was hot and sticky. After we saw the chateau and its magnificent gardens, we were walking toward the town to look for a hotel or a restaurant. At one point, Michael began to roughhouse with Stephanie, in a playful way, I thought. He was holding her up and suddenly she started crying, saying, "You're hurting me, stop, stop." He wouldn't, and she whined some more. "Stop, you're hurting me." Then he put her down. She was whimpering a little. I asked him to please apologize to her.

"You are spoiling these girls; they manipulate you with any little whine or cry."

"Maybe you were not aware you were hurting her. I am sure she was in pain."

"I was not hurting her at all. She is exaggerating. You are overreacting to her."

"Maybe you're pissed off because when you were little and got hurt, people around you thought you were overreacting, and you feel angry because they never acknowledged your pain."

"That's ridiculous."

"Well, if it's that way, then you go back to Anjou, and I'll spend the rest of the time here with the girls."

He didn't leave. He took us into Paris the next day. But we hardly spoke, and I stayed mostly with the girls. I certainly could not be with a man who did not understand my closeness and trust with my girls.

Yet, as the night moved into its silence, I missed his caresses. I got up and knocked on his bedroom door, and he let me in. We made love with the longing of innocent times. He spent a couple of days more with us and then went back to Anjou to meet up with his son. The girls and I got back to Miami and to the rhythm of school and days with sun and steamy tropical showers. He called often and sent fabulous flowers.

He invited me to Colorado Springs. We had a good time going up into the mountains on his motorcycle. I was shocked when he got angry in his apartment; he picked up one of his cats and threw it against the wall. The cats had become very obese, probably to protect themselves from his onslaughts of rage. Their fur was matted and dirty. I had never seen cats with such low self-esteem. Whenever we were at a crossing and he'd be waiting for a female driver in front to turn left, he exploded into a rage. "You are a goddamned bitch, you don't know how to drive. Get the hell out of my goddamned way."

In quieter moments, he said more than once that he blamed his mother for his father's cancer and early death. He never got around to explaining.

Even though it was balanced with some lovely moments and meeting his friendly family, I was on my guard.

I asked to meet his previous wife. He didn't like the idea. Finally, he acquiesced.

He showed me where she worked and called her to warn her I may be coming by to talk with her.

When I walked into the children's shop where she worked, I felt that magic scent of new clothes and tiny shoes. She was a beautiful brunette behind the counter. I introduced myself. She was a little cool at the beginning. After the usual polite phrases, she said, "Michael is a misogynist. He never allowed me to do what I wanted to do. If I found out about an audition, he invented a trip out of town. Of course, I surrendered. Who doesn't like a sailing trip in the Bahamas or a ski trip? He always had something better to offer me, so I never did anything for myself. That was okay until I found him so drunk he started seeing hallucinations and endangering the children. I could not stand it anymore."

"You know he still loves you," I said. He's told me several times. "How would you feel if he asked you to get back together?"

"No, it's over."

"I want to you to keep in mind that I feel he loves you."

"I thought he loved you," she retorted.

"He did ask me to marry him. Yet he has contradicted himself because every time I ask him if he would take you back, if you would come back, he has said 'yes.'"

She gave me a look with a tiny wisp of a knowing smile. Her black hair glistened so richly in the spotlight.

After a few more brief polite phrases, I left the store and walked back to Michael's studio. He wasn't there. When he got back, he was very eager to know what we had discussed. I suggested he speak to her. He soon took me to the airport.

When he left me there, part of me was sad, and another part was relieved. I don't think I could have handled all that enormous bundle of repressed emotions.

Within the next few weeks, he called to let me know they got back together. I was disappointed because he had asked me to marry him, and I had accepted. Now I knew I was strong enough to recognize what was not good for me.

I shed a few tears in a dark movie house. Mostly I was irritated with myself that I hadn't yet worked out whatever it takes to be ready for a lasting and fruitful relationship. I must have more forgiving to do. I wished I could take myself to a Laundromat, a spiritual and psychic one, where all my guilt and fear would be bleached away in one powerful cycle. Then I could come out fiercely radiant and powerfully healing.

A client of mine said I was guiding him into appreciation of women. I asked him to imagine what it would have been without any women in his life. He said it would have been so nothing, so dry. He said that he remembered a moment when he was fourteen and he entered a bar in Peru where there were a lot of prostitutes. There he noticed an older woman and thought to himself how disgusting she was, compared to the other young girls. He added:

"Maybe it showed on my face; she came up to me and with great kindness and affection told me never to look down on a woman just because of her appearance. I felt such warm tenderness; I understood that even though she seemed to be the least valuable person in the world, somehow now I was experiencing her as the richest one. This moment has come back to haunt me over and over again in my life at different moments, and I have grasped it each time in a different way."

51

Don't ask about caste or riches but instead ask about conduct. Look at the flames of a fire. Where do they come from? From a piece of wood and it doesn't matter what wood. In the same way a wise person can come from wood of any sort. It is through firmness and restraint and a sense of truth that one becomes noble, not through caste.
—Sutta Nipata

In a dream I was underwater and a ferocious black and silver shark was swimming straight at me. Frightened, I swerved away. Within the dream, I imagined myself protected by an invisible light. Awake, I debated whether to engage Phil Laut, the coach who wrote a book called *Money Is My Friend*. The first step was getting my files in order. I felt like a yo-yo, not knowing at what end of the space to stand still. To be still and focus, I had to trust in my ultimate safety.

Books and Books is the best bookstore in Miami. They organize talks with brilliant authors. There I heard Deepak Chopra. He filled me with wonder. He spoke of the subatomic level of existence where there is a sea of infinite possibilities. Focusing on those words all day gave me energy and enthusiasm for all that could be and can be and will be. I became so optimistic. Everything flowering. Even though it might not all flower the way I imagined it, it might in a better way. Dizzy with energy and fabulous expectations, I was a tornado of light, a powerhouse of existence, unstoppable, healthy, filled with loving kindness. I wanted to be an example of the awakening power we all have.

Tuned in to infinite energy, I meditated to immerse myself in the experiences I longed for. I thought, *I am big, I am strong, I am shining light. I am joy and laughter. I can feed, I can grow, I can soothe the aching heart aglow. Be in my prayer, I'll be in yours. I'll find you there where heaven heals your sores. Come to my arms, let me caress, let me feel the relief of your brow with an internal political coup.*

That Deepak, he turned us all on, what a beam of light. I felt so connected. Thank you, Deepak, goodnight.

52

"Let no one come to you without
leaving better or happier"
Mother Teresa

While Michaela was in Middle School in the French Magnet program, she complained crying: "my French teacher ignores me when I raise my hand to answer a question". I asked for a conference with the teacher and the Assistant Principal. While sitting at this meeting where I included Michaela, I explained the situation and asked Michaela to voice her complaint to her teacher.

The Assistant Principal said: "This is unprecedented, that a student complains to the teacher."

I replied, "Is this not a democracy?"

Michaela, in a very polite tone, said, "my experience is that you ignore me in class and do not allow me to participate."

The French teacher huffed and puffed. I don't remember how or if she defended herself.

All I know is that Michaela reported that since our meeting, her French teacher was allowing her to participate more in the class.

Another time, I confided in my girls about the abortion I had years before.

"I'm sorry, girls, you might have had a brother. Everything would have been different."

"Don't worry at all Mom", said Michaela," I was the soul of that first child. I just waited around until you were ready for me".

One day, just before Edward came to pick up the girls to take them to spend Christmas in Key West, where he was living, Michaela, fifteen, urgently grabbed me out of the kitchen and dragged me into her room. She closed the door and sat me on the bed.

"I've got to talk to you, Mom. I've got to talk to you."

"What is this about?"

"I've got to tell you, I've experimented with LSD, I smoke cigarettes, and I have a boyfriend." She rattled it off as fast as she could so as to get it over with.

"Okay," I uttered, shocked, as I nodded with my eyes wide open.

"You're not angry?"

"No. It's natural at your age to want to experiment and try different things. I did. At the same time, I know you love and respect yourself and want to take care of your body and your brain. You are a brilliant girl, and I know you will make the right choices. I know you are super careful. I also know that if you decide to have sex with your boyfriend, you will make sure he has a condom and you have a contraceptive."

"I've told him I'm not ready for sex at least until I'm sixteen."

"That's wise. That way you'll have more time to get to know him."

Michaela graduated, a few years later, with honors from an excellent science magnet high school called MAST and got a full scholarship to UCF.

After her prom she wrote me this letter:

Dear Mom,

I'm just writing to say thank you for all the stuff you've done for me over the past twelve years. Thanks for bringing me everything that I forgot at home, even though my school is really out of the way. Thank you for giving me lunch money almost everyday. Thank you for letting me play hooky all those times, and letting me sleep in when you knew I needed it. Thanks for letting me go out until really late so that I could hang out with my friends, even if it was on a school night. Thanks for giving me moral support when I had all those big projects I thought I was never going to finish. Thank you for everything. I hope you have fun while Stephanie and I are away at school, we know we will.

Lots of love,

Michaela xoxox

53

Your children are not your children.
They are the sons and daughters of
Life's longing for itself.
They come through you but not from you,
And though they are with you, yet they belong not to you.
—Kahlil Gibran, *The Prophet*

"Where is my Stephanie?" I cried out, staring at Maria Isabel, my friend. She was keeping me company.

"She always checks in," Maria Isabel said, nodding her oval face with a strong Roman nose and green eyes.

"I've been calling her since midnight. It's already noon. Why haven't I heard from her?" I poured my friend a cup of coffee, thankful to have her here to attend to. She followed me with worried eyes.

Maria Isabel never had children, only two abortions. She is Cuban. Her father was a priest who left the priesthood for her mother, a source of shame for Maria Isabel's recovering Catholic heart. She was my closest friend at that moment.

She loved to babysit my girls. She took them out to the movies and sent the right doctor to our house when they were ill. She took us to her favorite beach on Marathon Key. Despite her high blood pressure, we rented Jet-skis and zipped around a small harbor. When we shared one, we stopped and slid off for a swim. We laughed when I had to tug her roly-poly body back on.

My daughters and I lived in our 1940s house in Coconut Grove, Miami, in a development for World War II veterans. The swimming pool I had built was collared in brick and surrounded by coconut palms. Adjacent was the Merrie Christmas Park, "Our Park," as we called it, graced with gigantic banyan trees. Vines dropped from their branches, reached the ground, and took root. Wide canopies of emerald leaves were held high by clustered trunks. We celebrated many birthdays here, with piñatas, clowns, potato bag races, and scavenger hunts.

My girls' art, papers with many colors and shapes, quilted the main living room wall, a gallery for their art. The scent of gardenias wafted throughout the house with a spring breeze. We had bowls of them in every room and four corpulent flowering bushes outside, at one end of the pool. My friend Bob planted them before he died of AIDS.

Edward and I baby-proofed the house when we moved here from New York City. Stephanie was one, and Michaela was three. Bookshelves lined the walls of the dining area. They were filled with books on the mind-body connection, meditation, psychic, and healing research. There was French, American, Russian, Spanish, and Brazilian literature, drama, and art; a Lincoln rocking chair I found dilapidated on Canal St. in New York. When re-caned, it was perfect to rock Michaela and Stephanie and nurse them to sleep. An upright Steinway was the first object Edward and I bought together.

Now, Michaela was away at her first year of college at the University of Central Florida. I supported our little family of three with a private practice in hypnotherapy and a minimal child-support check.

"I've driven to the boy's house three times," I said to my friend. "I've been calling all night. No one picks up. At first, no one answered the doorbell."

"Maybe they are all asleep with ear plugs." Maria Isabel suggested.

She lit a cigarette, her eyes squinting. Was she thinking, *Where did Lili go wrong as a mother?*

"The third time I went over, the mother came to the door. She invited me in with a tired smile. She was dressed in a pink and red flower printed housedress. She moved so slowly, I wanted to scream. Did she know where her son was? She spoke Spanish, in a whisper, shrugging and shaking her head from side to side.

'Yo no se donde esta mi hijo.' (I don't know where my son is.)

"It was six a.m. I sat in his mother's living room-terrace, sipping matte tea. Yellow spider orchids clung to the balm yair.

'My husband is very ill,' she said in a monotone. 'He's dying of cancer. We shut off the phone in his room at night. I saw my son John leave in a car with some friends. There was a girl with them,' she added, as an afterthought."

"'That was my Stephanie,' I said, almost spilling my tea, disregarding her husband's illness. 'She told me they were staying here and that John's girlfriend was also coming.'

"'John and Mercedes broke up a week ago,' the mother replied."

Maria Isabel shook her head from side to side in disbelief.

"'John told me he wasn't going to spend the night here,' the mother continued, dragging one foot on the terracotta floor, to the phone. She could barely bend her knee. She called her son. No reply. Soon, she shuffled around to his room and found his cell phone."

I looked directly at Maria Isabel and told her, "I'm desperate. I'm praying…"

The clawing dread of not having been as careful a mother as I could have been was unbearable. What if my daughter were drugged or lost, raped, or kidnapped? What if she was hurt and couldn't get to a phone to ask for help? Why hadn't I demanded to speak to the boy's mother to make sure Stephanie had told the truth?

I always trusted her. She never lied to me: my sweet, wise, brilliant, beautiful Stephanie. At age five, after her father left, she declared, "Mom, you'd better find yourself another man. Dad loves you, but he doesn't want to spit it out."

Stephanie had gone once to a rave with her big sister and a group of older kids I knew well. They all knew the dangers of drugs. The following day she was wiped out. So we had agreed. She didn't need to go to any more raves. It was too much, those warehouses where drugs were passed around so the young could stay up all night, dance until dawn under the pulsing strobes. They liked to have breakfast together.

I don't dare call her father or her sister, until I know what is really going on, I thought at the time. *The police will not let me file a missing-person's report until twenty-four hours have passed.* Now, I know. If it's a child, they start the search immediately.

Maria Isabel kept saying, "I'm getting palpitations. All I can do is pray. *Ai, Dios Mio.*" She shut her eyes. Then she opened them, checked her pulse with her right hand over her heart, caressing her chest. "I have to go home soon."

She got up to leave and with a slight strut of indignation gave me a peck on the cheek and said, "Stay with God."

I understood how she felt. I realized she couldn't help, except pray. We agreed to talk later.

I collapsed on the couch and closed my eyes. When I was fourteen, I talked back to my mother. We spoke, diagonally across a rectangular inner patio, from her bathroom window to my bedroom window, on the second floor. She wore a bright orange red tailored shirt. We called it "Mummy's color." Fire-red lipstick lips contrasted with her ebony black hair and her large brown eyes.

"Mummy, I want to go to the slumber party at Chantal's with my friends tomorrow."

"Impossible, Charity's mother told me there would be boys and girls all night."

"I don't care what you think; I'm going with them anyway."

"How dare you speak to me this way! It is out of the question."

It was a totalitarian regime, no democratic debate.

54

She who loves roses must be patient and not cry out when she is pierced by thorns.
—Olga Broumas

Tomb silence set in. Fears of Stephanie hurt and needing help crept in. Was the indigo blue, gold, and crimson-patched Japanese silk skirt she had made for herself, last week, torn? Was she alone, robbed, or lost? I paced up and down in my living room; I called her cell phone ceaselessly, to no avail. I went to the bathroom mirror and gave myself a good talking to. Those big brown eyes, we all had them.

I took a different approach. After years of practicing and teaching meditation, my only recourse at this time was to test my skills and sit still and listen to my inner voice. This voice was my constant companion especially in the last nine years, since I'd become a single mom. I forced myself to sit and close my eyes.

I managed to calm my imagination with deep breathing. The coolness of the air came up my nostrils. It filled my lungs and stretched my diaphragm. I guided the breath to trickle into my stomach, and then as I exhaled, it rose up my spine out through my lips. I paused for a moment of stillness. I repeated the breathing cycle over and over again. My imagination went into slow motion. I envisioned a plush burgundy carpet covering a white marble staircase. After twenty-one steps, I arrived into a semi-circular living room filled with red poppies and very pale yellow velvet cotton sofas cushioned with down pillows. French doors opened out on to a brick veranda studded with turquoise and yellow painted Sicilian ceramic pots filled with outbursts of flowering wisteria. Over the worn marble balustrade down another curving staircase, I took a path to the left. Beyond, I could see a waterfall, jutting over gigantic rocks, splashing into a pond with pink and white quartz crystals and amethysts in its depths.

There I saw Buddha, Kuan-Yin, Abraham, Moses, Christ, and Mohammed bathing together, waiting for me to join them. I took another deep breath and plunged in with delight. I felt at one with them, Allah! A swim, droplets gleaming in the inner sunlight, eyes opened, the water tasted sweet, a scent of jasmine imbued the air. I took another breath.

"Is she all right?" I whispered.

"Yes, she is thinking of you right now." I heard inside my body.

"Please, ask her to call me. Thank you."

Slowly, remarkably relieved, I opened my eyes and waited in silence. That tenuous communication was the only link I had. How thrilled I will be as soon as I hear her voice. I imagined the sound of her voice in my mind. Her effortless, "Hi, Mom." I sat in a stupor, observing the dance of inkberry branches outside the living-room widow. They seemed to be greeting the intense midday sun. The phone rang.

The world switched from black and white to flaring color when I heard, "Hi, Mom."

"Where are you?" I said, in a whisper of profound relief.

She spoke in her cool teenager monotone. "We're here in Hollywood, where we had breakfast. My friends are bringing me home."

Holding back the torrent of emotions bubbling inside me, "Are you all right?" was all I could voice.

"I'm fine," she said nonchalantly.

"How come you didn't answer my calls? I've been calling you all night!"

"I left my cell phone in my bag in this guy's car, the guy who took us to the party. Then he decided to leave early without letting us know. My bag is still in his car. But I have some friends here; they are taking care of me."

"How come you didn't call me when you didn't have a ride back from the party?"

"I knew you were going to scream at me because I'd gone to a rave without telling you. So I hung out with my good friends."

"How soon will you be home?"

"In about an hour."

"We'll talk when you get here."

A few minutes later, she called again to ask me if I could pick her up near someone else's house because they were dropping off so many kids.

I was right there when their car drove up to the agreed place.

Stephanie climbed out and moved her lanky body. Her shoulders drooped. She plopped her slim frame onto the passenger seat.

"Okay," she said, "I know you're mad at me." Her cheeks were like white rose petals. There was a scent of stale smoke and dried perspiration.

"Why do you think I'm mad at you?"

"Because I didn't call you earlier." She mumbled without looking at me.

"So, if you knew you were meant to call me, why didn't you?" I didn't start the car. I was staring straight ahead.

"Because I knew you were going to yell at me." She combed her fingers through her hair as if to clear the air of the intensity. She finally looked at me through the endearing sweep of her long brown eyelashes.

"So rather than take the risk of being screamed at, or not, you're going to punish me and make sure I am tortured with fear, not knowing where you are?"

"No, Mom, I'm sorry, I didn't think of it that way."

I felt my chest unclench. I got the well-traveled Toyota running and started driving home.

"I realize that. Until you learn to think of it that way, you are not allowed to go out at night anymore for at least three weeks." Now I had to be quietly tough. I had never punished her so severely. We had always been able to talk and come to an understanding.

"What! I might as well kill myself. I need to see my friends."

"I didn't say you couldn't see your friends. You can invite them over to our house."

"Oh! Great."

"The ones who like you will be happy to come over."

We rolled into our driveway and came to a full stop.

"I might as well sleep for the next three weeks."

"Stephanie, there is something you have not understood. The one who is furious is me, not you. I'm the one who has not slept all night worrying, wondering if you were missing or worse. It's not fair that while you are out having fun and dancing the night away, I had to be here in a mortified frazzle of anxiety. You can't think of my feelings for one single moment, so I can relax and enjoy my life, too?"

"Mom, it's too noisy there to call."

I got a whiff of the scent of the dried eucalyptus leaves I kept on the shelf behind the back seat. "All I needed to know is that you are okay! You are the one who has to apologize to me. You are the one who has to understand that for you to ever be allowed to leave this house again I have to have complete confidence that you will always, and I mean always, answer my calls, when I call you. That if your ride leaves the party or wherever you may be, you will call me at whatever time it is and I will pick you up. I do not want you to depend on very nice people perhaps, but you don't know what they are on."

I moderated my fury. With steely firmness, I added, "You're going to have to get that through your beautiful brilliant head so clearly that I will never again doubt that you would do otherwise. You'll have to understand my anguish so thoroughly, when I don't hear from you, that you will, of your own initiative, call me for sure to let me know where you are and that you are all right. Do you understand me?"

"Don't you think you're overdoing it?"

"In your book I may be overdoing it, but that is not my concern. I must know where you are. I am responsible for you. I need to know where you are. It's a necessity as having to go to the bathroom or drinking water when I'm thirsty, or eating when I'm hungry. I need it from the depths of my body and soul, and you need to satisfy me."

"What about satisfying me? It's always about you. What about me?" she cried.

"I want you to be happy, but not at my expense. You can be happy and allow me to be happy, too. Until you are an adult, meaning until you are paying for all your needs, you answer to me. And that's final. Do you understand?"

She sulked. Climbing out of the car, she cried, "You're a domineering mother." Then, she marched to her room and slammed the door.

After a few hours, I knocked and peeked in.

"May I come in?"

"Yep, I slept," she said.

She was re-organizing her room, her Leika set on the dressing table, a note pad with scribbles on it. She seemed quite satisfied, nesting like a bird.

In the following days, we had many more conversations.

"What would you do if you lost your cell phone and the person you have a ride with gets sick?

"I find some other friends to take me home."

"What do you do before you do that?"

"Mom, stop being ridiculous."

"I want to know."

"I don't know."

"Yes, you do know. Whenever there is a change of plans, you call me to let me know so we can agree on what is the best course of action. Do you understand?"

She rolled her eyes and shook her head of brown silky curls. "Yeah, bro."

"What do you do, if someone drops you off at the wrong place and you don't know what to do next?"

"I call you and we figure it out together." She spoke in a nasal computer voice tone.

With more hindsight and study, I've realized teenagers are wired to take more chances than we would like them to. Compared to adults, they value rewards more than consequences. During these adolescent years, their brains undergo extensive re-modeling and wiring upgrade. Because of their biologically induced search for new thrills and sensations, they are able to get out of the house into new territory and connect more with their peers.

A year went by. Stephanie was not happy in her high school.

"We have a math teacher who tells us every morning she hates math. It doesn't make sense." Stephanie quipped.

"I want to go to Katie's school in Massachusetts." Katie was a friend from New York. "Katie says she can go to class in her pajamas if she wants, and the teachers are young and friendly."

First, we went to visit, to see if she liked it up close. She did, and so did I. Then we had to convince her dad to pay for half of it. It was an expensive progressive boarding school.

Her dad finally agreed after a lot of discussion. He dropped her off there in late August. I visited her in the fall and very early spring. She came home for Christmas. She was depressed the first winter away from home. I wish I had gone at least another time during the thick of winter. She only told me about her sadness later. She felt she had made such a big fuss to go there that now she couldn't complain. Knowing what a stretch it was for me to come up with half the tuition, she decided to get as much out of the school as she could: good grades, more art projects, and more clothes. She made a wonderful skirt all of men's ties stitched together. Yet, when I went to the Spring Arts show, she didn't have it out in the showroom.

"Where is your amazing skirt?"

"It's not good enough."

"What do you mean? Last week, I saw a very similar one in one of the center pages of the Italian *Vogue*!"

"Oh Mom, you don't understand. I don't feel like showing it."

"Okay." I was puzzled and asked a teacher to address it.

I suggested this affirmation to Stephanie: ". The universe supports and protects me in loving and unexpected ways."

She rolled her eyes.

I worked on my own self-esteem as I was helping them with theirs.

This was one part of myself speaking to another part of myself:

I want to share my transformations, confident in the work I'm doing.

I forgive my mother for wanting to control me. I forgive myself for allowing myself to be controlled.

When I returned home, I received the results of a bone density test. They said that I had osteoporosis. First, I was shocked at the implication of my fragility. I began to imagine my skeleton as that of a twelve-year-old girl, full of life. I looked up in Louise Hay's book *Heal Your Body* the emotional origin of osteoporosis. Feeling there is no support left in life, she suggests a new thought pattern: "I stand up for myself. And life supports me in unexpected, loving ways." I repeated all this. I also reminded myself that Deepak Chopra talked about the skeleton being replaced every three years. So in three years, I would have a whole new healthy skeleton. One that rocks, baby. Tomorrow, I was going to get myself some two or four pound weights and also some extra calcium and magnesium. The magnesium helps absorb the calcium. I had to eat a lot more greens and do more exercise.

My coach, Phil Laut, suggested that I sounded like a little girl waiting for my father to show up and protect me. No, I said. Those days were over now. I was surprised and defensive. I thought I had worked all that out. Yet within seconds of his mentioning it, my eyes began to water. As soon as I hung up with him, I sobbed.

In rewriting the affirmations and applying new ways to promote myself, I noticed more clients showed up. Conversations with friends and with my inner voice led me to embrace the word *competitive*. The competition was with myself.

55

At the heart of Buddhist meditation
are concentration and inquiry.
When you cultivate these two qualities
in meditation, you develop
your ability to be quiet and clear to
offer understanding and love.
—Martine Bachelor

My coach's way of making me write interactive evolving affirmations, from a doubtful retort to a more and more confident one, shifted my stance. The organization of my files improved.

I arranged to set up a table within the Whole Foods on U.S. 1, with brochures of my work and information about the Silva Method. The manager said it was fine as long as I only spoke to the people who came up to the table.

Decked in my blue suit, with a pleated skirt, Charles Jourdan heels, and pearls, I set my table near the bins of seeds, nuts, and cereals. People came. One of them, with a dwarfish quality, was a Cuban elderly man. "Oh Silva, I've taken Silva. I know lots of people who would like to take

Silva. I teach metaphysics. You must call me; I'll give you their names."

"Thank you," I said.

He took my hand and looked right above my head.

"You don't need to be here; you don't need to do this. A man loves you; he has a big house. He loves you."

I looked around. All I could see were the vegetables lined up and the containers of nuts. *Where? Who?*

A week later, I received an email from Emmanuel. We hadn't spoken in years. For two months we exchanged more emails, until I asked him, in talking about a new relationship, "Don't you think I can at least expect to be with someone who respects the way I think?"

His reply was, "The way you think is way out there. You can't expect people to understand you."

I wrote back immediately. I couldn't believe I had thought he understood me all along. Now I realized he thought I was completely out of the box in my thinking and that he had never understood me at all. It was a great liberation.

Stephanie and I arrived in New York on September 5th. We rented a car at La Guardia. The plan was to visit six different colleges, so Stephanie could form an idea of what her preferences might be.

The car rental gave me a new white Chevrolet. What intrigued me was the license plate: AWE 6223. I don't really know what the numbers meant. I felt the word "AWE", in capital letters, was related to our journey.

We enjoyed seeing the differences between the colleges and commenting about them. Bard University, right on the Hudson, was two hours from New York City. We felt welcome. Everyone was very willing to assist and guide the student. Skidmore was far up north. Mt. Holyoke and Smith were the most impressive. Clark was in such an ugly place, and we had such trouble finding the admissions office that by the time we got there, the secretary seemed rude and disgruntled. I can't tell if we had written the school off even before we got there. Boston University was varied and yet so large and unwieldy. Finally, we went to Brandeis where we got completely lost. Stephanie had an obnoxious interviewer. So when we were finished with that tour, we went back to Hampshire College where Katie, her great friend, was. We had dinner with her and drove all the way to Willliamstown late at night. It was September 10th. I wanted us to wake up near Buxton, Stephanie's school, for the eleventh. That was the day Stephanie was meant to arrive at school for her senior year.

September 11, 2001: We woke up at the Willows motel in Williamstown. As soon as I was dressed, I went up to the office to pay my bill and the man at the reception said, "Have you heard about the tragedy?"

I thought to myself that maybe someone had been murdered in Williamstown.

"An air craft has crashed into the World Trade Center."

"What?" I called my daughter from the front desk. "Turn on the TV."

By the time I got back into the room, we saw on the screen another plane plow into the other tower. That image was replayed on the television screen. It is branded into my brain. We were horrified. I was trembling inside. We huddled together, feeling so thankful that we were together. We called up Edward. He had already seen it. Michaela hadn't seen anything. I tried calling New York on the phone to reorganize my plans; no dial tone. Not only had both the towers crumbled into ashes like fragile sand castles, but all those people inside. What happened to them?

"My God, everything has changed, forever," Stephanie cried out, holding her head in the palms of her hands. "Everything is different, everything has changed." She kept repeating it as she probably saw in her mind's eye more new flashes of realizations. "I can't believe this is really happening; it's like a nightmare." She was only seventeen. "Fashion design seems such a superficial endeavor now. I think the world needs something else," she added.

We were soon to find out that not many survived. A lot of our mental structures and our priorities also disintegrated at that moment, and it would take us months and years to realize it. It was the most pivotal point in history that I had ever lived through.

When we got to Stephanie's school, everyone was stunned and troubled. I could feel heaviness in their eyes. I asked if I could spend the night there with her, and they were very understanding. The next morning I drove into New York City. I felt so frazzled that I kept taking the wrong turn, and when I did take the right turn, I was never sure that it was the correct one. I didn't trust what I remembered I had just read on a map. Nonetheless, I arrived. As soon as I stepped out of the car, a stench of burning acrid smoke overwhelmed my senses. How reassuring to find Petunia my cousin and her husband and my mother all well and very concerned. My mother was visiting for a week.

Providence provided the moment to spend time with my mother. The tragic events closed down all the airports.

The intensity of the emotional and physical vulnerability brought us closer together. For the next few days, we were practically inseparable. We were sharing the same room and stayed up talking into the wee hours of the morning. I was able to ask her point blank if I was Bertrand Smye's daughter. She denied it.

I explained, "Daddy had said he wasn't sure I was his daughter. My stepmother confirmed that he had that doubt, when she and I and spoke after he died."

"But, he recognized you in his will as his daughter," she replied.

"You often joked around saying how funny it was that Uncle Ogilvy wasn't sure who my father was. I thought maybe you had an affair with Bertrand Smye, and that I am his daughter."

"No," she said, "he had a crush on me, but that was the extent of it. He was married anyway."

"As soon as I got to New York, he instantly gave me a job and placed me in his private office. I kept staring at his nose wondering if I had his nose."

"No, absolutely not," she repeated. "You had your grandfather's nose. I joked with him when he was alive that if you ended up with his nose, he would have to pay for the plastic surgery."

"Okay," I said, wanting to believe it. "But," I added, "why didn't you want me to tell my father I had had the operation?"

"I don't remember that!"

"Well, you didn't, and I always wondered why." I didn't let the question hang in the air too long. I interrupted myself with “Anyway he never noticed; neither did most other people.”

How we yearn for and fear the truth.

56

No pessimist ever discovered the secret of the stars or sailed to an uncharted land or opened a new heaven for the human spirit.
—Helen Keller

Every time I returned from a trip, it took me at least two weeks to get my business revved up again. This slow take-off was always anxiety ridden for me. The one time it didn't happen was when I boasted to my parents that I always had three to four clients a day. As soon as I got back, that's exactly what happened.

This lady called me up. "My husband has had terrible pain all his life and is addicted to pain killers. Can you help him?"

"I'm sure I can help him with the addiction. I'm not sure about the pain. Why don't you have him come in for a complimentary consultation? Then, he can decide what he wants to do."

"All right," she said.

After his first session, the husband called to report he felt more at ease in social situations. Yet, with respect to his addiction and pain, nothing had changed. We talked for a while. He asked me if I felt I could help him because his addiction had been so intense for so long. I replied that the power of our subconscious mind is much greater than what we can imagine and that we must give it the benefit of the doubt. He returned for a second session. We worked on transforming uncomfortable feelings of his inner child into supportive ones. During a regression, he found himself at age two feeling unrelenting pain in his feet. His mother gave him pain killers. She didn't know what else to do. Doctors had found no physical cause for the pain.

He was feeling pain in his feet, right then and there. A teacher had told me that when the pain was in the upper part of the feet, while the subject is in a deep state, it related to past lives. When the subject feels pain on the sole of the feet, it relates to feeling a lack of understanding about a certain moment in his or her present life.

I asked him if he would be willing to go into a past life. "Yes," he said. I guided him into another reality. He found himself as a woman in an indigenous culture in South America, living in the jungle in a hut. She vividly experienced herself dropping some very hot greasy liquid onto her legs and feet. From then on, she always walked with great difficulty. The sores did not heal well. Then I guided him to find himself or rather herself, one hour before her death. She saw herself lumbering along a river. Now she was an older woman. Her feet and legs were so sore it was very hard to walk. When she splashed into the river to catch a fish, she stumbled on a rock. She could not get up any more. She drowned.

"Feel the death, go through it, and completely let go of that body." I insisted he let go of this body of pain. His frame shook in undulating spasms for an interminable minute as I kept encouraging him to let go of this body and of this pain once and for all and to feel his true spirit emerge as a witness.

Then, we wrapped up the session tying up the loose ends. I guided him out in perfect health.

Three days later he called me and reported that since that session he had felt no more pain in his feet, pain that he had endured daily for more than forty years. For a few mornings, I awoke with pains in my feet. They only lasted a few minutes and then disappeared.

He returned for another session where we dealt further with him letting go of the addiction to the painkillers, and he reported having success in reducing the dosage every day.

Every day, I invoked the highest masters and teachers of the universe to help and guide me in this work. I allowed them to work through me. I surrounded myself in purple light, the color of forgiveness, and became the channel that I am. I said to myself, *I am a healer.* My inner voice responded: "You are protected."

Yet the world was changing rapidly. In Afghanistan, we helped the Northern Alliance overthrow the Taliban, and a new Afghan tribes' coalition created a new government. The threat of terrorism was still very present in the United States. I felt the media and the government were playing it to the hilt to be able to change the laws and revoke more and more civil liberties. We needed to be vigilant. At the same time, the American policies in the Middle East were going to have to take into consideration the anger and frustration of many Muslims with no jobs. It was a very complicated situation; as a result, everyone was feeling much more vulnerable and uncertain. I felt the experience of being alive was so much more precious. This intensity never arose before. Buried emotions were surfacing, and I found myself feeling uneasy and sobbing for ancient feelings of abandonment.

Time was so short. I looked at myself in the mirror and said to myself, *I love you just the way you are. What can I do to make you happy?* Then I quieted my mind and heard an answer come from within me. It could be the simplest answer: "Take a shower," "Go and meditate," or "Pay your bills." I heard it more and more and wanted to live within the moment of now as much as possible. A bomb, a wave or anything could hit at any moment. I heard a voice inside:

"Make sure you stay in touch with your daughters."

"Is that you, Joan?"

"Yes, I'm right here, with you, always part of you, always letting you know that you deserve heaven on earth, and that you can feel it happening to you."

"I want to go see my mother, for her birthday. Do you think she and I can have real conversation?"

"It's worth a try. What do you mean, a 'real conversation'?"

"One where we could admit to our true feelings."

"She has to keep up her version of the story. That is the basis for her sanity.

Just as you keep up yours; if not, you would have to declare that all your memories are false and that you are crazy. You'll have to accept each side of the story as belonging to each one of the characters. Go and see her and envision your desired end result."

When I arrived in Pittsburgh, where they both live, my sister and mother were happy to see me. Settled in the car, they asked: "How are you? What have you been doing?"

"I'm well. I've been learning about digital video editing. This is very exciting because I have so much footage from over the years."

"What are you going to do with it?" my mother asked.

"Edit and put it into CDs. I am working on Michaela's graduation. What have you all been doing?"

"We've been gardening and playing with Mummy's new puppy.'

"Yes, Ilona comes by to see me twice a week, sometimes more. In the morning, she takes me with her in the car, and so we do errands together."

"Hee hee, I keep her on her toes!"

"She reminds me of what I forget."

"Yes, darling, you just stick with me, I'll take care of you, baby."

My mother, delighted with Ilona's jocular and protective tone, looked at me to let me know how much fun they were having together.

Mummy's house was an attractive old stone house built in the 1920s, with an acre of lawn and a slope down to a ravine threaded with a stream.

I recognized the worn leather chairs and the matte damask covered sofas. The nineteenth-century German inlaid wood grand piano, graced with many silver framed brides, also had a few photos of Victor's parents: his father in full military regalia, his mother, an elegant beauty. The soft terrier puppy sauntered around asking for attention. My mother's tone with him was so sweet and endearing, I felt jealous of him. With me, her tone was distant and matter of fact.

We talked little by little with more trust. Could I really open up? I could stay the polite and humoring and tender daughter or I could show her more of myself.

After fourteen years on my own, I had met someone wonderful and profound in so many ways. After a year of getting to know each other I moved in with him, soon thereafter we married. This was the first time I visited my mother since the wedding.

The next morning after breakfast, my mother and I talked. I told her a bit about my challenges in adapting to my new life in Massachusetts. I felt the courage to say I was writing this book. That the whole purpose was to understand and forgive as best I could, also to attempt to see the events from other points of view.

We got to when Victor beat me because of the dirty pictures that someone else had shown Charity and how no one ever said they were sorry.

"We never put a hand on you. Certainly not Victor." Her brittle tone became more distant. She moved her body further back onto the wrought-iron love seat with white stiff sailcloth cushions.

"I have a letter from you where you admit that he did and that you were proud of it. You cannot deny it," I retorted.

She got flustered; there was a silence. She got up and stepped into the living room, and I followed her. "Oh my

God, I've been a monster. I'm so sorry," she said as she sat herself down in an upholstered chair.

"Oh Mummy, it's all right; we all make mistakes." By this time I was crying. "It's fine. I just want my mommy." And I hugged her.

At that very moment, my sister walked in. We explained what had happened. Ilona chimed in saying: "My God, I've also made mistakes. We have to move on."

I got up to hug her. Then I went to hug my mother again. "Lilizinha, I am so sorry," she repeated.

Both my sister and I did all we could to let her know that we can let go of the mistakes of the past.

"Why don't we let you rest for a while? Get dressed quietly and recuperate from all this drama. I'll take Lili out for a while."

As soon as we were back, my mother said she had almost killed herself while we were out, and then she took a librium and now she was better.

After Ilona left, I showed my mother how to get onto and explore a few sites on the Internet. Then, I took her out to dinner for her birthday.

"My whole life has been hell," she admitted to me at the table. I knew she was implying her life with my step-father. He had been so insensitive, having affairs with so many women, including his secretary, almost right before her eyes. This was why he lost the position in Brussels and was sent back to Chicago years ago. She felt she had to bear with it. She said in Brazil she had too many small children and did not know how to handle it alone.

Recently, he had told her to meet him outside a department store where they were both shopping. He would pick her up in half an hour. She waited for him all afternoon. He never showed up. She had to call the police to find him. He was home. He had forgotten. He had a drink too many and fell asleep.

After dinner, we went to my sister's for cake and more presents. It was jolly and calm.

The next morning, as soon as I got downstairs, my mother's first words were: "Everything you said yesterday were *calumnias*, all calumnies."

I called the dog and took him out running, all the while trying to convince myself to stay calm although I didn't feel calm at all. How could she deny everything she had admitted the day before? She could, and she had to. Unfortunately, I was not able to control my anger.

"You will only hurt yourself by writing the book. I am going to write my own book," she said outraged, as I stepped back into the living room.

"I'd like to see you do that. Sit down and write and write some more, day after day, night after night, as if your life depended on it," I responded heatedly.

"All lies. Where did you get all these stories from?"

"It's what I lived through. Maybe you don't remember because you were all drinking a lot. I wasn't."

She threw her coffee cup on the floor. It cracked and broke into many pieces. Then she picked them up.

"Do you want me to leave?" I asked.

"You always do what you want anyway. Why do you ask me?" she thundered and stomped her way up the stairs and shut herself in her room.

I didn't know what to say.

I called my sister and could not find her. I left her a message relating the essence of what had happened. I asked her to come over as soon as possible. I told my mother I was sorry I had raised my voice at her. I don't know if she heard me or not.

By the time my sister arrived, we had calmed down. My mother signaled to her that she had taken a pill. Ilona helped our communication by showing she understood both points of view, or so it seemed to me. Whatever I said, my mother took it as an attack rather than a statement of fact. I said, "I guess you didn't leave Victor because you didn't have the courage." This could sound like an attack.

"No," she said. "What was I going to do with three small children, on my own in Brazil?"

"I guess you didn't think it was bad enough to leave. Had he been chopping our fingers up with a knife, you would have had to leave."

We talked until my sister left to feed her children.

My mother and I spent a quiet evening watching a bit of TV. There was a documentary on Bob Dylan. I told her that for a while I had pretended he was my father. She looked at me as if I were crazy and left the room to let me watch it alone. Later we watched a bit of FOX News, her favorite and my least favorite channel, together. By the time it was bedtime, we were able to say goodnight in a gentle way.

My sister's husband took me to the airport. I called my sister to get her perspective on what was happening. She didn't reply. When I called her again and found her, she was furious with me for having been so cruel to my mother. She gave me a rampage of anger, and I just backed out as gently as I could. I didn't need to defend myself. I didn't like it but I knew she had too much on her plate.

During her senior year, Stephanie found out that several design schools were holding interviews at FIT in New York City.

"I'd have to show up with my portfolio, Mom. Do you think I should do it?"

"Absolutely!" I replied.

She got on a bus at dawn from Massachusetts and was the first one in line to speak to the interviewers from the Rhode Island School of Design.

"Do you think I should apply?" She asked them after they viewed her portfolio.

"You must apply!" They replied.

Stephanie graduated. She was chosen to be the first senior to speak to the community of the school at the graduation. She looked like a Greek goddess: brown curls framing her face, gold paillette epaulettes and an empire ribbon on the high waist of her long white crepe dress made by her paternal grandmother in the 1950s. Each senior was asked to give a half-hour talk about any subject they felt was relevant to the occasion. Graced with regal posture, she spoke about how when she came to the school she thought it was important to be cool. Then, with time, and some suffering, she got that what is truly important is to be real. I was proud of her. She was accepted at the Rhode Island School of Design.

57

Moreover, one has to know oneself. I am really best when I can focus on one thing at a time.
—Eric R. Kandel

Two years later, I convinced my mother to let me accompany her on a trip. Where would she want to go? She often told me how she and her mother travelled to the Holy Land where Grandmaman wanted to go before she died. My mother was eighty-five. Her mother was ninety when she died. As time passed, Mummy only had a longing to see Luz, my friend Amanda's mother and her friend of many, many years. At first, she said she was afraid to travel. Then she proved to herself she wasn't so afraid to travel because she went to see Tanti Lili and managed very well on the train to NY. When I asked her, "Wouldn't you like to go visit Luz?"

"Yes, but I'd be scared to travel alone."

"I'll go with you."

"All right, let me think about it."

A few weeks later, she called me.

"Darling, I think it would be a wonderful trip if we could go and return together."

We met at Tanti Lili's on Long Island, spent a couple of days with her, and then flew to Santiago, Chile.

We stayed with Luz, in her spacious apartment in La Providencia, a part of town with worn down streets. She had imposing views of the Andes, on one side, and a glimmering expanse of the lights of Santiago, on the other. The terrace off the dining room was filled with tall bamboo plants that served as a natural shade from the sun. There was a Chinese and Philippine flavor to the style of the furniture. The living room had two puffy white canvas loveseat sofas perpendicular to each other and a lot of her paintings on the walls.

I found so much warmth and recognition in Luz. She was a tiny woman with tamari roasted almond eyes, almost as wide as her cheekbones. She had the majestic nose of an Inca and a pointed chin. She twisted and pinned, on the back of her head, her long silver hair, evocative of a musical cleft. The timbre of her voice had depth of sonority and melodious freedom. Her laughter climbed effortlessly different notes of two octaves as she spoke and chuckled simultaneously. Her posture regal, the fluid grace of her manner showed a generous spirit. The expression in her face for us was so open and full of pleasure. She dressed simply in black pants and a black or white tunic. When it was chilly, which it was, she wrapped herself in bright colorful shawls. Pearl earrings and necklace framed her face with a classic touch.

It was so endearing to hear my mother and Luz reminisce about their young days in New York giving dinner parties with Stokowski and Gloria Vanderbilt.

"I was having an affair with him. After I introduced them, they sort of took off, and I didn't see them very often after that. I loved having your mother there; she was always so interesting and such a striking beauty."

"And how is Amanda?" I asked.

"She is better because she isn't taking any more drugs. She likes the woman who is taking care of her, and she is in her own apartment. I have been able to put aside some money from the sale of the house in trust for her expenses. The only thing I worry about when I die is to leave her too lonely. Nobody in the family cares about her. My other two children at times have felt jealous of the time and energy she has demanded of me and away from them."

When, inevitably, the conversation moved into the political arena, I was relieved to hear Luz also felt this war in Iraq was a great tragedy and disaster. My mother was as always defending the President and his administration. I kept quiet because I did not want to get into a political discussion with my mother.

At the dinner table after realizing what my mother's views were, Luz did say: "But, Josette, how can you be so much in denial? This war has been a disaster for the United States and for the world."

"Well, I still think President Bush is a good man."

"He may be a good man, but he is totally ineffective."

"I know you think I am wrong, but I have my opinions on the situation."

As the conversation went on, my mother said how Tanti Lili is always criticizing her, and then she mentioned that Tanti Lili wouldn't criticize me.

"She used to, plenty of times, until you got married respectably. It's also that your husband is a darling person. Before you weren't doing respectable things, so you couldn't be treated respectably."

I wondered silently what were the things I had done that were not respectable. I was able to let the tentacle fall away.

One day we went to photograph the cathedral and took Luz to lunch in a bohemian part of town. Another day, Mummy and I went to the pre-Columbian museum.

I planned to visit Amanda. Luz's chauffeur took me to her apartment. A very gentle girl, Valentina, received me at the door. When I stepped into her bedroom, I could feel the dank stuffy air. It was warmer than the small sitting room with a painting hanging askew on its nail. Amanda was lying in the bed naked. Her shoulder joints prominently protruding over the edge of the sheets. Her face was more chiseled than I remembered it, the last time I saw her in Marbella, ten years before. At that time, she was very negative about everything. Now she seemed more relaxed, although she did receive me by saying, "Are you comfortable at my mother's? It is so noisy and cold in that apartment. I can't stand that place."

"I am very comfortable. It's a beautiful apartment. I love seeing all her wonderful objects and paintings. All the views from the windows are marvelous."

"Oh, I agree," she said. "The views are beautiful."

We had a lot to catch up with. I told her a bit about my new life with Robert, my husband.

She told me how she had been in and out of the hospital many times. How they had insisted she take certain drugs and all the harm they did. Now she was on nothing. She felt very pure.

I took in her raw beauty and saw her stringy and greasy long hair as part of her style. Her mother had told me she didn't like taking baths nor washing her hair. Then she said, "Maybe I'll let Valentina cut my toenails." She pulled out her tiny skeletal feet, and I noticed her dark toenails curled over her toes.

"Whatever you feel is right for you," I replied, wanting to respect her right to have two or three inch long curling toenails. I touched her bony feet and caressed them and held them, allowing our energies to merge. With wide-open eyes, she spoke slowly, "I didn't know the difference between acting and being."

"Amanda, what you just said has explained a lot to me about what you have gone through."

"What did you understand?" she replied.

I didn't tell her that during the past year, I had become aware of how we all have a mask we use to hide feelings we are ashamed of. What I did say was:

"You didn't know how to show your true feelings. Perhaps when you had, they were rejected. You were always 'dramatic' and that was your creation. So you had to go through all these years of experiencing all your greatest fears and torments, maybe they were attached to you. Now that you are off all the drugs, you experience the calmness of your being. Almost thirty years of torment to discover whom you are. Amazing."

She nodded. There was a long silence. Then she said: "Show me some pictures of your life."

I pulled out the computer and started clicking through iPhoto.

58

Only he who attempts the absurd is
capable of the impossible.
—Miguel de Unamuno

My mother came to Stephanie's fashion show and graduation dinner. We picked her up at the train station in Providence. She is eighty-six and traveled alone all the way from Pittsburgh. She looked very elegant in her black watch tweed suit and a shawl to match. She was happy to be there and friendly with everyone. The fashion show was gorgeous and professional with beautiful girls, all friends and acquaintances from Rhode Island School of Design and Brown, modeling the astonishing creations of students. There were light effects, music and rhythm. Stephanie's designs were chosen to be the "grand finale." We were all so proud of her. Her father and his wife were also there. I said to him, as we were leaving, "It felt as if we all had died and re-met in heaven."

I wanted to embrace everybody and pray that we all find a way to start fresh, luminous as we are. Original goodness and common humanity were the realities to expand.

The greatest success in my life so far is the radiance and recognized burgeoning talents of my two daughters. Michaela has been accepted in a graduate Ph.D. program in molecular and cellular biology at Harvard University. Stephanie is graduating in fashion and apparel design from Rhode Island School of Design. One of her designs was photographed for the *Boston Globe*. She is heading for New York City to find a job.

In learning to be an example for my daughters, supporting their sense of self, I have found that true beauty is not in the shape of my nose nor in the smoothness of my skin, but in the radiance of the inner spirit I can allow to flow through me.

I've returned to Pittsburgh more times and had a chance to feel more at peace with my sister. She is an immeasurable support to our parents. She visits them every week, brings them food and takes my mother on little errands.

My sister urged us, her siblings, to help her convince them that it was time to move into assisted living. My parents resisted at first. Their inability to drive, to protect themselves from predatory callers and their gaps of memory, made it imperative. My brothers came at different times. My mother was offering pieces of her furniture and art to whichever of my siblings wanted them. My sister got the largest amount of objects because she was there helping them in the same city. I didn't need any furniture or paintings. I told my mother there was only one belonging of hers I wanted. It was the gold bracelet made of little moving bricks of gold with a buckle of rubies and diamonds. It was an icon of my early years with her, when it was just the two of us. When I could see it, it meant she was near. My mother said she didn't remember where it was or whether she had given it to my sister. She added "I will ask her if she has it."

My sister confided she could not stay in her marriage anymore. She went through a difficult divorce. She found a good place to live and created a new life. She oversaw the care my mother and stepfather might need. I came as often as I could to support her and to understand what were their essential needs and help a little. During one of those visits, I asked my sister about the bracelet and explained what it meant to me. My sister tensed up and said:

"But that's one of my favorites too."

"You have all the rest of her jewelry, except for the diamond ring my father gave her." We let those remarks just hang in the air.

The next day when I went to spend the night at my sister's, I said,

"I really like that bracelet, too. We could share it."

She promptly reached into a paper shopping bag and brought out a thin, red leather case embossed with gold leaf and handed it to me.

"You keep it, it's yours."

After a lot of deliberations, they moved to an assisted living facility. My older brother came to help. My mother was diagnosed with beginning of Alzheimer's and has gaps of memory. Sometimes, she holds a conversation and seems fine. When there is a specific reference to the past, she searches in her mind and says; "Remind me". There is no point in talking about the past anymore. For her, it's mostly gone.

59

Even after all this time
The sun never says to the earth
"You owe me."
Look what happens with a love like that,
It lights the Whole Sky.
—Hafiz

Recently, I stayed with my sister. It was catch-up time, so nourishing and healing for us both. Then, we went to visit them. My stepfather had been for several weeks in the hospital side of the facility. When we reached my mother's little suite, she was just getting out of bed. It was almost noon. Her hair was greasy and long and she was in a bit of a daze. My sister, as soon as we stepped in, sprayed some generic sweet air freshener, in all directions. "I always come prepared," she said.

I turned the air conditioner on low to see if a little clean air would come in. The windows do not open in this place.

While my sister went to talk with some people in the administration of the senior community, I encouraged Mummy to get into the shower and promised I would be right there to help her wash her hair. First, I gave her a little privacy in the bathroom to undress. Then, while she was wrapped in a dry towel, I found some discarded towels in the bin for carpeting the floor, so we could keep the shower curtain open and they would soak up any rogue drops or squirts. I had to adjust the temperature and pull off the handle of the telephone shower. Mummy said it was stuck. With a little effort I pulled it off. I realized that for her, it was too much of an effort, or maybe she had just gotten depressed having my stepfather in the hospital for so many weeks. My sister underscored this concern to the people in charge: they have been so long together, they are very co-dependent and they begin to fade when they are apart. When I had seen my stepfather the day before, his eyes were sunken into his sockets and surrounded by a haunting gray. He was thin. His flesh draped as white sheets on furniture.

When she sat on the white plastic seat in the shower, she was the size of a ten-year-old girl. I held the showerhead handle over her back and neck to keep her warm while reaching for the shampoo bottle. "You can put some shampoo on. Here's the bottle. Put your head down forward. I'll wet your hair."

She lifted her arms and scrubbed her soapy scalp with the tips of her fingers. A scent of marzipan from the shampoo reminded me of celebrations.

"It feels so good to scratch my scalp. I want to do it again."

Her full head of hair, a lot of black mixed in with the gray. She sighed as she relished the pouring warm water over her head.

Then she grabbed the soap and bent over and scrubbed other parts of her body. Surprised at the tenderness I felt for her fragile figure, her skin so smooth in spite of sagging, I let her revel in the pleasure of the warm water as long as she wanted. The echoing pitter-patter shower splashes felt like a rain blessing.

"I'm ready," she said.

"Okay, I'll shut the water off. Here is your towel."

I helped her stand and wrap the towel around her hunched body. Once she was safely out of the shower, I gave her privacy.

Dressed, she sat at her dressing table in front of her mirror. I wrapped a towel around her shoulders, reached for the scissors, and asked her how she wanted me to trim her hair.

"I like it when it's no longer than my chin."

I divided her hair into two levels and pinned the higher level on top of her head.

I cut two inches off all around the bottom. Then I trimmed the top layer at a slight angle so it curved in as a pageboy. She seemed pleased.

When I called a few days later to ask how the haircut was holding up, she giggled and said she got a few compliments. Then she added,

"I'm tired, Lilisinha, if you call sometime and I'm gone, know that you have been a sweet perfume in my life."

Epilogue

Today, I live in Groton, Ma. This is the eleventh year of my deepening marriage. Through a committed relationship, I discover more about myself and define better how I want to evolve. I am grateful for my new family, my private practice, my video making, my reading and writing, my singing and cooking and my children. My mother is still alive and we have sweet conversations over the phone or when I visit.

34305984R00243

Made in the USA
Charleston, SC
06 October 2014